NOTTINGHAM FOREST
the 80's

THE CONTINUING SUCCESS OF OLD BIG HEAD!

MMP
Max Media Publishing Ltd

ANDREW S. DOLLOWAY

MMP

Max Media Publishing Ltd.

First published in Great Britain by:
Max Media Publishing Ltd 2019

ISBN 978-0-9954783-4-3

www.maxmediapublishing.com

Max Media Publishing Ltd
49-51 Bancroft Lane, Mansfield, Notts, NG18 5LG
Edited and written by Andrew S Dolloway

Associate design by Simon Meakin at In House Design, Mansfield, Notts.

INTRODUCTION

It's July 1980 and Nottingham Forest have just been crowned European Champions, but in truth, their period of dominance was coming to an end. This is the story of the team's gradual decline before Brian Clough once more took the Reds back to the top of the domestic game. Continuing on from my previous books; 'Nottingham Forest in the 1960's, the Forgotten Decade' and 'Nottingham Forest in the 1970's, a Decade of two Halves', this book charts the journey from European Cup success in 1980, right through to the new young vibrant team that represented the club in the late eighties.

It was a decade that saw many fall out of love with the game, as first there was tragedy at Bradford City and Heysel, before we witnessed the unbelievable scenes at Hillsborough. I was fortunate to be working at the club for three of these years and witnessed first hand the emergence of Nigel Clough and the rest of Clough's 'bairns' as he liked to call them.

Once more, in this book I have tried to capture the excitement of the decade, with lots of unseen photographs, memorabilia and memories of players involved in this era.

I hope you get as much enjoyment out of this book as I did putting it together. COYR.

Andrew S. Dolloway, September 2019

CONTENTS

SEASON 1979-80

Back Row: L to R: John Robertson, Martin O'Neill, Ian Bowyer, Tony Woodcock, Frank Clark, Kenny Burns, Trevor Francis. Middle Row: L to R: Ken Smales (Secretary), Colin Barrett, Dave Needham, Peter Shilton, Chris Woods, Viv Anderson, John O'Hare, Jimmy Gordon (Trainer) Front Row: L to R : Garry Birtles, John McGovern, Peter Taylor (Asst. Manager), Stuart Dryden (Chairman), Brian Clough (Manager), Larry Lloyd, Archie Gemmill.

How do you top winning the European Cup? Go and win it again, perhaps with a bit more style, after all the final against Malmo itself wasn't the best of games.

Brian Clough once more played down the 'Cup', preferring to stay with his usual line that his 'bread and butter' was the league, and that would be the club's main focus. Peter Taylor was clear: "We need at least two new faces to compete," he said, and that was before the departure of several stalwarts.

Frank Clark had been offered another year, but he himself realised that he was unlikely to get much game time and when the chance to begin a managerial career as assistant to Ken Knighton at Sunderland came up, it was too good an opportunity to pass up. Chris Woods who had been content to learn his trade under the tutelage of Peter Shilton, also felt that it was in his best interests to move on, Queens Park Rangers paid a fee of £200,000 to secure his services.

Perhaps the most surprising transfer was that of Archie Gemmill. Harsh words had passed between him and the manager over his omission from the European Cup Final team. Archie had been adamant that the boss had promised him that he would play, if he proved his fitness. However, when he hadn't even got on as a substitute, that was the end as far as the player was concerned, but in spite of this, it was not until just a few weeks before the start of the season that Gemmill made the switch to Second Division Birmingham City. It was a move that both parties would regret to some extent. Clough, because Gemmill's replacement Asa Hartford turned out to be wholly unsuitable, and for the player, because he was to miss out on the opportunity to play in a European Cup Final. After all, hadn't Martin O'Neill found himself in exactly the same situation in Munich? But in his case, Martin had bitten his tongue and was to earn his reward twelve months later. Forest received £150,000 for the 32 year old Gemmill.

Peter Taylor had already earmarked the replacements. Frank Gray arrived at the City Ground as the new left back from Leeds United, joining for £450,000 and he was followed by Asa Hartford for the same fee from Manchester City. Chris Woods' replacement turned out to be the veteran keeper Jim Montgomery from Birmingham City.

Despite the economic troubles facing the country, (the new Conservative government under Margaret Thatcher had just announced £3.5 billion of cuts), football itself seemed oblivious, with clubs spashing more cash than ever. As an example of the madness pervading the game, Manchester City spent £1,450,000 on Wolves mid-fielder Steve Daley....who?!!

As the season started, ITV would be on strike, the Times newspaper had not been published for a year and bank interest rates had reached 17%. The Queen's own art historian, Anthony Blunt had been revealed as a Soviet spy, but worse still, the IRA were still committing atrocities, the latest being the murder of Lord Mountbatten.

The Professional Footballers' Association won a landmark case against the Football Association, in a move that was to signal a change in the balance of power between club and player. Players would now be free to seek a new club at the end of

Slow going with the new East Stand development.

their contract. There would still be a transfer fee to pay, agreed between the clubs or if that was not possible, after arbitration. No longer could clubs hold on to a player's registration if the player wished to leave.

As European champions, the club were very much in demand and this meant a change from the favoured normally low key build up to a season, that usually consisted of a series of matches against humble European opposition. Now, they were expected to take on more high profile and lucrative games,

After an opening match against Holsterbro from Denmark, only noteworthy because the two keepers swopped sides at half-time to give Shilton something to do, Forest were pitched into an encounter with Bayern Munich back in the familiar surroundings of the Olympic Stadium, against an outfit whose preparations were several weeks ahead of theirs. The 5-0 defeat did nothing for the team's reputation.

A further weeks training though, meant that by the time they reached Bilbao for a four team tournament with the hosts Athletic, Botafogo of Brazil and Dynamo Bucharest of Rumania, most of the cobwebs had been blown away and they were ready to do themselves justice. They duly won the competition and were awarded a magnificent trophy.

John McGovern, with the Bilbao Trophy.

When the club had signed Trevor Francis from Birmingham City the previous season, they knew that he had already committed himself to return to Detroit Express for the summer. They had been unable to talk him out of this and feared that playing continuously for eighteen months would be detrimental to the player. This surely contributed to the injury Francis picked up in America and when the manager found out that he would miss at least the first two months of the season, rather than just a couple of games, he was fuming and he vowed that he would not be caught out again.

Clough particularly thought that the player had been badly

Peter Taylor, alongside new signings Frank Gray and Asa Hartford.

advised by his agent, and the manager really did not like agents.

The season began with a difficult looking away game at Portman Road against Ipswich, on the usual bakingly hot opening day. The one pen allocated to the Forest fans behind the goal, was always going to be inadequate and fans climbed over the fences to take over the sterile area that had been left between rival fans. Chants of, 'Champions of Europe', greeted the players, who responded with a superbly professional performance and a win courtesy of a Tony Woodcock goal.

The City Ground had resembled a building site throughout the summer as Norwest Holst the construction company entrusted with delivering a new east stand, had tried to keep up with the demanding time schedule, but the project had fallen behind after a series of delays, notably a strike by steelworkers. You perhaps would have thought that Brian Clough might have been more supportive of his fellow workers, but he caused anger when he described the steelworkers as slower than his back four and then had to smooth things over by explaining that the statement was said firmly with tongue in cheek. The ground capacity was set at only 28,000 until the stand was completed.

The first home game against Stoke City took place against this unusual backdrop, and as the night grew darker during this mid-week game, the harsh shadows cast by the steelwork became even more exaggerated. A goal from Martin O'Neill continued the fine start and when John McGovern scored twice against Coventry in a 4-1 win, (the first double for the player in nine years), the early league table had the Reds top of the pile.

By the time Forest travelled to Blackburn Rovers for the first leg of the first round League Cup game, the management had already made up their minds that Asa Hartford was not their type of player. Peter Taylor commented on the player: "I wished that I had listened to Malcolm Allison who had told me that the player only 'lends you the ball'. The player was blinkered, he could only see twenty yards, his passes were accurate, but too short."

By now opposing teams were switched on to Robbo and Forest needed the option to switch play quicker. Hartford himself said that he was struggling to find space between Frank Gray and John Robertson.

When the players reached Ewood Park, they were told the news, skipper McGovern was not surprised.

Forest were able to recoup their money though, Brian Clough contacted Gordon Lee, the Everton Manager (who had been trying to sign Hartford when he joined the Reds) and told him he was now available. As Taylor explained it: "We were decisive, when we realised we had made a mistake, we acted." Once again though, Forest were left with a bare minimum squad of fourteen players, to compete on four fronts. This had been a significant factor in not retaining the league title the previous season.

As Forest began their attempt to win the League Cup for a third successive season, they came up against an old friend in Duncan McKenzie, a fine player whose career seemed to be on a downward path at Third Division Blackburn Rovers. After a hard fought away draw, the Reds progressed through comfortably, after a 6-1 second leg home victory, that saw Frank Gray net his first goal for the club. The signing of Gray had been criticised by some, after all, he was considered to be far more proficient going forward than he was at defending.
Preceding the thrashing of Blackburn, the Reds had travelled to the Hawthorns to face West Brom and produced perhaps their best league performance since Old Trafford in December 1977. They were simply awesome, despite going behind early in the game. Leading 3-1, they weren't even bothered by referee Neil Midgley chalking off a thirty yarder from Burns that entered the net as he blew for half-time. The subsequent decline in league form after this 5-1 victory was inexplicable.

The home draw with Leeds might have appeared insignificant, but events happening off the pitch were to have an effect on the club. Tony Woodcock had been 'tapped up' before the season had started, to see if he was interested about following Kevin Keegan to Germany. Cologne, who Forest had beaten on the way to winning the European Cup, were the team making overtures to the player. Woodcock was interested, and it was after the home game against United that he left for Germany with his agent to tie up the details. Although this sort of behaviour was common in football, it was also illegal and when Woodcock bumped into a Forest committee member Geoffrey McPherson at the airport, he was forced to lie and say he was just meeting a friend.

Losing 3-1 to lowly Norwich was not the best way to prepare for your defence of the European Cup. Fate decreed that their first round opponents in this competition, would again be Swedish, Oesters Vaxjo who had been surprise winners of the Swedish title. They were to prove to be unexpectedly tough opposition. A lowly crowd of only 21,000 turned up for the

IAN BOWYER
NOTTINGHAM FOREST
FOREST
adidas

Another 8 pages of our 'CAPTAINS' booklet
SHOOT!
20p
22nd SEPTEMBER, 1979
CAN FOREST RETAIN THE EUROPEAN CUP?
PREVIEWS OF FIRST ROUND EURO~TIES
Plus
IN COLOUR
MAN. CITY
TEAM GROUP
+Club Spotlight
FOCUS ON
FRANK McGARVEY
Liverpool
Forest winger John Robertson talks about the European Cup campaign inside.
Australia — 45c; New Zealand — 45c; South Africa — 45c; Malaysia — $1.30; Italy — L.800; Denmark — Kr.6.00; Canada — 55c.

FOREST Win Adidas European Team of the Year award

Europe's best line-up with their awards. From left to right: Laszlo Fekete (Silver Boot), Thomas Mavros (Silver Boot), Kees Kist (Golden Boot), Ruud Krol (who received the Ajax trophy), Andre Bord (the Strasbourg President) and Forest's Trevor Francis.

TREVOR FRANCIS received a trophy for Nottingham Forest this season before he had played a League game for them.

The England midfield star, earlier troubled by a deep-rooted groin injury, was at a special ceremony in the famous Lido Night Club in Paris recently with Forest chairman Stuart Dryden and secretary Ken Smales to collect the France Football/Adidas European Team of the Year award on behalf of the club.

The trophy is awarded for performances throughout the whole of last season, in both domestic League and European competition.

This year Forest, the current European Cup holders, finished ahead of Ajax Amsterdam, with French Champions Strasbourg third.

It was the second year in succession that an English club had carried off the award.

Last season it was Liverpool, who had previously won it in 1976.

The only other British clubs to have won the trophy were Celtic in 1970 and Arsenal, who tied with Ajax in 1971.

Apart from the clubs, Europe's top scorers were also honoured by France Football/Adidas in Paris.

Winner of the superb Golden Boot for 1979 was Kees Kist of AZ Alkmar 67.

Kees, the top scorer in the Dutch League for the past two seasons is the first player from that country to win the award.

Greek international Thomas Mavros (AEK Athens) and Laszlo Fekete of Ujpest Dosza and Hungary tied for second place and won the Silver Shoe trophy.

FRANCE-FOOTBALL/ ADIDAS AWARDS

How The Clubs Finished

		Points
1	NOTTINGHAM FOREST	27
2	AJAX AMSTERDAM	21
3	STRASBOURG	19
4	SERVETTE	17
	LIVERPOOL	17
	RANGERS	17
7	BARCELONA	16
	W.B.A.	16
	PORTO	16
10	MONCHENGLADBACH	15
	ANDERLECHT	15
	BEVEREN	15
	MILAN AC	15
	BENFICA	15

THE TOP SCORERS

		Goals
1	KIST (AZ 67)	34
2	MAVROS (AEK)	31
	FEKETE (Ujpest)	31
4	KRANKL (Barcelona)	29
5	ALBERT (Beveren)	28
6	BIANCHI (Paris SG)	27
	FAZEKAS (Ujpest)	27
	GNOMES (Porto)	27
9	CLARKE (Ajax)	26
10	GEELS (Anderlecht)	25
	NENE (Benfica)	25

Francis stoops to head Forest's winning goal in last season's European Cup Final against Malmo.

Burns on the spot to open the scoring.

ROUND ONE FIRST LEG...
Wednesday 19th Sept. 1979
Forest 2
Oesters Vaxjo 0

Woodcock fires home the second goal from close range.

Our camera captures Garry Birtles in two aerial challenges with the Oesters Vaxjo defence.

Viv Anderson stands firm in this challenge.

ROUND ONE SECOND LEG...
Wednesday 3rd Oct. 1979
Oesters Vaxjo 1
Forest 1

Gary Mills goes close in Sweden.

FOREST EASE PAST OESTERS...

FOCUS ON

GARRY BIRTLES

NOTTINGHAM FOREST

FULL NAME: Garry Birtles
BIRTHPLACE: Nottingham
BIRTHDATE: 27th June, 1956
HEIGHT: 6ft 1in
WEIGHT: 11st 6lbs
PREVIOUS CLUBS: None
MARRIED: Yes to Sandra
CHILDREN: No
CAR: Capri 2000
FAVOURITE PLAYER: Former Manchester United star, George Best
FAVOURITE OTHER TEAM: Manchester United
MOST DIFFICULT OPPONENT: Bristol City defender, Norman Hunter
MOST MEMORABLE MATCH: Beating Liverpool in the first-leg of this season's European Cup
BIGGEST THRILL: Being picked for my First Division debut
BIGGEST DISAPPOINTMENT: Being turned down by Aston Villa at the age of 15
BEST COUNTRY VISITED: Austria
FAVOURITE FOOD: Steak
MISCELLANEOUS LIKES: Squash and good friends
MISCELLANEOUS DISLIKES: Losing and false people
FAVOURITE T.V. SHOWS: Monty Python's Flying Circus and any programme which stars Leonard Rossiter
FAVOURITE SINGERS: Alice Cooper, David Bowie and Bryan Ferry
FAVOURITE ACTOR/ACTRESS: Clint Eastwood and Susan George
BEST FRIEND: Digby, my Pyrenean Mountain Dog
BIGGEST INFLUENCE ON CAREER: My wife and family, Geoff Barrowcliff and Long Eaton Rovers
BIGGEST DRAG IN SOCCER: When I'm not scoring goals
INTERNATIONAL HONOURS: None yet
PERSONAL AMBITION: To be happy and honest in everything I do
PROFESSIONAL AMBITION: To keep scoring goals for Nottingham Forest
IF YOU WEREN'T A FOOTBALLER, WHAT DO YOU THINK YOU'D BE? A floor layer, my profession before I joined Forest
WHICH PERSON IN THE WORLD WOULD YOU MOST LIKE TO MEET? Pop star Alice Cooper or tennis player Jimmy Connors

Garry Birtles

Garry Birtles fires under the body of Ray Clemence, the Liverpool keeper.

Burns in action against Leeds United.

ACTION FROM THE CITY GROUND!

Harvey, Leeds keeper saves his team once more.

Martin O'Neill crashes home the winner against Stoke City.

home leg, a combination of increased prices, disappointment at the draw and confidence of progression contributed to this. The foul weather made it unpleasant for fans sitting in the lower east stand, still without a roof. The Reds struggled to overcome their dogged visitors and it wasn't until the 62th minute that Ian Bowyer broke the deadlock, quickly followed by a second from the same player, although this shot benefited from a wicked deflection.

Further progress was made in the League Cup, 3-1 at the expense of Middlesbrough, before the visit of Liverpool to the City Ground. Injuries already meant that Clough had to call on John O'Hare and once again he didn't let anyone down, as Forest won 1-0 thanks to a thirty fifth minute winner from Birtles.

If Forest had hoped for a nice easy stroll through to next round of the European Cup, they were in for a shock, as the Swedish team battered them during the return leg, and when an untypical slip by Viv Anderson presented them with a goal, it really was backs to the wall. Luckily, Gary Mills who had come on as an early substitute for O'Neill, fashioned a goal for Woodcock, and Forest were then able to see out time.

The big story however came off the pitch, when in an explosive press conference, seemingly out of no-where, Brian Clough attacked the Forest Committee saying: "I have been having a running battle with the Forest hierarchy since the day I arrived. If they don't think that Peter Taylor and I are handling their affairs to the best of our ability, I suggest they get someone else. If they wish to shake hands and part company, they can do so with pleasure. I've never been in love with directors, our chairman Stuart Dryden is fantastic, but he is outnumbered. Unfortunately the game attracts a certain percentage of people who are nobodies in their own walk of life and want to become somebodies through football."

Football League chairman Jack Dunnett presents an award to the managerial duo celebrating the 42 game unbeaten run.

The manager couldn't have predicted the storm that this statement produced. He had always been one to needle the directors, but on this occasion it looked as if he might have gone too far. After a committee meeting he was placed in the embarrassing position of having to apologise to save his job, so he did: "What I said was unbefitting for a manager of a successful club, I bitterly regret what I said, and I am just glad it's all over."

As a side note, on the day that Forest progressed in Europe, Liverpool were knocked out of the same competition by Dynamo Tbilisi after conceding three second half goals.

There was the welcome sight of Trevor Francis returning to the line-up against Wolves and he didn't waste any time, scoring in a regulation 3-1 win. In fact Forest were to return to the top of the table after drawing at Stoke, but a run of away defeats was soon to impact on the league position.

The 5-2 victory over Bolton on the 20th October meant that Forest had completed fifty home league games in a row unbeaten, a run stretching back to the 1-0 home defeat to Cardiff City in Division Two, that at the time, looked to have scuppered any promotion hopes.

Forest had drawn Arges Pitesti the Rumanian champions in the second round of the European Cup, with the first leg again at home. They came with a reputation for rugged play and didn't disappoint as they amassed 31 free kicks and a sending off. Despite scoring two early goals, Forest were unable to achieve any sort of rhythm and couldn't add to their total, but there was total confidence in the camp that they could handle them in the second leg and this proved to be so. The match was an afternoon kick off, as Arges did not have floodlights and the result was a comfortable 2-1 victory. In fact the main fear for the players was expressed by Larry Lloyd, who on hearing that Arges played in Trannsylvania, hoped that the players wouldn't come across any Draculas! Brian Clough declared that Pitesti was, 'like Middlesbrough, but without the glamour'.

Still on the trail of a third League Cup trophy, the Reds travelled to Bristol City, without Brian Clough, who was on holiday. On the journey down, Peter Taylor instructed Albert the coach driver to pull in at the motorway services just past Birmingham. After a few minutes, the cries came up asking: "What are we waiting for?" "We've arranged to meet Trevor Francis here," said Taylor. "He is on the back here with us playing cards," came the reply followed by laughter. "Well he has been as quiet today as he was at Norwich," came back Taylor.

The Reds' performance against Bristol was considered so poor, that the headline in the Daily Express the following day was, 'Sagging European Champions'. Ken Smales, who didn't often enter the dressing room, reported what he had witnessed after that game. Peter Taylor had laid into the players saying: "You've got a nice house Robbo, so have you John, do you know how you got them? Because we've played possession football for two years."

There was a school of thought put about by several players, that performances often dropped off when Clough wasn't there, Colin Barrett particularly was of this opinion: "As far as I was concerned, Clough was the main man, I didn't listen to Taylor at all."

There was exciting news off the pitch as Forest's debut single, 'We've got the whole world in our hands', hit number one in the Dutch pop charts, only eighteen months after it was first released!

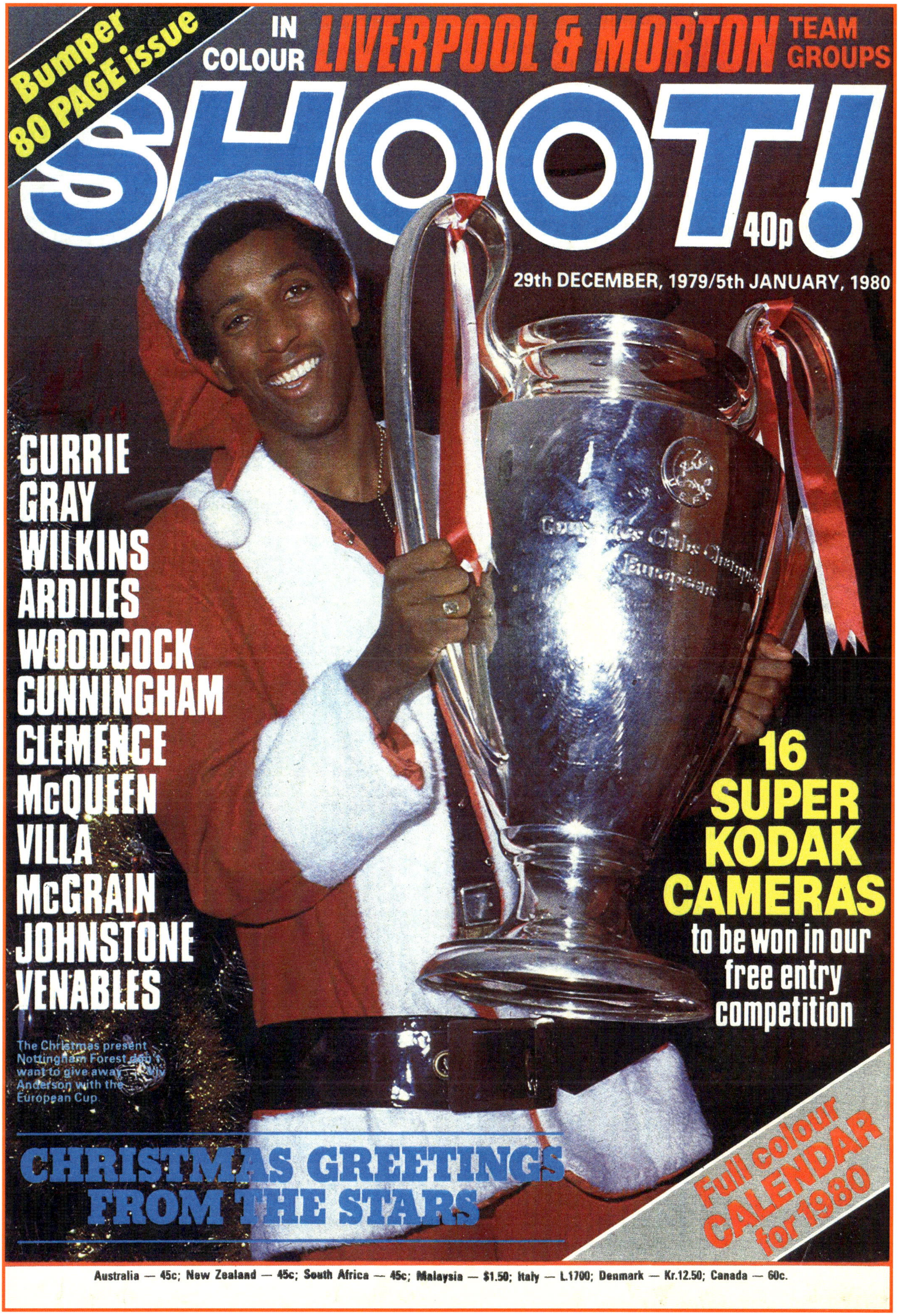
Bumper
80 PAGE issue
IN COLOUR
LIVERPOOL & MORTON
TEAM GROUPS
SHOOT!
40p
29th DECEMBER, 1979/5th JANUARY, 1980
CURRIE
GRAY
WILKINS
ARDILES
WOODCOCK
CUNNINGHAM
CLEMENCE
McQUEEN
VILLA
McGRAIN
JOHNSTONE
VENABLES
The Christmas present
Nottingham Forest
want to give away
Anderson with the
European Cup.
16
SUPER
KODAK
CAMERAS
to be won in our
free entry
competition
CHRISTMAS GREETINGS
FROM THE STARS
Full colour
CALENDAR
for 1980
Australia — 45c; New Zealand — 45c; South Africa — 45c; Malaysia — $1.50; Italy — L.1700; Denmark — Kr.12.50; Canada — 60c.

This fine left foot effort from Garry Birtles, goes under the body of Bradshaw from Wolves.

FOOTBALL POST

SATURDAY NOVEMBER 17TH, 1979

BRIGHTON END THE REDS' LONG UNBEATEN HOME RUN!

Woodcock adds the second against Bolton.

Moseley, the Brighton keeper guesses correctly and keeps out this penalty from John Robertson.

A fine study in concentration as Trevor Francis curls a beauty in to the Ipswich net.

In a sign of further developing defensive frailties, Forest suffered their worst defeat in three years, going down 4-1 to Southampton and this was followed by another 4-1 defeat in their next away game to hated rivals Derby, who up until that game couldn't buy a goal.

In between those two performances, Forest knocked out Bristol City in the League Cup replay, before Brighton became the unlikely team to lower the club's colours for the first time in three years at a home league game. Without an away win, Brighton left with a 1-0 win courtesy of a Gerry Ryan goal, but Forest missed the chance to keep their record going when John Robertson missed a late penalty. This also proved to be Tony Woodcock's final game for the club, two days later he signed for Cologne, Forest receiving £650,000 for a player who had been available for only £10,000 three years previously. Woodcock's record was 176 appearances and 62 goals.

Although the squad was now beginning to look really threadbare, they reached the semi-finals of the League Cup, after disposing of Second Division West Ham United, after yet another replay had added an unnecessary burden on a small squad. The manager continued to moan about the demands on his players, but it was he who had dragged them all the way down to Plymouth, for a testimonial game, so he didn't really have a point. The squad was desperate for re-enforcements, the club had the money and the lure of European football, so the fans were entitled to ask questions.

Peter Taylor had long fancied Peter Ward at Brighton to be Woodcock's replacement. After Brighton had initially seemed open to a deal, they then began asking for 'silly money'. Looking back, Peter Taylor remembered this as perhaps the first moment that Clough had begun to doubt his judgement: "When he said are you sure Pete? I was floored and insulted." Anyway the deal didn't go through, so the pair turned their attention elsewhere.

Despite a congested fixture list, the club managed to squeeze in another lucrative trip to Cairo, where they had originally been scheduled to play two games, but in the event they only played one, allowing the players not only extra rest, but the chance of some time off sightseeing. The club and it's supporters were put under a severe media spotlight after Arsenal goalkeeper Pat Jennings was hit by a dart thrown from the Trent End. The Forest supporters to their credit, were quick to point out the culprit and this prompt action probably saved the club from punishment.

There was finally activity on the recruitment front. Stan Bowles was one player who did deserve to be called a maverick. Supremely skilled, it was usually his off the pitch persona that counted against him. Stan liked a drink, liked to bet and liked the ladies. Not bad you might think, but perhaps not the best attributes for a footballer no matter how skilful. Peter Taylor who was renowned for the thoroughness of the checks he made into a player's background, didn't have to do much digging on this occasion. Taylor was prepared to accept one vice if the player was honest about it, but three!

Stan tells the story about how the transfer came about: "I was sitting at home when the chairman of QPR, Jim Gregory rang. How would you fancy a transfer he said, not really I replied, I was hanging on for a testimonial. You might be interested if you know who it is, Tottenham, Arsenal I said, no it's Old Big Head and his mate, well I'd better go and see them I said." So the unlikely alliance was made. Stan thought he might have a chance of picking up a medal and Forest were introducing more flair to a team that looked to have gone stale.

The same week that the Bowles transfer went through, Martin O'Neill was placed in an impossible position by the management. Forest wanted to sign Mick Ferguson, the Coventry City centre forward, a player very much in the Peter Withe mould, and as part of the deal, City had enquired about O'Neill and were surprised when they were told he was available. Ferguson came over to Nottingham to discuss terms, the Coventry manager met O'Neill and it looked as if time was being called on the popular Irishman's career at the City Ground. All of a sudden, Clough did a complete about turn, told Coventry that Forest wouldn't be completing the signing of Ferguson and that there was no way O'Neill would be leaving. In a statement to the press

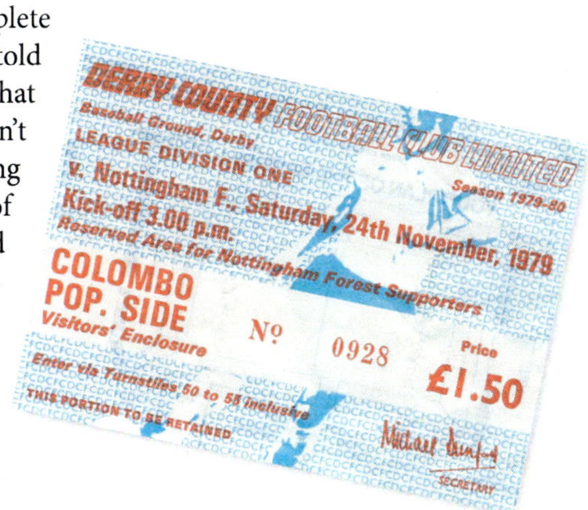

Robertson drives this effort against the upright!

ROUND TWO FIRST LEG...
Wednesday 24th Oct. 1979
Forest 2
Arges Pitesti 0

Kenny Burns just fails to add to the Reds' lead.

Goal number one for Tony Woodcock.

Birtles adds the second goal five minutes later,

ROUND TWO SECOND LEG...
Wednesday 7th Nov. 1979
Arges Pitesti 1
Forest 2

John Robertson in action in Romania.

Birtles knocks home from close range.

Ian Bowyer scores early against Arges.

BOWYER AND BIRTLES STRIKE!

FOREST 6
BLACKBURN 1

No 1: Bowyer.

No 2: Robertson.

No 3: Bowyer.

FOREST 3
BRISTOL CITY 0

O'Neill scores against Bristol City.

THREE TIME

FOREST 3
WEST HAM 0

Martin O'Neill completes the rout of the Hammers.

No 4: Gray.

No 5: Woodcock.

No 6: Robertson.

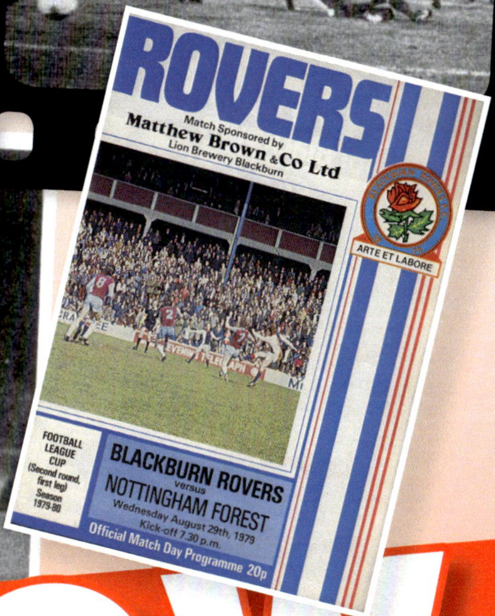

Viv Anderson left foot goal against Bristol.

S IN A ROW

O'Hare opens the scoring against West Ham.

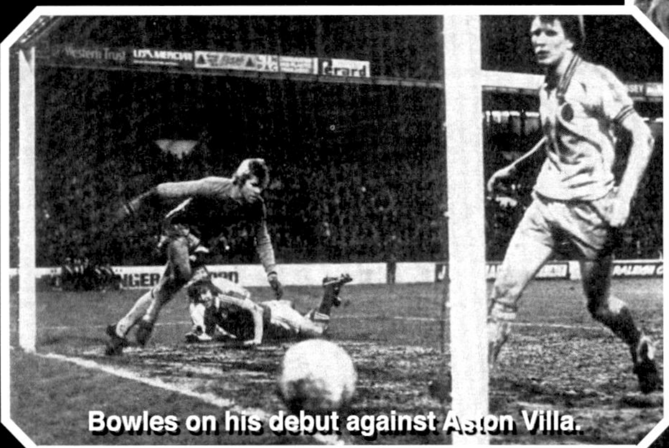

Bowles on his debut against Aston Villa.

Peter Shilton scrambles to keep out this effort from Stapleton of Arsenal.

More action from the Villa game.

Dave Needham just beats O'Neill to the ball and fires home against West Brom.

A fine action shot of Birtles and Lloyd challenging at a corner kick.

What a MUD bath...

Stan Bowles pictured outside the City Ground, after signing for Nottingham Forest.

Clough said: "I am concerned about the number of players leaving this club, it has to stop." So O'Neill was staying, still in the team, whilst Ferguson managed to negotiate himself a wage rise with Coventry. Just another day in the often bizarre world of Brian Clough. The next day Forest dropped to an unheard of thirteenth place, after a 3-0 defeat at Old Trafford, a game that was littered with defensive errors, before Stan Bowles made a scoring home debut in the Boxing Day victory over Aston Villa. Stan's goal was an unlikely header. Bowles then scored for the second successive game as Coventry were well beaten 3-0.

Forest began their FA Cup campaign with a very tricky looking tie at Elland Road against Leeds United. In fact it turned out to be just the opposite, the team returning from Yorkshire with a 4-1 win under their belts.

The draw for the fourth round was to pit them against Liverpool in Nottingham. This was to come only three days after the two teams would meet at the same venue in the first leg of the League Cup semi-final, meaning a total of at least four games between the arch rivals in only a month.

Meanwhile, Brian Clough showed his support and loyalty for his friend and Forest Chairman Stuart Dryden, as he was in court accused of financial irregularities at the Post Office that he ran. Even as a guilty verdict was passed, the manager was there beside his friend.

Peter Taylor had tried to sign Charlie George whilst the player was still at Derby. Understandably the Rams were worried about the fans' reaction if they let him go to their closest rivals, but when Taylor heard that the player might be available from Southampton, who Derby had previously sold him to, they moved swiftly. Charlie had missed many months with an injury, so Forest were reluctant to splash out £500,000 without testing the player's fitness. An initial month's loan deal was arranged and Charlie made his debut in the league encounter at Elland Road, in an exciting looking Forest outfit. Flair players Bowles and George augmenting Francis, Birtles and Robertson. John McGovern himself was surprised at these particular two additions to the squad. He remembers them both as 'good lads, no trouble', but not the type of player he thought they needed at that time. It seemed to be the defence that needed looking at.

The club had been asked by UEFA to find time for a two legged Super Cup, to be played between the winners of the two major European competitions, Forest and Barcelona. The club were obviously keen, but with a backlog of fixtures, finding a date was a problem. In the end the second leg had to be played when England were on international duty, and several players had to be given permission to miss them.

Before this however, there was the little matter of two home encounters against Liverpool and two sell out games.

The first, the League Cup semi-final, was a tense affair, finally settled in Forest's favour by a last minute penalty kick from Robertson. The FA Cup tie on the Saturday was a different story, Liverpool fully deserving their 2-0 win.

The way was now clear for the showdown with Barcelona. Heavy rain in the run up, meant that there was a real possibility of the game being postponed. In the end, heroic efforts meant the game could go ahead, but it was on a mud bath that was not conducive to the style of either team. Charlie George scored the only goal with a fine header, although the Reds did have opportunities to extend their lead. The only disappointing aspect of the evening was the size of the crowd, less than 24,000 turned up, although the club reported record programme sales of 15,000.

In preparation for the game, Barcelona had asked if they could use Forest training facilities. Martin O'Neill remembers the astonishment of the Spaniards when they had to use the public park that passed for the training ground of the European champions.

If Forest were to reach Wembley again in the League Cup, they were to be punished by a reduction in the number of tickets allocated to them. In the usual rush for tickets for the final the previous season, some had found their way on to the 'black market'. Subsequent to this, Mr T Parkinson, of the Old General Pub had complained to the league and this in turn led to the punishment.

Six days after the Super Cup first leg, it was a very different atmosphere that greeted the players of Nottingham Forest as they stepped out at the Nou Camp, Barcelona, before 90,000 spectators. As was usual, Forest had been written off before they had even arrived in Spain. Brian Clough was bemused: "According to some, I don't know why were even boarding the

LEAGUE CUP SEMI FINAL

NOTTINGHAM FOREST v LIVERPOOL

FIRST LEG 1-0

Forest try and penetrate the Liverpool defence.

Francis tries to round Clemence.

The wall stands firm as Case fires in this free kick.

Robbo keeps his nerve to outwit Clemence with this last minute winner.

SECOND LEG 1-1

AGG. SCORE 2-1

No room for Dalglish with this close attention from Ian Bowyer.

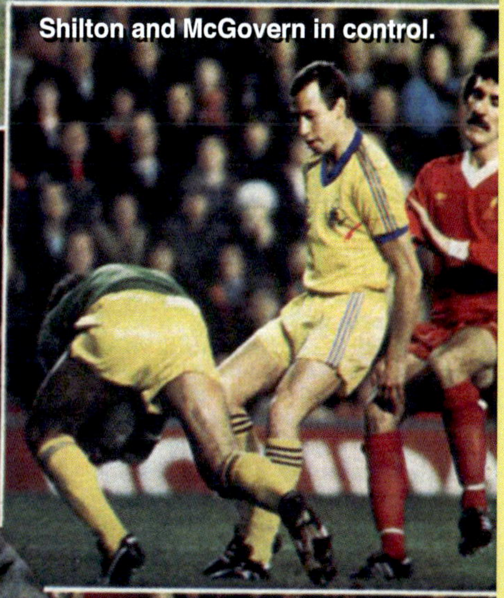

Shilton and McGovern in control.

Peter Taylor and Brian Clough are so proud of their players.

BARCELONA

SUPER FOREST

European Champions NOTTINGHAM FOREST recently added the European Super Cup to their collection when they beat Barcelona over two legs. Charlie George (left, partly hidden) scored the only goal at the City Ground

SUPER CUP FIRST LEG 1-0

Kenny Burns goes close.

Charlie George heads home.

John McGovern points out it will be a third trip to Wembley, as the players are pictured in the Anfield dressing room, after completing the 2 - 1 aggregate win over Liverpool in the League Cup semi-final.

plane." And as usual, the players of Nottingham Forest rammed the critics comments back down their throats. It seemed as if they would never learn. How much more would the club have to achieve before they received the true acclaim that was theirs?

In an exciting game, Kenny Burns equalised after Barcelona had gone ahead from the penalty spot. The game finished in a draw, but it could have been even better, the usually reliable John Robertson missed from the spot after Bowles had been tripped. The Barca fans were gracious in defeat, applauding the players off. John McGovern who had been rested for the first leg, vividly remembers the pride of the players as they made their way to the bus after the game, through a mass of Barcelona fans chanting 'Forest'.

Stan Bowles had joined Forest to win medals and he hadn't had to wait long. The player was proudly photographed on the pitch, with the first and as it turned out, the only one of his career.

The following Saturday's 0-0 draw with Bristol City was an anti-climax for most, but to a young Steve Hodge, an apprentice, from a Forest supporting family, it was memorable occasion, as the manager told him to take the Super Cup out and parade it around the ground.

The away game in Barcelona had proved to be the fourth and last appearance in the Garibaldi for Charlie George. The way the fixtures had fallen meant that the management felt they needed him to stay for a further month, before they made their mind up on his fitness. George initially refused and by the time he had changed his mind, Clough had changed his, and there was no way back for the player.

Liverpool were super confident about turning round the one goal deficit in the second leg of the League Cup. Forest were again down to the bare bones, with no George, cup tied Bowles or injured Francis, they once more dug deep and in fact took the game to Liverpool more than they had recently. With O'Neill playing up front alongside Birtles, the encounter was evenly matched. Forest went ahead after only 23 minutes, when Clemence in the Liverpool goal pulled down O'Neill. Robertson nervelessly tucked away the penalty despite missing one the previous week in Barcelona. Robbo remembers those penalty duels against Ray Clemence: "It got to the stage when it was just a battle of wits. He always seemed to guess the right way, but I always managed to beat him. In that semi-final I thought I had missed it, but it just squeezed in." Despite conceding a late equaliser, Forest held on to secure a 2-1 aggregate victory.

With another trip to Wembley now booked, the games continued to come thick and fast, including the resumption of the European Cup, where the Reds had been drawn against Dynamo Berlin from East Germany.

The difference between the team's home and away form was now like chalk and cheese. If the players had been able to find any form on the road, they would have been challenging for the title. As it was, the team could thump Manchester City and Tottenham 4-0, whilst losing alternate games 1-0 away at Bolton and Brighton. Were the players having trouble getting 'up' for mundane matches? Surely a team capable of going toe to toe at Liverpool and Barcelona should be capable of at least grinding out a draw at Burnden Park.

Dynamo Berlin at home seemed eminently winnable. The Germans were flying straight in for the game and then leaving immediately afterwards. Bryn Gunn came in for a rare start, replacing the suspended Anderson, but otherwise it was a full strength team. Berlin had the giant 6'7" Bodo Rudwaleit in goal, and a useful forward in Hans Riediger, but apart from them, they were very much an unknown quantity. Brian Clough and Ken Smales had made a quick dash over to Berlin to watch them in action, but the manager reported back that he didn't feel there was much to fear.

Did this feeling get through to the players? Because the team produced a tepid performance, rarely threatening the Berlin defence. There was even very little response when they went behind to a goal from Riediger in the 63rd minute and if it wasn't for a smart last minute save from Shilton, the tie could have been out of sight.

Brian Clough was once more called upon to show his confidence about progressing, in an after match interview: "I don't think we can possibly play as badly over there as we have done tonight," he said, with echoes of the bravura he had shown after the Cologne game the previous season.

When Forest lost to Wolves in the League Cup final at Wembley, the season was in danger of falling apart. Larry Lloyd missed the game after picking up too many disciplinary

John McGovern and Juan Asensi

Forest on the attack.

THE REDS CLINCH ANOTHER TROPHY

AS THEY WIN 2-1 ON AGGREGATE, AFTER THE 2ND LEG TIE FINISHES ALL SQUARE IN THE NOU CAMP.

Kenny Burns heads home the equaliser.

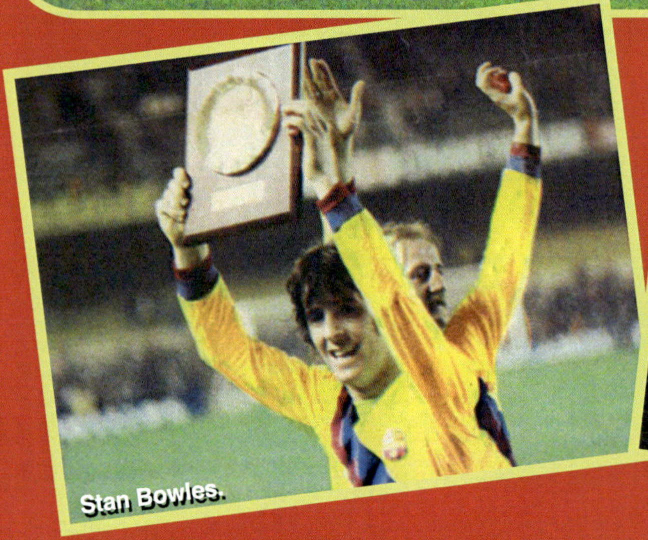

Stan Bowles.

Shilton, George and Burns

NOTTINGHAM FOREST

Back Row L to R: Ian Bowyer, Dave Needham, Trevor Francis, Kenny Burns, Martin O'Neill (hidden), Peter Shilton, Larry Lloyd, Charlie George, John O'Hare.
Front Row L to R: Frank Gray, John Robertson, Garry Birtles, Viv Anderson, Stan Bowles.

Robertson with a free kick.

Garry Birtles flying high.

Last ditch defending by the Germans.

No way through for the Reds.

No luck for Garry Birtles.

ROUND THREE FIRST LEG...
Wednesday 5th March. 1980
Forest 0
Dynamo Berlin 1

LEAGUE CUP FINAL 15TH MARCH ...WEMBLEY STADIUM

WEMBLEY WOE'S

IT may not have been the best of games, but Wolves fans won't care too much. Their team beat Nottingham Forest 1-0 in the League Cup Final and that's all that really matters.

The youth team proudly show off the cup they won in Germany. A young Steve Sutton holds the trophy.

points, although the club did take the matter to appeal, saying that in light of the number of games he played his record was good, but the committee, although understanding the situation, were unable to overturn the decision.

Wolves had more luck however. Andy Gray, their talismanic centre forward was also due to miss the game, but the Football Association raised no objection when they hurriedly re-arranged a fixture so that he would miss that game instead.

Wolves' manager John Barnwell also pulled a stroke when he booked the hotel that Forest usually stopped at when they went to Wembley. Clough in return arranged for a coach party including players' wives and children to stop there for lunch on the way to the game, causing the Wolves' manager to demand that the restaurant be sectioned off. It got worse, at Wembley, Barnwell was determined to get his own back, making Brian Clough and his team wait extra long in the players' tunnel, whilst he held his Wolves squad back. As Barnwell admitted, the effect was somewhat lost when his team finally emerged to find that Brian Clough wasn't standing there, he had given the honour of leading the team out to veteran trainer Jimmy Gordon, whilst he and Taylor had already made their way to their pitch side seats.

John Barnwell was to have the last laugh though, his team won the cup after a comical collision between Shilton and Lloyds' stand in, Dave Needham, had left Andy Gray with an unguarded net to fire into.

In truth Forest were the better side but couldn't score. Trevor Francis was used as an unfair scapegoat, he was again forced to play wide right, though, hadn't he scored the winning goal in Munich from that position? In reality the player was unhappy, within the Forest team, the position was considered to be the graveyard role, due to the team's preference for using the other wing and the skills of Robertson.

On the Boeing 737 taking the players and officials to Berlin for the second leg of the European Cup, nerves were already tight, many on board didn't like flying, particularly the manager who had to have a 'couple' to help. So when the pilot announced that the autopilot had failed and that he would have to fly the plane manually, there was a collective groan, after all, the Munich air crash in 1958 was still fresh in the memory. Anyway the team arrived safely, but there would still be red tape at customs to navigate. Firstly, German officials wanted to know why Kenneth Burns who was on the passenger manifest was not there. Secretary Ken Smales had to explain that because he was suspended, he had been left behind in Nottingham, Then John Robertson was pulled to one side and asked why he was bringing subversive literature into the country, Robbo can't remember now what the title of the book was, but it was confiscated.

Forest had a mountain to climb. Records showed that no other team in the history of the European Cup had lost a home first leg and still gone through. Several hundred Reds' supporters made the trip, those on coaches were dropped off in the Eastern Zone and given half a day to look around. Back then Communist Eastern Europe, really was something else. Shops that had window displays, but once inside, no products, just an area where you put your name on a list, in case a fridge or something similar might become available. It was grey, it was dark and more than anything it was COLD. Many players, including Larry Lloyd said it was the coldest they had ever experienced when playing football.

At the ground, Peter Taylor went through his usual act, relaxing the players, threatening to throw Robbo's shoes over the Wall, picking holes in the opposition. After watching the Dynamo players warming up, he returned to the dressing room to declare that they: "Were scared to death, like zombies. If there was a Ladbrokes here, I would get a bet on."

Before the match, Clough pulled Trevor Francis to one side: "Now where would you like to play?" "Up front," the player replied, and he then went on to justify this decision with two first half goals, complimented by a penalty from Robertson, that turned the tie on it's head. Viv Anderson says that the Berlin game was the team's greatest performance, adding that: "We were on the floor before it."

Back to mundane league matters, where the outside hopes of qualifying for Europe through league position, were finally extinguished after a 3-2 loss away at Aston Villa. It was 100% clear, that the club must now win the European Cup.

Only Ajax of Amsterdam stood between Forest and another European Cup final. Once again they were given the least favoured home leg first. Ajax were not the same team that had stormed through Europe in the early 70's, but there was still plenty of talent such as Ruud Krol and Soren Lerby, to ensure that they were still a force to be reckoned with.

Forest and in particular Francis came out quickly. Sharply constructed attacks put the Dutch visitors on the back foot, and they rarely looked capable of even getting out of their own half. Almost constant pressure finally brought it's reward in the 33rd minute. Birtles and Lloyd contested a corner kick, and the ball bounced invitingly for Francis to fire home from

McGovern and Taylor in determined mood.

ROUND THREE SECOND LEG...
Wednesday 19th March. 1980
Dynamo Berlin 1
Forest 3

Trevor Francis pokes home to bring the aggregate score level.

NOTTINGHAM NEWS
No. 18. FRIDAY 21st MARCH, 1979 8p
FANTASTIC FRANCIS FIRES FOREST!!

Robertson scores from the spot...

and then turns away to celebrate...

THE GOALS START FLYING IN!!

Burns scores against Tottenham.

Francis nets against Spurs.

Trevor Francis rises to head in his first against Man City.

Burns nods home against Man City.

The goal that gave Francis his hat-trick against City.

A piledriver from Francis before he went off injured against Palace.

The Reds celebrate as Garry Birtles scores against Southampton.

AS THE RED'S HIT FORM

close range.

The Reds extended their lead fifteen minutes into the second half. Francis chasing what appeared to be lost cause as the ball headed over the line at the Trent End, suddenly managed to hook the ball over his shoulder and on to the hand of Ajax defender Zwamborn.

"Penalty," said the referee. "Goal," shouted the fans as Robbo dispatched the penalty.

There were further chances to extend the lead, but again the Reds were grateful to a smart save from Shilton as they almost fell to an away goal sucker punch.

To the press, Clough put on a confident front that two goals would be enough, whilst in private confiding to local journalist John Lawson, that he would have felt safer with another goal.

Only one league game before the return leg in Amsterdam, and it was a good one. Frank Gray's winner against Derby, helped to ensure that they would be relegated in the same season Forest won the European Cup, sweet revenge for 1972.

Forest were always going to take thousands to the game in Amsterdam. In the end over 8,000 officially made the trip. The game had been transferred to the Olympic Stadium, where the capacity was 65,000. Ajax always did this for big games, as their own stadium surprisingly, was an old fashioned small ground that only accommodated 20,000.

The team arrived in Amsterdam on the Monday before the game and things did not immediately go to plan, when the coach driver taking the team to their hotel firstly got lost, then followed this by taking them to the wrong training ground as well. Brian Clough was then criticised for holding his press conference in a bar, the media thought he was disrespecting them.

Larry Lloyd, player of the year.

Before the game the players followed the usual routine of relaxing and taking in the sights. On this occasion a tour of the Red Light District gave Peter Taylor the chance to try and negotiate a group discount, before the players found a quiet bar to have a few beers. As the clocked ticked past 10.00 o'clock on the eve of the game, Martin O'Neill turned to Brian Clough and said: "I wonder what the Ajax players would make of this, they will all be in bed." "But none of them will be getting any sleep," said the manager.

The game itself was a throwback to when Shilton, Lloyd and Burns were unbeatable. Burns in particular was immense. Lerby pulled one back, but the Reds held firm. The closest Ajax came to equalising was when Francis broke off from the end of wall when facing another Lerby free-kick. Francis shouted: "It's going in," but Shilton flung himself to his left to keep the ball out. It may have been the team's first defeat in a European away leg, but who cared. Later that evening they found out that they would face Hamburg and Kevin Keegan in the final to be played in Madrid on May the 28th.

There were still six league games left to play before the match of the season was to take place. Five clean sheets were to follow, until a final game 3-1 defeat at Molineux brought the curtain down. But it was during the 4-0 rout of Crystal Palace that disaster struck. Trevor Francis whilst sprinting down the right wing, suddenly pulled up and it was clear from the player's reaction that it was serious. He had torn his Achilles tendon and would be out for months, meaning that he had no chance of making the Hamburg game.

On top of this, Stan Bowles was getting restless. He was being picked for the home games, but being left out for the big away games, where the management preferred the more workmanlike Bowyer or O'Neill. Things came to a head when the player asked to see Peter Taylor before the John Robertson testimonial game. Stan thought that the manager didn't rate him either as a player or a person, and that if he couldn't even get in the team for a testimonial game, what future was there for him. Taylor advised him not to do anything rash, but to remember that he was only weeks away from potentially the biggest game of his career, although he didn't go as far as telling him that he would definitely start in Madrid.

The management team were so concerned about the loss of Trevor Francis, that they even thought about pushing Kenny Burns up front, but after experimenting with this against Notts County in the County Cup, they quickly dropped the idea.

A few weeks later, Brian Clough gathered the players around and announced he had a question for them: "Who won two international caps in one day?"

"Larry Lloyd, his fourth and last," he said.

Lloyd who at the age of 32 had long given up on an England recall, had surprisingly been called up for a home international against Wales. It turned out to be a nightmare for the defender who had recently been voted Player of the Year by the Reds' supporters. Not only were England thrashed 4-1, but a crude tackle by Terry Yorath had injured the player's ankle, making him a doubt for the final.

Larry Lloyd was forced to miss the end of season trip to Majorca, staying behind in Nottingham for treatment, however, he wasn't the only player not to travel, Stan Bowles had already made his mind up and walked out on the club, meaning that there was no way back for him. As for Larry, it wasn't looking promising, although the player was determined to play. As the game got closer, the manager wasn't sure. He asked him: "Are you fit?". "Yes boss," came the answer, then the manager kicked him on the ankle. As Larry puts it: "Every time he saw me he kicked me, and I had to smile, even though it hurt like hell."

Missing from the Forest party setting off to Madrid was Trevor Francis, who had been told by Brian Clough not to travel to the game. Francis was gutted, he was part of the team and wanted to support his team mates, but the manager's aversion to having injured players around, meant that he was forced to stay behind, and this incident soured relations between them.

Eighteen year old Gary Mills was told on the Tuesday that he would be in the starting line-up, but because Bowles had

THE EUROPEAN CUP

MARCH…

SEMI FINAL FIRST LEG...
Wednesday 9th April. 1980
Forest 2
Ajax Amsterdam 0

Robbo keeps his cool to slot home this penalty.

Francis on the spot, and the net bulges.

UPPER EXEC"N" EAST C/PARK
FOREST
v
AJAX AMSTERDAM
WEDNESDAY 9TH. APRIL
KICK-OFF 7:30 P.M.
EUROPEAN CUP
SEMI-FINAL 1ST. LEG
ROW 08
SEAT 198
RESERVED SEAT (including V.A.T.)
£7.00
Secretary
THIS TICKET IS VALID FOR THE ABOVE MATCH ON WHATEVER DATE PLAYED
NOTTINGHAM FOREST FOOTBALL CLUB
CITY GROUND NOTTINGHAM NF2 5FJ

Oh so close!!

Another view of the Robertson penalty.

McGovern with Ajax captain Ruud Krol.

Forest in a rare attack on the Ajax goal.

Shilton in control.

It's in Shilt's!..
...But no, the Forest keeper swoops to save .

EVENING POST

No. 31,374 A

FOREST THROUGH TO THE FINAL!!

O'Neill and Bowyer battle for control.

SEMI FINAL Second LEG...
Wednesday 23rd April. 1980
Ajax Amsterdam 1
Forest 0

The players can relax, a job well done, and it's on to Madrid next.

John McGovern battles with Gerry Daly of Derby.

not travelled, the team would only name four substitutes rather than the five permitted.

Unlike most of the other players, Peter Shilton felt he needed to train, he needed to feel the ball. The story of the player finding some grass in Madrid to dive on, is not only outrageous, but true. Along with trainer Jimmy Gordon, Shilton was seen on a roundabout near the team's hotel, going through his pre match routine. The player also, unknown to anyone, was also receiving treatment for a leg injury, that required a pain killing injection shortly before the final.

The coach journey to the stadium was a quiet one. Peter Taylor was pleased, he sensed the players were focused. Forest were underdogs for the final, and privately the management duo were concerned. They had decided to alter their tactics for the first time, stringing five across the midfield and playing with Birtles as a lone striker. But the pressure was on, only a win would keep them in European competition for the following season.

Hamburg also had injury problems of their own. Horst Hrubesch, the giant centre forward nicknamed the 'Heading Monster', hadn't fully recovered from his own injury and was left on the bench. There was also the Keegan factor. The player had been popular and successful in Germany, but he had perhaps surprisingly decided to return to England after just two seasons, and even more surprisingly had signed for Southampton. So there were many neutrals who would have liked a Hamburg victory for him.

What really happened in the tunnel before the game, fact, fiction or embellishment? Did Larry Lloyd really warn Keegan that Burns was mad with him? What we do know for certain is Hamburg came out quickly and had Forest on the backfoot, though Burns did manage to land a couple of heavy challenges on the Brit.

After twenty minutes of German pressure, Forest finally managed to get the ball forward. Robertson in his adopted casual manner collected the ball wide on the left, before injecting some urgency with a sharp pass to Birtles, the player struggled, but managed to lay the ball back, Robertson stretched, shot and the deadly accurate effort beat Kargus in the Hamburg goal. The Reds were one up with their first attack.

With seventy minutes remaining, the Germans weren't about to panic. Back on the attack, they had a goal disallowed when Reimanns' effort was ruled offside, then Burns was booked for yet another foul on Keegan. The combination of rough and tight marking, plus frustration with his team mates had the desired effect, as Keegan dropped deeper and further away from where he was most dangerous.

Half-time. 1-0, it had been one way traffic, but the Forest supporters who made up the majority of the 50,000 crowd were confident, they had seen this scenario played out many times before.

Hamburg couldn't wait any longer, Hrubesch was thrown on and the bombardment intensified. Wave after wave of attack, Burns and Lloyd magnificent, with Shilton looking unbeatable behind.

Half way through the second half, unsung hero John O'Hare replaced Mills, what a reward for the player who had loyally served Brian Clough for thirteen years. The minutes ticked agonisingly by, another Shilton leap to keep out a Kaltz blockbuster. Four minutes to go, Frank Gray couldn't continue, Peter Taylor turned to the bench to look at his options, someone shouted: "Bryn's warming up." "F**k me," said Taylor, "we're

'Carry On' star Barbara Windsor, dropped in to the Jubilee Club.

definitely in trouble now." But Bryn Gunn took the field and earned his place in the club's history as his replacement. Suddenly Birtles broke clear as Hamburg over committed, but the player was exhausted and could not finish. Then the whistle went, it's over, but it's not, the referee was just blowing for an offence, but thirty seconds later it really was. On the touchline, Clough breathed out deeply, one can only imagine the pressure he felt under. Nottingham Forest European Champions 1980.

Post match, Clough planted a kiss on Branko Zebec the Hamburg manager and then declared: "This is probably the greatest moment in my career, I cannot remember being so emotionally involved in a game, it seemed to go on for hours, not just ninety minutes."

Kevin Keegan said: "I thought we had done enough, but the clever thing about Forest is that they make you play to their strengths and then you get picked off by Burns and Lloyd."

The newspaper reports, apart from the local ones obviously, were generally consistent in decrying the defensive way that Forest had played. The fact that they had lost two star attacking players in the build up to the game, held no water. That a club the size of Nottingham Forest had won the European Cup twice seemed to have put the noses of the so called big teams out of joint and they never truly received the recognition that they deserved until many years later.

It was unfortunate though, that the way post match celebrations were handled by the manager, soured the evening for the players. The team were staying at a hotel way outside the city, whilst players wives and girlfriends were local. The manager insisted that the players return as one to their hotel, leaving several players disgruntled. Worse still, after a meal and a few drinks, Clough and Taylor went to bed, leaving the players fuming. Several players including Lloyd and Robertson decided they would go anyway and paid the son of the hotelier to take them into Madrid, and damn the consequences.

As in the previous year, Clough and Taylor decided not to attend the civic reception back in Nottingham, preferring to go away on a family holiday instead. But once more the city of Nottingham turned out in their hundreds of thousands to welcome the boys home, the Market Square was ablaze with colour as a jubilant Larry Lloyd along with his fellow players soaked up the adulation.

Had success in Europe merely papered over the cracks? Or could Clough and Taylor take Forest on to further glory.

FOREST Champion

s of Europe...again

Let the CELEBRATI

Repitió el Nottingham

Hamburgo, un digno rival

Un gol de Robertson y las paradas de Shilton decidieron

as

PEREIRA. CUATRO PARTIDOS DE CASTIGO

RUPEREZ (que no cede) A LA ESPERA DE SU OCASION

ONS begin!!

NOTTINGHAM NEWS
No. 18, 8p

A CHAMPIONS WELCOME HOME...

FOREST

APPEARANCES TEAM LINE-UPS

Aug 18th, A, v Ipswich Town, W, 1-0, Scorer Woodcock, AT 27,237, Shilton, Anderson, Gray, McGovern, Lloyd, Needham, O'Neill, Hartford, Birtles, Woodcock, Robertson.

Aug 22nd, H, v Stoke City, W, 1-0, Scorer O'Neill, AT 26,147, Shilton, Anderson, Gray, McGovern, Lloyd, Needham, O'Neill, Hartford, Birtles, Woodcock, Robertson. SUB Bowyer.

Aug 25th, H, v Coventry City, W, 4-1, Scorers McGovern (2), Woodcock, Robertson (P), AT 23,025, Shilton, Anderson, Gray, McGovern, Lloyd, Burns, O'Neill, Hartford, Birtles, Woodcock, Robertson. SUB Bowyer.

Aug 29th, LC, A, Blackburn Rovers, D, 1-1, Scorer Lloyd, AT 20,458, Shilton, Anderson, Gray, McGovern, Lloyd, Burns, Mills, O'Neill, Bowyer, Woodcock, Robertson.

Sept 1st, A, v West Brom, W, 5-1, Scorers Birtles (3), Lloyd, Gray, AT 26,135, Shilton, Anderson, Gray, McGovern, Lloyd, Burns, O'Neill, Bowyer, Birtles, Woodcock, Robertson.

Sept 5th, LC, H, v Blackburn Rovers, W, 6-1, Scorers Bowyer (2), Robertson (2) (1P), Woodcock, Gray, AT 21,244, Shilton, Anderson, Gray, McGovern, Lloyd, Burns, O'Neill, Bowyer, Birtles, Woodcock, Robertson.

Sept 8th, H, v Leeds United, D, 0-0, AT 26,914, Shilton, Anderson, Gray, McGovern, Lloyd, Burns, O'Neill, Bowyer, Birtles, Woodcock, Robertson.

Sept 15th, A, v Norwich City, L, 1-3, Scorer Woodcock, AT 18,056, Shilton, Anderson, Gray, McGovern, Lloyd, Burns, O'Neill, Bowyer, Birtles, Woodcock, Robertson.

Sept 19th, EC, H, v Oesters Vaxjo, W, 2-0, Scorer Bowyer (2), AT 21,974, Shilton, Anderson, Gray, McGovern, Lloyd, Burns, O'Neill, Bowyer, Birtles, Woodcock, Robertson.

Sept 22nd, A, v Bristol City, D, 1-1, Scorer Mills, AT 22,767, Shilton, Anderson, Gray, McGovern, Lloyd, Burns, Mills, O'Hare, Birtles, Woodcock, Robertson.

Sept 25th, LC, A, v Middlesbrough, W, 3-1, Scorer Woodcock (3), AT 29,869, Shilton, Anderson, Gray, McGovern, Lloyd, Burns, Mills, O'Hare, Birtles, Woodcock, Robertson, SUB O'Neill.

Sept 29th, H, v Liverpool, W, 1-0, Scorer Birtles, AT 28,262, Shilton, Anderson, Gray, McGovern, Lloyd, Burns, O'Neill, O'Hare, Birtles, Woodcock, Robertson.

Oct 3rd, EC, A, v Oesters Vaxjo, D, 1-1, Scorer Woodcock, AT 14,772, Shilton, Anderson, Gray, McGovern, Lloyd, Burns, O'Neill, Mills, Birtles, Woodcock, Robertson. SUB Bowyer.

Oct 6th, H, v Wolverhampton Wanderers, W, 3-1. Scorers Francis, Birtles, Robertson (P), AT 27,569, Shilton, Anderson, Gray, McGovern, Lloyd, Burns, Francis, O'Hare, Birtles, Woodcock, Robertson.

Oct 10th, A, v Stoke City, D, 1-1, Scorer Birtles, AT 28,514, Shilton, Anderson, Gray, McGovern, Lloyd, Burns, Francis, Mills, Birtles, Woodcock, Robertson.

Oct 13th, A, v Manchester City, L, 0-1, AT 41,683, Shilton, Anderson, Gray, McGovern, Lloyd, Burns, Francis, Mills, Birtles, Woodcock, Robertson.

Oct 20th, H, v Bolton Wanderers, W, 5-2, Scorers Anderson, Lloyd, Francis, Woodcock, Robertson (P), AT 24,564, Shilton, Anderson, Gray, McGovern, Lloyd, Burns, Francis, Mills, Birtles, Woodcock, Robertson.
SUB Bowyer.

Oct 24th, EC, H, v Arges Ptesti, W, 2-0, Scorers Birtles, Woodcock, AT 24,828, Shilton, Anderson, Gray, McGovern, Lloyd, Burns, Mills, Bowyer, Birtles, Woodcock, Robertson.

Oct 27th, A, v Tottenham Spur, L, 0-1, AT 49,038, Shilton, Anderson, Gray, McGovern, Lloyd, Burns, Mills,Francis, Birtles, Woodcock, Robertson.

Oct 30th, LC, A, v Bristol City, D, 1-1, Scorer O'Hare, AT 25,695, Shilton, Anderson, Gray, McGovern, Lloyd, Burns, O'Hare,Francis, Birtles, Woodcock, Robertson.

Nov 3rd, H, v Ipswich Town, W, 2-0, Scorer Francis (2), AT 24,593, Shilton, Anderson, Gray, McGovern, Lloyd, Burns, Francis, O'Hare, Birtles, Woodcock, Robertson. SUB Mills.

Nov 7th, EC, A, v Arges Ptesti, W, 2-1, Scorers Bowyer, Birtles, AT 25,000 Shilton, Anderson, Gray, McGovern, Lloyd, Burns, O'Hare, Bowyer, Birtles, Woodcock, Robertson. SUB Mills, Gun.

Nov 10th, A, v Southampton, L, 1-4, Scorer Birtles, AT 22,072, Shilton, Anderson, Gray, McGovern, Lloyd, Burns, Francis, Bowyer, Birtles, Woodcock, Robertson. SUB Needham.

Nov 14th, LC, H, v Bristol City, W, 3-1, Scorers, O'Neill (2) Woodcock, AT 20,462, Shilton, Anderson, Gray, McGovern, Lloyd, Needham, O'Neill, Francis, Birtles, Woodcock, Robertson.

Nov 17th, H, v Brighton, L, 0-1, AT 25,837, Shilton, Anderson, Gray, McGovern, Lloyd, Needham, O'Neill, Francis, Birtles, Woodcock, Robertson. SUB Bowyer.

Nov 24th, A, v Derby County, L, 1-4, Scorer Robertson (P), AT 27,729, Shilton, Anderson, Gray, McGovern, Lloyd, Needham, O'Neill, Mills, Birtles, Francis, Robertson.

Dec 1st, H, v Arsenal, D, 1-1, Scorer Birtles, AT 27,925, Shilton, Anderson, Gray, McGovern, Lloyd, Burns, O'Neill, O'Hare, Birtles, Francis, Robertson.

Dec 4th, LC, A, v West Ham, D, 0-0, AT 35,856, Shilton, Anderson, Gray, Bowyer, Lloyd, Burns, O'Neill, O'Hare, Birtles, Francis, Robertson.

Dec 8th, A, v Crystal Palace, L, 0-1, AT 34,840, Shilton, Anderson, Gray, Bowyer, Lloyd, Burns, O'Neill, O'Hare, Birtles, Francis, Robertson.

Dec 12th, LC, H, v West Ham, W, 3-0, Scorers O'Neill, O'Hare, Birtles, AT 25,462, Shilton, Anderson, Gray, Bowyer, Lloyd, Burns, O'Neill, O'Hare, Birtles, Francis, Robertson.

Dec 22nd, A, v Manchester United, L, 0-3, AT 54,607, Shilton, Anderson, Gray, McGovern, Lloyd, Burns, O'Neill, Bowles, Birtles, Francis, Robertson.

Dec 26th, H, v Aston Villa, W, 2-1, Scorers Bowles, Robertson (P), AT 32,072, Shilton, Anderson, Gray, McGovern, Lloyd, Burns, Bowyer, Bowles, Birtles, Francis, Robertson.

Dec 29th, A, v Coventry City, W, 3-0, Scorers Bowles, Robertson (2) (1P), AT 24,722, Shilton, Anderson, Gray, McGovern, Lloyd, Burns, Francis, Bowles, Birtles, Bowyer, Robertson.

Jan 1st, A, v Everton, L, 0-1, AT 4,622, Shilton, Anderson, Gray, McGovern, Lloyd, Burns, Francis, Bowles, Birtles, Bowyer, Robertson

Jan 5th, FAC, A, v Leeds United, W, 4-1, Scorers Gray, Birtles, Bowyer, Robertson, AT 35,945, Shilton, Anderson, Gray, McGovern, Lloyd, Burns, Francis, Bowles, Birtles, Bowyer, Robertson.

Jan 12th, H, v West Bromwich Albion, W, 3-1, Scorers Anderson, Needham, Francis, AT

1979 - 1980 DIVISION 1 TABLE

TEAMS	P	W	D	L	F	A	W	D	L	F	A	PTS
1 Liverpool FC	42	15	6	0	46	8	10	4	7	35	27	60
2 Manchester U	42	17	3	1	43	8	7	7	7	22	27	58
3 Ipswich T	42	14	4	3	43	13	8	5	8	25	26	53
4 Arsenal	42	8	10	3	24	12	10	6	5	28	24	52
5 Nottingham F	42	16	4	1	44	11	4	4	13	19	32	48
6 Wolverhampton W	42	9	6	6	29	20	10	3	8	29	27	47
7 Aston Villa	42	11	5	5	29	22	5	9	7	22	28	46
8 Southampton	42	14	2	5	53	24	4	7	10	12	29	45
9 Middlesbrough	42	11	7	3	31	14	5	5	11	19	30	44
10 W.B.A	42	9	8	4	37	23	2	11	8	17	27	41
11 Leeds U	42	10	7	4	30	17	3	7	11	16	33	40
12 Norwich C	42	10	8	3	38	30	3	6	12	20	36	40
13 Crystal Palace	42	9	9	3	26	13	3	7	11	15	37	40
14 Tottenham H	42	11	5	5	30	22	4	5	12	22	40	40
15 Coventry C	42	12	2	7	34	24	4	5	12	22	42	39
16 Brighton & H.A	42	8	8	5	25	20	3	7	11	22	37	37
17 Manchester C	42	8	8	5	28	25	4	5	12	15	41	37
18 Stoke C	42	9	4	8	27	26	4	6	11	17	32	36
19 Everton	42	7	7	7	28	25	2	10	9	15	26	35
20 Bristol C	42	6	6	9	22	30	3	7	11	15	36	31
21 Derby Co	42	9	4	8	36	29	2	4	15	11	38	30
22 Bolton W	42	5	11	5	19	21	0	4	17	19	52	25

WHO? WHAT!

FACTFILE

RESULTS LEAGUE TABLE

27,724, Shilton, Anderson, Gray, McGovern, Lloyd, Needham, O'Neill, Bowles, Birtles, Francis, Robertson. SUB Mills.

Jan 19th, A, v Leeds United, W, 2-1, Scorers Francis, Birtles, AT 29,816, Shilton, Anderson, Gray, McGovern, Lloyd, Needham, Francis, George, Birtles, Bowles, Robertson.

Jan 22nd, LC, H, v Liverpool, W, 1-0, Scorer Robertson (P), AT 32,220, Shilton, Anderson, Gray, McGovern, Lloyd, Needham, O'Neill, Bowyer, Birtles, Francis, Robertson.

Jan 26th, FAC, H, v Liverpool, L, 0-2, AT 33,277, Shilton, Anderson, Gray, McGovern, Lloyd, Needham, O'Neill, Bowyer, Birtles, Francis, Robertson. SUB Burns.
Jan 30th, SC, H, v Barcelona, W, 1-0, Scorer George, AT 23,807, Shilton, Anderson, Gray, O'Neill, Lloyd, Burns, Francis, Bowyer, Birtles, George, Robertson.

Feb 5th, SC, A, v Barcelona, D, 1-1, Scorer Burns, AT 90,000, Shilton, Anderson, Gray, McGovern, Lloyd, Burns, Francis, Bowles, Birtles, George, Robertson. SUB O'Neill.

Feb 9th, H, v Bristol City, D, 0-0, AT 23,421, Shilton, Anderson, Gunn, McGovern, Lloyd, Burns,O'Neill, Bowles, Birtles, George, Robertson.

Feb 12th, LC, A, v Liverpool, D, 1-1, Scorer Robertson (P), AT 50,880, Shilton, Anderson, Gray, McGovern, Lloyd, Burns, O'Neill, Mills, Birtles, Bowyer, Robertson.

Feb 16th, H, v Middlesbrough, D, 2-2, Scorers O'Neill, Robertson (P), AT 23,889, Shilton, Anderson, Gray, McGovern, Lloyd, Burns, O'Neill, Bowles, Birtles, Francis, Robertson. SUB Bowyer.

Feb 19th, A, v Liverpool, L, 0-2, AT 45,163, Shilton, Anderson, Gray, McGovern, Lloyd, Burns, O'Neill, Bowyer, Birtles, Francis, Robertson.

Feb 23rd, H, v Manchester City, W, 4-0, Scorers Burns, Francis (3), AT 27,225, Shilton, Anderson, Gray, McGovern, Lloyd, Burns, O'Neill, Bowles, Birtles, Francis, Robertson.
March 1st, A, v Bolton Wanderers, L, 0-1, AT 16,164, Shilton, Gunn, Gray, McGovern, Lloyd, Burns, O'Neill, Bowles, Birtles, Francis, Robertson.

March 5th, EC, H, v Dynamo Berlin, L, 0-1, AT 27,946, Shilton, Gunn, Gray, McGovern, Needham, Burns, O'Neill, Bowles, Birtles, Francis, Robertson.

March 11th, H, v Tottenham Hotspur, W, 4-0, Scorers Burns (2) Francis (2), AT 25,733, Shilton, Anderson, Gray, McGovern, Lloyd, Burns, Francis, Bowles, Birtles, O'Neill, Robertson. SUB Bowyer.

March 15th, LC, N, v Wolverhampton Wanders, L, 0-1, AT 100,000, Shilton, Anderson, Gray, McGovern,Needham, Burns, O'Neill, Bowyer, Birtles, Francis, Robertson.

March 19th, EC, A, v Dynamo Berlin, W, 3-1, Scorers Francis (2) Robertson (P), AT 27,000, Shilton, Anderson, Gray, McGovern, Lloyd, Needham, O'Neill, Bowyer, Birtles, Francis, Robertson.

March 22nd, H, v Southampton, W, 2-0, Scorers Birtles, Robertson (P), AT 27,675, Shilton, Anderson, Gray, McGovern,Lloyd, Burns, O'Neill, Bowles, Birtles, Francis, Robertson.

March 29th, A, v Brighton, L, 0-1, AT 25,128, Shilton, Anderson, Gray, McGovern, Lloyd, Burns, O'Neill, Bowles, Birtles, Francis, Robertson.

April 2nd, H, v Manchester United, W, 2-0, Scorers Birtles, Robertson (P), AT 31,417, Shilton, Anderson, Gray, McGovern,Lloyd, Burns, O'Neill, Bowles, Birtles, Francis, Robertson.

April 5th, A, v Aston Villa, L, 2-3, Scorers Birtles, Bowyer, AT 29,156, Shilton, Anderson, Gray, McGovern, Lloyd, Burns, O'Neill, Bowles, Birtles, Francis, Robertson. SUB Bowyer.

April 9th, EC, H, v Ajax, W, 2-0, Scorers Francis, Robertson (P), AT 31,244, Shilton, Anderson, Gray, McGovern, Lloyd, Burns, O'Neill, Bowles, Birtles, Francis, Robertson.

April 19th, H, v Derby County, W, 1-0, Scorer Gray, AT 32,266, Shilton, Anderson, Gray, McGovern, Lloyd, Needham, O'Neill, Bowles, Birtles, Francis, Robertson.

April 23rd, EC, A, v Ajax, L, 0-1, AT 65,000, Shilton, Anderson, Gray, McGovern, Lloyd, Burns, O'Neill, Bowyer, Birtles, Francis, Robertson.

April 26th, A, v Middlesbrough, D, 0-0, AT 17,021, Shilton, Anderson, Gray, McGovern, Lloyd, Needham, Mills, Bowyer, Birtles, Francis, Robertson.

April 30th, H, v Norwich City, W, 2-0, Scorers Francis (2), AT 21,242, Shilton, Anderson, Gray, McGovern, Lloyd, Burns, Mills, Bowles, Birtles, Francis, Robertson.

May 3rd, H, v Crystal Palace, W, 4-0, Scorers Lloyd, Francis (2), Robertson, AT 24,529, Shilton, Anderson, Gray, McGovern, Lloyd, Burns, O'Neill, Bowles, Birtles, Francis, Robertson. SUB Mills.

May 5th, A, v Arsenal, D, 0-0, AT 34,632, Shilton, Anderson, Gray, McGovern, Lloyd, Burns, O'Neill, Bowyer, Birtles, Mills, Robertson.

May 6th, CC, A, v Notts County, W, 2-1, Scorers O'Hare, Robertson, AT 8,339, Montgomery, Anderson, Gray, Bowyer, Lloyd, Needham, O'Neill, O'Hare, Burns, Bowles, Robertson.

May 9th, H, v Everton, W, 1-0, Scorer Anderson, AT 22,122, Shilton, Anderson, Gray, McGovern, Lloyd, Burns, O'Neill, Bowles, Birtles, Mills, Robertson. SUB Bowyer.

May 12th, A, v Wolverhampton Wanderers, L, 1-3, Scorer O'Neill, AT 21,725, Shilton, Anderson, Gray, McGovern, Lloyd, Burns, O'Neill, Bowyer, Birtles, O'Hare, Robertson. SUB Needham.

May 28th, EC, N, v SV Hamburg, W, 1-0, Scorer Robertson, AT 50,000, Shilton, Anderson, Gray, McGovern, Lloyd, Burns, O'Neill, Bowyer, Birtles, Mills, Robertson. SUB O'Hare, Gunn.

John McGovern and Kenny Burns pictured after the game in Barcelona.

WHERE! WHEN!

SEASON 1980-81

Back Row: L to R: Gary Mills, Ian Bowyer, Garry Birtles, John O'Hare, John Robertson.
Standing: Jimmy Gordon (Trainer),Bryn Gunn, Dave Needham, Peter Shilton, Jim Montgomery, Larry Lloyd, Martin O'Neill, Kenny Burns.
Seated: Trevor Francis, John McGovern, Peter Taylor (Asst. Manager), Brian Clough (Manager), Geoffrey Macpherson (Chairman), Frank Gray, Viv Anderson.

The management clearly thought that there had been major issues with the team during the previous season, despite retaining the European Cup. They had always built their teams from the back, but on many occasions the team had succumbed to inferior opposition, not just conceding goals, but being heavily defeated. Indeed, thirteen away league defeats for a team with such a powerful looking defensive line up was unacceptable.

The first sign of cracks in the team's spirit of unity also appeared, Trevor Francis had been upset about being excluded from all the build up to Madrid, even to the extent of being told to stay away completely. The manager's aversion to having injured players around was well known, but it did seem extreme to not even allow the player to travel to Spain and watch the game, after all he had played a major part in the team getting to the final.

It also appeared as if Garry Birtles had succumbed to flattery whilst away with the England squad for the European Championships. It was well known that when players gathered for international duty, that they often could be unsettled when they heard what other players were earning.

So when a row broke out between the player and the manager, publicly, over whether the player was entitled to ask for extra time off to complete a house move (after all, the player had had no close season, representing England at the European Championships), was it really about this issue, or about contract negotiations, you will have to make your own mind up. Whilst Taylor, although recognizing that Birtles was a fine player, thought that he still had much to learn.

This argument resulted in the player being placed on the transfer list. Peter Taylor remained convinced that Birtles was getting bad advice from his own family, telling him that he was already a superstar. After all, the player had been a late entrant into the professional game and had only completed two seasons. As many Forest players who left the club found out, the system that they played in was suited to them, so when they changed clubs, their form seemed to decline as they were forced to adapt their game.

Viv Anderson himself thought that it, 'just felt different' when they returned in July. Pre-season preparation again wasn't ideal, as the team set off on an exhausting two week tour of North and South America, that included a painful 5-0 thrashing by virtually the national team of Columbia. Inexcusably the players had been expected to drop in and play at high altitude without any preparation whatsoever. This was no way to maintain the team's high reputation.

There were also the usual gripes about bonuses and the daily allowance. When English teams were touring abroad, clubs had a duty to pay the players a little extra. It might seem old fashioned that players who were receiving a decent wage would get this, but if it was supposed to be paid it should be. The PFA had negotiated a standard fee of $10 per day for the players, on top of their usual wage, and whilst everything else was of course sorted for the players, it was none the less embarrassing that they had to keep asking for their money. The squad also held serious discussions amongst themselves about bonuses based on performances in the league and various cup competitions, many felt that they hadn't benefited from the club's success and Clough often seemed to outsmart them on various occasions.

The players' requests for bonuses to be written into their contracts continued right up to the eve of the new season and they were not happy about the amount being offered either. So when without anything being resolved, the players were handed forms about bonus amounts that had not been agreed and told that they could 'take it or leave it', there was mutiny in the air.

However skipper John McGovern believed that they had taken the negotiations as far as they could and would only be spiting themselves if they entered the season with no scheme in place whatsoever, so he duly signed his, but he was held in contempt by several of his team-mates for 'selling out'.

Despite the club spending out almost £3.5 million on ground improvements over the past twelve months, including the building of the new stand, money was still available for team building, and Taylor was casting his eye around for players who could improve the squad. If they had been able to sign a couple of the targets that were mooted, things might have turned out differently. Liam Brady from Arsenal was number one on the list, but he was determined to go to Italy, whilst Dutch masters Neeskins and Krol were also the subject of enquiries.

In reality the list of players that Taylor settled on and told Clough to sign, turned out to be inadequate. They needed players who would fit into their system, not the other way round. In later years Clough was to comment that Taylor had got lazy, preferring to sit in his office rather than doing the hard miles that he used to, in search of players.

First in was Ian Wallace, he was a surprise signing from Coventry City, mostly because it had seemed that Taylor had fancied his strike partner Mick Ferguson far more. Although a decent player, Wallace was more of a predator than an all round forward in the mould of Birtles or Woodcock, and after all, one of the first requirements of a Nottingham Forest striker, was the ability to run diagonally onto the carefully crafted balls played behind the defence by Robertson. He had also spent his whole career playing off a 'big man', a player that Forest didn't possess at that time.

The other major signing turned out to be Raimondo Ponte, who had caught Taylor's eye when playing for Zurich Grasshoppers against the Reds in the European Cup, though Clough had preferred the Grasshoppers forward Claudio Sulser. On the face of it, this signing looked like another challenger for Martin O'Neill to see off. Ponte was not a citizen of the EU, and therefore the club had to jump through hoops to get the deal done. It was almost scuppered when the Home Office insisted that Forest provide details of why a suitable home grown player wasn't purchased instead, and also the club must provide names and evidence. Clough wasn't prepared to give out such sensitive, confidential information and the club were forced to argue their case in court instead. Eventually though, the authorities relented and Forest were allowed to sign the player for a fee of £230,000.

Brian Clough also had a quiet word with John McGovern and Larry Lloyd about their futures. McGovern was told that he was not certain to be an automatic selection and would have to fight for his place, whilst Lloyd who had just enjoyed an exceptional season, that had culminated in him receiving the player of the year trophy, was told he was unlikely to be first choice and was asked how he felt about moving and taking up a player/manager role somewhere. Clough said that he could talk up the player through his media contacts. This seemed strange to the player and although he had aspirations to move into management, he was in no hurry and thought that he had several playing years at the top left in him.

Ian Wallace in action against Arsenal.

Clough and Birtles may still have been at loggerheads as the season approached, but it was the whole squad that he was aiming at when he was quoted as saying: "I hope we can win something, so that we can pay our greedy players the bonuses they want before a ball is kicked."

It was revealed in August, that unemployment had passed 2 million, the highest since 1936 and was set to go higher. The country was officially in recession and the economy was creaking and inflation rising. The miners were on strike asking for a 37% pay rise and the Yorkshire Ripper had claimed his thirteenth victim.

Forest had reached the top, but events in the country were conspiring against them maintaining that position. Along with a series of self-inflicted wounds, a club that should have been looking to build a dynasty was now looking shaky, morale was

Colin Walsh (right) with the trophy captured by the youth team.

After rows with Brian Clough...

ROBBO'S HAPPY NOW

JOHN Robertson was ready for a winter of discontent after a summer snarl-up with Brian Clough.

Nottingham Forest's brilliant Scottish international winger, the man whose goal won the European Cup for Cloughie against Hamburger SV in Madrid, has signed a new contract that will tie him to the club for the rest of his career.

Yet a few months ago it seemed Robbo was as determined as Garry Birtles to get as far away from the City Ground and the Clough-Taylor partnership as he could.

The 28-year-old wing wizard asked for a transfer over a contract row and spent a lot of time in Clough's bad books.

Robertson even had an argument with his boss the day Forest arrived back in England with the European Cup, claiming that he and other players were undervalued due to the publicity which perpetually surrounds Clough and Taylor's deeds.

But he says: "All that is behind me now. I'm glad to say I'm staying with Forest and I want to help get us back into the European Cup again.

"I must admit that in the past Brian Clough has said things about me that have annoyed me. But, having said that, I have just as often over-reacted.

"When I said I wanted to leave, it was a spur of the moment thing that developed. Really my heart has always been with Forest and I know that if it had not been for the manager I would not have enjoyed the medals and international recognition I have had.

"Now we are all getting down to some real work at Forest. It's been a pretty disappointing season so far, because of our defeats in the European Cup and the League Cup. We are a far better side than our Cup results have indicated.

"I'm glad I'm still with the club. At one time, after Tony Woodcock's move to Cologne, I fancied trying out Continental football myself.

"But that was just part of my dissatisfaction with things generally at the club. Now I can see where my future lies and just want to get stuck in and forget all my past problems.

"Young Colin Walsh has done a very good job for Forest since he came into the side, and now I know I face a stiff challenge for a place in the team. It is just the sort of competition I need to keep me on my toes and make sure that I never take my place in the side for granted. And the return of Trevor Francis has also helped revive my enthusiasm."

Robertson was a member of the side that could manage only a 0-0 draw with Portugal at Hampden. Like the rest of his Scots teammates, he was disappointed with the result.

RIGHT: Nottingham Forest manager Brian Clough.

BELOW: Forest's winning goal in last year's European Cup Final, scored by John Robertson.

But he maintains: "Scottish teams of the past have attacked opponents for 85 of the 90 minutes and lost 1-0 because of a stupid error. At least that did not happen to us.

"We have taken three points from a possible four, which would have been perfectly acceptable before our games against Sweden and Portugal. That is a good solid start and if we can pick up at least a point when we play Israel next month we'll be on our way.

"Anyway, we will get our revenge against Portugal. We are all convinced that we'll beat them in the return game over there."

Aside from his new-found determination at Forest, Robertson's ambitions have quite naturally spread to helping Scotland reach the World Cup Finals in Spain.

JOHN
ROBERTSON
Nottingham Forest

OUR CAMERA CAPTURES THE EARLY SEASON AT THE CITY GROUND

Birtles opens the scoring against Manchester City.

Goal mouth action from the Peterborough cup game.

Ian Wallace, with this brave header against Stoke City.

Ian Wallace grabs the third and decisive goal against Man City.

Birtles from a tight angle against Stoke.

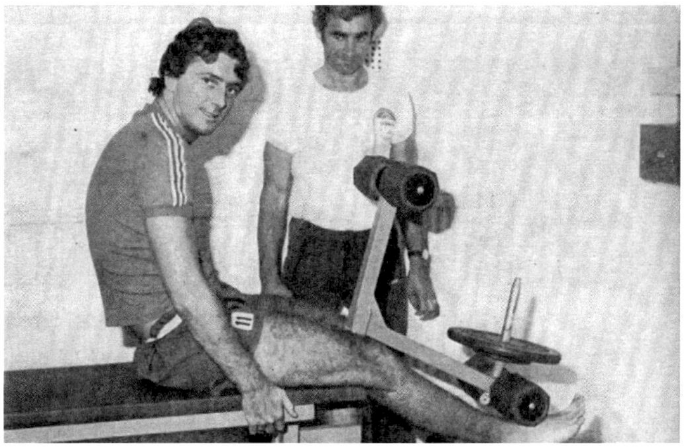

Trevor Francis watched by club physio Tony Verity, fights his way back to fitness,

low and several players were fearful about their futures. The team that began the season away at Tottenham, certainly didn't look like a harmonious outfit and an underwhelming display resulted in a 2-0 defeat, the problems that the team had experienced on the road the previous campaign were just as evident again.

A decent crowd of almost 27,000 attended the first home game of the season against Birmingham City. Pre-match, the European Cup was paraded around the ground by the club's younger players. On the pitch, there was a first win of the season, 2-1, and a first goal for Ponte, who impressed fans with his all action style. Clough wasn't so pleased with Martin O'Neill, as he allowed himself to be dragged into an argument with City's self styled hard man Mark Dennis, that led to both players receiving their marching orders. O'Neill himself was applauded off by the fans, but afterwards the manager called supporters idiots for doing so.

After a goalless draw at Everton, Forest followed this up with a couple of goal sprees, beating Peterborough United 3-0 in the League Cup, before slamming five past Stoke City. Ian Wallace opening his Reds' account with a couple against the Potters. Garry Birtles meanwhile looked like he was just getting on with business, he had notched up four goals himself already.

Before the return game against Peterborough, a storm erupted at the City Ground, with the publication of Peter Taylor's autobiography, called, 'With Clough by Taylor'. Clough was angry, because his partner had not informed him about the project and also because he felt that by having his name on the cover, he was being exploited. That both of them liked money was no secret, and Taylor often thought that he didn't get his fair share, so when he was given the opportunity to tell his side of the success story and make a few bob, it seemed too good an opportunity to pass up.

Because Taylor was seen as the junior partner in the relationship by the club, Clough always led the negotiations and Taylor was never totally certain that he was getting his dues. After the dust had settled, to those around them, it seemed as if there was a subtle change in their relationship.

Crowd trouble was to mar the next two games. Forest fans had infiltrated the home end at Peterborough and as they were being led out around the pitch, they had to walk past Brian Clough in his dugout and they were left in no doubt about how he felt regarding their behaviour. Worse still after the next game away at Middlesbrough, clashes between supporters resulted in the death of a 'Boro fan, Craig French, who died of a brain injury, having hit his head on the pavement after being punched.

Despite any off the field problems, form seemed to be fine and the Reds travelled to Bulgaria where they were due to meet CSKA Sofia in the first round of their defence of the European Cup. This was clearly a tie that should have held no fears. The CSKA stadium was very basic. 65,000 fans, all standing, with no cover. The pitch was 4 inches of grass rolled flat and the goalposts were square, this perhaps was the reason why a Robertson effort came straight back off the upright, rather than going in, but even after losing this away tie 1-0, it was still thought that they would have too much for them in the second leg After the game, Clough earned the thanks of reporters, when he delayed the return flight in order to allow journalists to file their match reports home, using the solitary telephone available.

There were another couple of goal blitzes on their return from Bulgaria, local rivals Leicester City were hammered 5-0, followed by a 7-0 League Cup victory at Gigg Lane, Bury, including a hat-trick for Ponte. Garry Birtles was interviewed on Star Soccer after the Leicester game about his contract situation and his face said more than words could, as he explained that his circumstances had not changed and also, that he had not been pleased with an article Clough had written about him in a football magazine.

The defending champions at home to CSKA, surely they could overcome the 1-0 deficit. Ticket sales had been sluggish after the draw had initially been made, and Taylor was entitled to feel aggrieved when he learnt that there had been a rush for them after the first leg defeat: "Why weren't they coming anyway?" he said.

The second leg turned out to be a complete anti-climax as Forest relinquished their crown with little more than a whimper. They huffed and puffed, but in truth rarely threatened to score and after Kerimov had extended the Bulgarian's lead in the 34th minute, there was to be no way back. This glorious chapter in the club's history had ended, would it ever be repeated? Taylor was apoplectic after the game, angry with the performance and when he was asked about Birtles' future with the club he replied: "He can leave now as far as I am concerned."

In fact Birtles would wear the Garibaldi one more time, against Manchester United, ironically the team he was soon to join for a fee of £1,250,000, not a bad return for a player who had cost virtually nothing. The transfer itself was a complicated affair, because it in fact involved three clubs, (bear with me); Manchester United had wanted Birtles, whilst Taylor wanted Peter Ward from Brighton, who in turn wanted Andy Ritchie from United. When all three parties and the players agreed, the transfers went through. Peter Taylor was basically putting his reputation with Clough on the line with the signing of

IAN
WALLACE
Nottm. Forest

END OF AN ERA

Ian Wallace challenges the CSKA goal keeper.

DISAPPOINTMENT AT THE THE CITY GROUND AS...

FOREST CRASH OUT.

No way through the massed ranks of the Bulgarian defence for Frank Gray.

John Robertson is deadly accurate from the spot, as the ball flies past Wallington in the Leicester goal.

Mills in action against Brighton.

Ian Wallace is captured from an unusual angle scoring the winner against Brighton.

SOME HIGHLIGHTS FROM THE WINTER MONTHS!!...

Kenny Burns goes for goal.

Birtles lunges to score against Leicester.

Brian Clough officially opens the new Executive Stand.

Ward. He had been forever singing the player's praises and the deal went through with an almost, 'on your head be it', feel to it. However, when Ward made his debut a few weeks later, alongside the also vertically challenged Wallace, supporters realized, that they now had a 'midget' strike force, and even with Trevor Francis to return, they offered no aerial threat whatsoever.

Tampa Bay Rowdies from the USA were touring the United Kingdom and finalizing opponents. Soccer in America appeared to be taking off and there was a certain glamour worldwide associated with the developments taking place over there. The fact that they had been able to attract stars such as Pele, Beckenbauer and Cruyff to play in the league certainly helped with game. The players that made up the Rowdies roster were not of that quality, names such as Lorimer and Hankin were well known to English fans, but Forest were persuaded to squeeze in a game against them. Playing on a Sunday, they had no real expectations about a large attendance, but acting on the advice of promoters accompanying the Rowdies, they threw the proverbial kitchen sink at it, and slashed prices. They were rewarded with a crowd of almost 19,000, who were treated to a range of other novel ideas, such as an organist who played whenever Forest mounted an attack, cheerleaders, pre-match entertainment and much more. Oh and a 7-1 win. Was this a sign of the way the game would be marketed in the future?

For those who love trivia, Forest gave a trial to an unnamed Argentinian international in this game, there was not even an announcement made to the crowd. Who was he? It turned out to be Claudio Marangoni, who had been released by Sunderland. Forest didn't take him on, but he went back to his home country and played successfully for Boca Juniors.

More and more it seemed as if Peter Taylor was now becoming the voice of the management, as he launched into yet another tirade, when despite a 2-1 home win against West Brom, he called the performance: "A disgrace and not of the standard expected. If they can't raise their level, I will have to replace them with players who can."

John McGovern commenting about this period recalls that it was around this time the aura of invincibility the team had was lost. "It was clear in the run up to Christmas we were a team in decline, particularly evidenced by a 4-1 defeat in the League Cup at the hands of Watford." After making his debut at Norwich, Steve Sutton was then unlucky enough to find himself making his second appearance four days later behind this leaky defence. He could not be blamed for any of the goals conceded.

To outsiders, it must have seemed strange that Clough and Taylor were so animated and angry about the team's failings, yes it was true that they had been eliminated from both the European Cup and League Cup, but after an away draw at Anfield, Forest were still handily placed in third position, but in a sign of further changes ahead, McGovern was dropped after a defeat to Birmingham. The decline in performance levels can be levelled directly at the management, they were in sole charge of team matters and recruitment and as much as they took credit for success they must take the blame when things go wrong. The team appeared unbalanced and low morale was also a factor, but they in truth just needed a couple of new players of the right quality to sort the situation out, but would they be found and brought in?

Clough softened the blow to McGovern's ego, by inviting him to sit on the bench alongside him for the game against Tottenham Hotspur. As it turned out it was a poor 3-0 defeat, but McGovern came away with an insight into the manager's thoughts, as Clough asked: "Do you know what's wrong with that Raimondo Ponte?" "I bloody signed him, that's what's wrong with him." Clough even refused to name a man of the match for the feature in the club programme.

Clough and Taylor decided, it was pace that was missing, but until Francis returned, their hands were tied. In the meantime there was another glamorous Super Cup tie with Valencia to look forward to, but when only 12,000 turned up, you might have been forgiven for thinking, Forest fans did not appreciate how lucky they were to be following the club during this era. Nottingham Forest had history with Valencia, they had been the club's first ever opponents in competitive European competition back in 1961, and they had also provided the opposition in the Centenary celebration match in 1965. On this occasion, a couple of goals from Ian Bowyer were enough to give the Reds a 2-1 victory, his second, helped by a wild deflection in the 87th minute proved to be the winner.

Eighteen year old winger Colin Walsh had been pushing for a first team opportunity for several months, and he did finally get his chance in the 1-1 draw away at Coventry, when he came on to replace the injured Robertson. He retained his place for the following game against Crystal Palace and scored in a 3-0 victory, a game that also saw Peter Ward on target as well.

Trevor Francis had spent months on his rehabilitation, he had played a couple of friendly games and thought that he was ready. He couldn't have chosen a better game or venue for his comeback, the Mestalla stadium in Valencia, for the Super Cup second leg. It was a tough re-introduction, he spent the whole game being man marked by the Spanish full back Botubot, who dished it out, but comically, the one time Francis caught him, he rolled theatrically around. On this occasion Forest were unable to cling on to their lead, losing the game 1-0 and the cup on away goals, after a 2-2 aggregate draw. Making a rare appearance for Valencia that night, was Mario Kempes, the Argentinian World Cup winner of 1978.

Amidst the gloom there was also humour, when the club reproduced a letter on the front cover of a home programme from a Mr P.D. Prebble. The letter was quite harsh but made a few

Robertson thwarted at St. Andrews.

Peter Ward celebrates a rare goal.

Action from the Ipswich game.

Ian Wallace at home to Tottenham.

GOALS AND ACTION... AS THE REDS FIGHT BACK

A spectacular effort from Peter Ward.

A trademark overhead kick from Ian Wallace.

FOREST v VALENCIA

Ian Bowyer puts Forest ahead at the City Ground.

SUPER CUP FIRST LEG 2–1

Ian Bowyer with a late strike clinches the first leg.

SUPER CUP SECOND LEG 0–1

No joy for the Reds in Spain.

Francis pops one in against the Villa.

Frank Gray against Crystal Palace.

Francis again, this time against Manchester United.

O'Neill completes the scoring against Villa.

LEAGUE AND CUP ACTION AT THE CITY GROUND

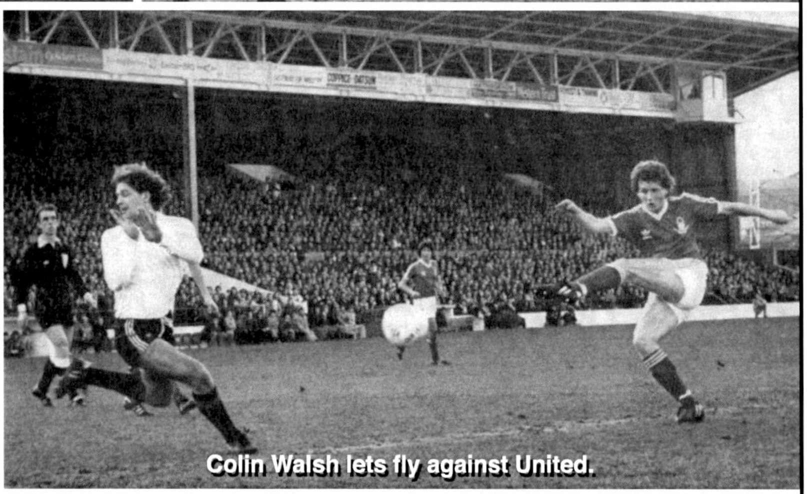

Colin Walsh lets fly against United.

Bailey the United keeper punches the ball into his own net.

Wallace goes sprawling against Palace.

salient points, claiming that the team's poor form was due to internal wrangling about contracts, constant re-shuffling of the line-up, and a management team more interested in personal gain. 'Spot on', replied Mr B.H. Clough. Spirits were also lifted for a time by a couple of good results, wins against Sunderland and Wolves with seven goals scored, followed by a creditable 2-2 draw with champions elect Aston Villa, that meant Forest were still in fifth place, within touching distance of the top.

Brian Clough had won every other trophy except the FA Cup, in fact he had never managed a team past the quarter finals, but a home tie with Second Division Bolton Wanderers in the third round seemed a perfect start to rectify this. However, the Reds twice had to come from behind, to earn a replay with a 3-3 draw, Ponte snatching a late equaliser in the 83rd minute. The Bolton keeper that day was ex-Forester Dennis Peacock. It then took extra time for Forest to progress at Burnden Park, this time Francis scored in the 113th minute to set up a mouth watering home clash with Manchester United and an early return to the City Ground for Garry Birtles.

Meanwhile Nottingham Forest had been asked to play in the World Club Championship by FIFA, to be competed for by the winners of the European Cup and the winners of the Copa Libertadores, the South American equivalent. The cup had fallen into disrepute over the years, after ill tempered affairs in the 1960's between Celtic and Racing Club, Manchester United and Estudiantes. And more recently when Ajax had been kicked off the park. Multiple sending offs and mass brawls had soured relations between the two continents. However, this time they came up with a new idea, a one off game played on neutral territory. Tokyo put up the money, so all that was needed was the will. Forest were keen to participate, the money would be welcome and also the prestige, but with a crowded fixture list, they would need some help from their own Football Association. Unlike the Uruguayan FA, who re-arranged fixtures to allow Nacional to not only travel, but arrive a week early to acclimatise, the English FA would not budge, insisting that Forest fulfil all their fixtures. A date of February the 11th was agreed and Forest desperately hoped that the Manchester United cup match would not go to a replay, otherwise they would be in a tight spot.

Unbeknown to several Forest players, their City Ground careers were about to end. Firstly, Frank Clark and Ken Knighton from Sunderland swooped to take Ian Bowyer to Roker Park in the week before the United cup game. A fee of £250,000 was agreed. Larry Lloyd was to be the second out of the door, although he was asked to stay on for a short while, as the club were short of defensive cover.

The FA Cup fourth round tie with Manchester United turned out to be a rip roaring encounter. Played out in front of a capacity crowd, it was settled by just one goal, when the blonde haired United keeper Gary Bailey, punched into his own net whilst under pressure dealing with a Robertson corner. The Reds had avoided the necessity of a replay and earned themselves another home tie against Bristol City in the process. The only problem was, that this was due to take place only 72 hours after the Reds were due to face Nacional on the other side of the world.

Another Forest youngster, Stuart Gray was drafted in for his debut against Manchester City, replacing the injured McGovern. Alongside Gary Mills and Colin Walsh, they formed a mid-field with an average age of less than twenty.

Forest set off for Tokyo on the same plane as Queen (the rock group), although the Forest party weren't in first class with them. The players helped themselves to plenty of drinks to pass the time on the long journey, having to change planes in Canada. This was to be the last appearance for Larry Lloyd, who was to take up the position of player manager with Wigan shortly afterwards. The player himself thought that he could still do a job in the First Division and wanted to stay really, so it was a real culture shock for him, when his next game was to be in front of only 3,000 spectators at the decrepit Springfield Park, home of Wigan

FOREST

FOOTBALL LEAGUE DIVISION ONE

SUNDERLAND

SATURDAY, 20th DECEMBER, 1980

Letterbox
Forest Review
Nottingham Forest Football Club
City Ground
Nottingham

23 Westhorpe
Southwell
Notts.

24th November 1980

Dear Sirs,

I doubt if you will print this but here goes (our over-priced Season Tickets are surely good for something!). The main thing wrong with Forest this year is a basic lack of confidence caused by:

internal wrangles over pay and contracts,
a constant reshuffling of the team pack,
a management team who appear to have more interest in squash, politics, book and record publishing and ill-judged public statements than putting out a settled team.

Let's be fair; Francis won't change what's going on, good as he is. Nor will Kempes, Fashanu or any number of ageing Dutchmen. Withe, Birtles and to a certain extent, Woodcock, were forced out, two midgets were brought in with no big target man and now even Robertson is unsettled. Who can blame him? As for Ponte, I feel downright ashamed for the lad at the way he has been treated here.

No, it will take more than the brilliance of Francis or the whatever (?) of McGovern to keep this squad in the top six. **It will need some realisation from the dynamic duo that the problem (and the solution) lie directly in their hands or are they really trying to go one up on the Grand Old Duke of York?**

Yours faithfully,

P. D. PREBBLE
(Block B, Row R, Seat 42, Main Stand)

● **Mr. Clough's reply to Mr. Prebble — "I think you are smack on, you have held your present seat for four years — I hope you keep it for another four."**

OFFICIAL PROGRAMME 25p

Volume 13, Number 16

Tokyo torment for Forest

Despite having most of the game, Forest were beaten 1-0 by Nacional of Uruguay in the World Club Championship played in Tokyo.

ABOVE . . . Martin O'Neill, Trevor Francis and Ian Wallace cause an anxious moment in the Nacional defence.
BELOW . . . Nacional display the trophy that has never been won by a British club.
RIGHT . . . Man of the Match Waldemar Victorino, who scored the only goal, with his prize: a new Toyota Celica, donated by the sponsors.

Back Row L to R: Viv Anderson, Martin O'Neill, Larry Lloyd, Kenny Burns, Peter Shilton, Trevor Francis.
Bottom Row L to R: John Robertson, Ian Wallace, Frank Gray, Stuart Gray, Raymondo Ponte.

HE would never admit it, but Brian Clough is sweating a bit on the ability of Norwegian international Jan Einar Aas to adapt to the demands of the First Division.

If Nottingham Forest's star capture from Bayern Munich succeeds in making the transition, the £150,000 deal will go down as another enterprising bargain for Clough.

If Aas fails to make the grade, those who claim the Forest manager is losing his Midas touch will be pointing a critical finger again.

They claim that cracks are appearing in the previously impregnable Forest set-up, and that Clough and his trusty side-kick Peter Taylor have made some unsuccessful and uncharacteristic probes with the cheque-book in the past year.

Jan Einar Aas

The big question asked is: HAS CLOUGH LOST HIS TOUCH?

It becomes imperative for Aas to succeed if Forest are to recapture the thrilling form which won them the European Cup twice.

Their First Division form of late suggests that the Norwegian's arrival, allied to another major buy this summer, could restore Forest to the top next season.

Brian Clough's activity in the transfer market since he took over at Forest in January, 1975, is worthy of close study before allegations are levelled about any diminishing powers in his ability to buy the right players.

We chart Brian Clough's major buys in alphabetical order and rate their contributions out of a maximum of ten points.

STAN BOWLES

BRIAN CLOUGH shook football by signing 'bad-boy' Bowles from Q.P.R., in December, 1979, for £250,000. He scored a goal in his second game and wore the number eight shirt for most of the season, scoring only one more goal. He never produced the inventive midfield artistry which gained him five England caps in the mid-70's. He ruined his future at Forest by refusing to accompany the team to the 1980 European Cup Final in Spain. Clough never forgave the indiscretion and happily sold Bowles to Orient for £100,000 last summer. A brave buy, which became a misguided one.

RATING: (out of 10) 4

KENNY BURNS

ANOTHER tempestuous player until tamed by Clough's soothing influence. Burns cost Forest £135,000 — a record Forest buy at the time — when he signed from Birmingham City four years ago. A former striker, Clough has converted him into one of the best central defenders in the First Division. He reached his peak in 1978 when he was granted the "Footballer of the Year" title. Burns' contribution helped Forest achieve miracles in Europe and gain the First Division title for the first time in 1977-78. There is no greater competitor in Forest's ranks. A courageous and inspired buy.

RATING: 8

TREVOR FRANCIS

ONE player, a striker, was needed to complete the great team Clough built in the first phase of his career at Forest. Lesser men would have frozen at the £1 million price Birmingham were asking for Francis. Clough got his man in February, 1979, to shatter the British transfer record. The money was well spent, never better illustrated than when the England striker scored Forest's winning goal against Malmo in the 1979 European Cup Final. A serious Achilles tendon injury suffered last May has done nothing to impair his acceleration, ball control, and shooting power. At a time when stylish players are in short supply, Francis is a diamond.

RATING: 10

ARCHIE GEMMILL

CLOUGH was heavily criticised for selling Gemmill to Birmingham in August, 1979. No player did more than Gemmill to clinch the Championship for Forest in 1977-78. A veteran of more than 500 League games for Preston, Derby, Forest and Birmingham, the Scottish international combined fierce but

Clough's good and

Brian Clough and Peter Taylor (left) have made some mistakes in the transfer market, but they came up trumps with the signing of Trevor Francis (above). Asa Hartford (right) failed to make such a favourable impression and was quickly sold to Everton.

fair aggression with the energy of a marathon runner to take charge of Forest's midfield after signing from Derby for £130,000 in September, 1977. Gemmill's non-stop involvement 'made' things happen for Forest, a fact which became abundantly clear after his departure and a decline in the club's performances. An absolute 'snip' at the money Clough laid out.

RATING: 8

FRANK GRAY

SCOTTISH international Gray had been at Leeds United ten years when Clough signed him for £400,000 on July 20th, 1979. Flaws were exposed in Gray's defensive technique, but there was no denying his speed of thought and eye for an opening going forward. Gray played a major part in helping Forest win the European Cup in 1980 after an outstanding season in which he had clearly shored-up any weakness in defensive play. A model professional ... and another bargain.

RATING: 7

ASA HARTFORD

THREE appearances, no goals, and trouble all the way. That sums up Asa Hartford's brief encounter with Forest after signing in the summer of 1979. Controversy raged from the moment Clough saw Manchester City's midfield star as a replacement for Gemmill. On August 24, 1979, Clough told the newspapers: "Asa is finding it extremely difficult to fit into the side. He is running all over the place without any discipline in his play. He has never played disciplined football in his life. If he is no good he will go." He went, after 63 days with Clough's last rites ringing: "Forest are too big to change their pattern for one player." A disastrous transfer deal, Forest losing £100,000.

RATING: 2

LARRY LLOYD

LARRY LLOYD marshalled Forest's defence superbly through all their glory times.

Yet he looked big, ponderous, a carthorse in a field of stags. In truth, he became a pillar of reliability, never better demonstrated than when Forest were up against it in European competition. Clough freed Lloyd to follow a management career this season after the old war-horse had shed buckets for Forest.

RATING: 8

JOHN McGOVERN

FOREST'S captain McGovern has been as quietly efficient for Clough as Martin Peters was for Alf Ramsey. He has none of Francis' crowd appeal, but McGovern is full of stealth, hallmarked by a "now-you-see-me-now-you-don't" routine in midfield. There are few club men as valued as this pedigree performer.

RATING: 8

bad buys

Kenny Burns (left).

John McGovern (above), one of Clough's most reliable signings but Peter Ward (left) has struggled.

DAVE NEEDHAM

REGULAR first teamer at Notts County and Queens Park Rangers, Clough has never guaranteed the big central defender First Division football. Needham has played more for Forest than Rangers, but could have expected more from the Midland club after making more than 400 appearances for Notts County. It is a tribute to Clough's handling of players that Needham has accepted his utility role without complaint. A shrewd purchase by a manager aware of the importance of cover.

RATING: 7

JOHN O'HARE

ANOTHER tried and trusted lieutenant devoted to his commanding officer's whims. O'Hare has spent most of his time in the reserves, grabbing any opportunity of first team action. He has turned on the magic in several Cup-ties. Clough bought security when he purchased O'Hare.

RATING: 6

RAIMONDO PONTE

SWISS star Ponte was signed from Zurich Grasshoppers at the start of the season. Many Forest fans were hoping for a bigger name after Clough had combed Europe. It is only in recent weeks that Ponte has begun to justify the £250,000 expenditure. His effectiveness remains in question. He tends to pose with the ball rather than probe and ferret in the true Forest traditions. At the moment he has not proved his worth.

RATING: 5

PETER SHILTON

AS secure as the Bank of England. He, and England colleague Trevor Francis, are the two Forest players who provoke the threat from Clough that "they leave over my dead body." He bought Shilton from Stoke for £270,000 in September, 1977. He is arguably Clough's most astute buy. Now, Shilton wants to leave Forest. How can a club compensate for his loss? It is a problem only Clough could solve. A magic buy.

RATING: 10

IAN WALLACE

CONSIDERING the eulogies which greeted his £1 million capture from Coventry City, Wallace has not produced the goods. Wallace (below) took 34 League games to score ten goals this season, an unconvincing record. The Scot could be excused for not producing his best after playing alongside a series of different strikers caused by Francis' prolonged injury. Hopefully, he will justify the huge sum Clough splashed out, but as yet he has been a disappointment.

RATING: 6

PETER WARD

PETER TAYLOR wanted to buy Ward from Brighton, Clough didn't. Taylor's powers of persuasion tilted the balance. Forest paid £500,000 for a striker rated a new "Jimmy Greaves". Ward has not fulfilled his potential, despite the chance he was given during Francis' absence. Clough will do his utmost to turn Ward into a First Division player.

RATING: 3

PETER WITHE

THE most underrated striker in the First Division. Withe was the ideal front man for Clough, blending superbly with Tony Woodcock. The Forest boss could be criticised for selling Withe to Newcastle United, yet the success achieved by Birtles and Francis since his departure stifles that argument. An inspired buy from Birmingham.

RATING: 7

VERDICT

BRIAN CLOUGH has made 15 major buys in six years at Forest. Asa Hartford's transfer was a dreadful mistake. Peter Ward, Raimondo Ponte and Ian Wallace have much to do before they justify their price.

Norwegian international star Einar Aas has made a promising start to his Forest career but the best of him will not be seen until he has settled into the club's system and come to terms with the First Division.

The rest prove that when it comes to spotting talent, Brian Clough is one of the best managers in the business.

Keep on waving the chequebook Cloughie!

Athletic in a run of the mill lower league game.

Forest were travelling across several time zones to contest this game and they would have to play another fixture immediately on their return to England. After consulting with various experts, the club had come up with what they thought would be the best solution to overcome jet lag. They would simply ignore it and stick to British time, which was nine hours behind. They would simply sleep during the day and have breakfast in the evening.

John McGovern was out injured, and in time honoured fashion at the club, would usually have been left behind. However, the manager told his skipper that the agent who arranged all of the club's lucrative foreign games, would be there to hand over some cash to be distributed amongst the players. They had all been demanding this money for months, so McGovern was told he could come along and sort this out as club captain. He was also pleased to not miss out on attending such a prestigious event.

Before kick-off, the players were introduced individually to the crowd, similar to the entrance made for the Super Bowl in America, in front of 60,000 Japanese football fans, most of whom appeared to be supporting the Reds. Despite going behind to a tenth minute goal from the extravagantly named Waldemar Victorino, Forest more than held their own and on the balance of play, probably deserved to win. The best chance fell to John Robertson in the last minute, when he struck a shot against the keeper, when he himself admitted he should have scored.

Einar Aas pictured with Ken Smales outside the Football League offices at Lytham St. Annes.

There was even more bad news for the players, when John McGovern called to see the manager about the player's cash, he was told: "I haven't got it, the agent didn't turn up," but it was eventually sorted out a couple of weeks later.

Meanwhile the players arrived back at Heathrow late on Friday with an FA Cup fifth round tie against Bristol City to be played less than 24 hours later. Understandably the players looked jaded. Trailing to a fortieth minute goal from Kevin Mabbutt, it wasn't until the last ten minutes that they turned the game on it's head. First Robbo equalised from the penalty spot, then Ian Wallace came up with the winner in the 88th minute.

It was at this time that stories about Trevor Francis and Peter Shilton wanting to leave, first began to circulate. Shilton himself said he fancied a new challenge, he knew the team was getting weaker by the number of saves he was having to make. But it turned out to be Martin O'Neill who was next out of the door, joining Norwich City in a deal worth £250,000, and this just days after scoring two goals in the 3-1 defeat of Arsenal. John Robertson thought that this was the strangest transfer of all, and wondered whether the manager had been influenced by the often fractious relationship he enjoyed with the player. As Martin himself said: "I thought I went on to play some of the best football of my career when I joined Norwich." Larry Lloyd commenting on the situation says: "The players all thought that the side was broken up far to quickly, we knew that we had more to offer, but Peter Taylor in particular, seemed in a hurry to dismantle the team."

Forest had been drawn at home to Ipswich Town in the sixth round of the cup. Ipswich who were vying with Aston Villa for the championship were a formidable team. The tie turned out to have almost everything, as they shared six goals in a game of constantly changing fortunes. The new look Forest team, with three youngsters across midfield and Kenny Burns now operating as a centre half, fell two goals behind, before a stirring fight back. Goals from Francis, Walsh and Robertson put the Reds ahead by the 51st minute. It was then end to end action, before a deflected shot from Franz Thijssen wrong footed Shilton to earn the visitors a replay.

Nottingham Forest's season virtually ground to a halt three days later in Suffolk, as they undeservedly exited the competition after the replay. Backed by thousands of fans, some of whom had climbed in after the gates were locked, saw Forest miss chance after chance, before falling to a sucker punch from Arnold Muhren. Alan Brazil recalls an incident from the game. He was playing wide trying to avoid Kenny Burns, when the manager Bobby Robson shouted:

"What are you doing out here?"

"You told me to play wide."

"Yes, but not that bloody wide."

Watching from the stand that night at Portman Road was Einar Aas, a Norwegian international defender who was to join the club from Bayern Munich. As with the Raimondo Ponte situation, Einar was also not a citizen of the EU and once again the club was forced to wait for his international clearance to come through. The style of football was to be a real culture shock for the player, but he quickly adjusted in a very short space of time and became a firm fan's favourite.

The title might now have been out of the question, but there was a definite possibility of qualifying for the UEFA Cup through a high league position. They bounced back after the Ipswich defeat with a 4-1 victory over Brighton, followed by a well deserved point from a 1-1 draw at Old Trafford. They were in third spot and it was theirs to lose with only eight games remaining.

There was another debutant at West Brom, keeper Lee Smelt taking over from Shilton, but he couldn't prevent Albion from winning 2-1. The game was overshadowed however by another row between the manager and the press. One newspaper had reported that the manager had ejected Trevor Francis from the team bus in the pouring rain onto a lay-by on the way back from an away game, before making sure that the player's lift was there. Francis seemed to corroborate the manager's version that he was perfectly okay to be dropped off, but Clough hated to be stitched up by the press, particularly on this occasion as it seemed there was an agenda to widen a rift between the manager and his player.

TREVOR FRANCIS
Nottingham Forest

GOALS! GOALS! GOALS!

1. O'Neill shoots against Arsenal.

2. Jennings dives.

3. But it's a goal.

Act

John Robertson strokes the ball past old adversary Jan Moller, the Bristol City keeper.

Wallace against Middlesboro.

Burns prepares to turn the ball into the Boro' net.

...m the Ipswich Cup game.

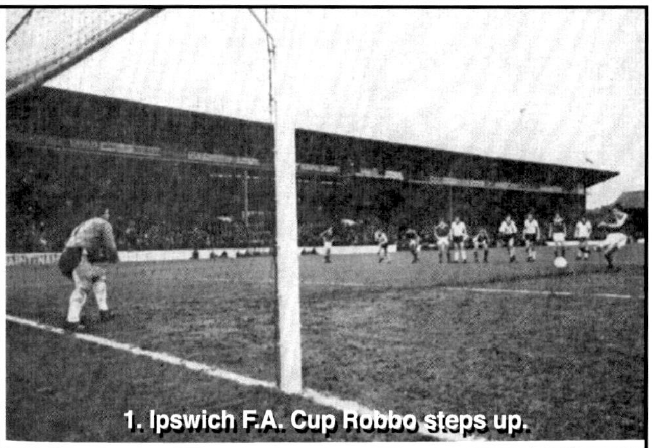

1. Ipswich F.A. Cup Robbo steps up.

2. Cooper dives the wrong way.

3. Bang it's in...

Frank Gray with a free kick against Boro.

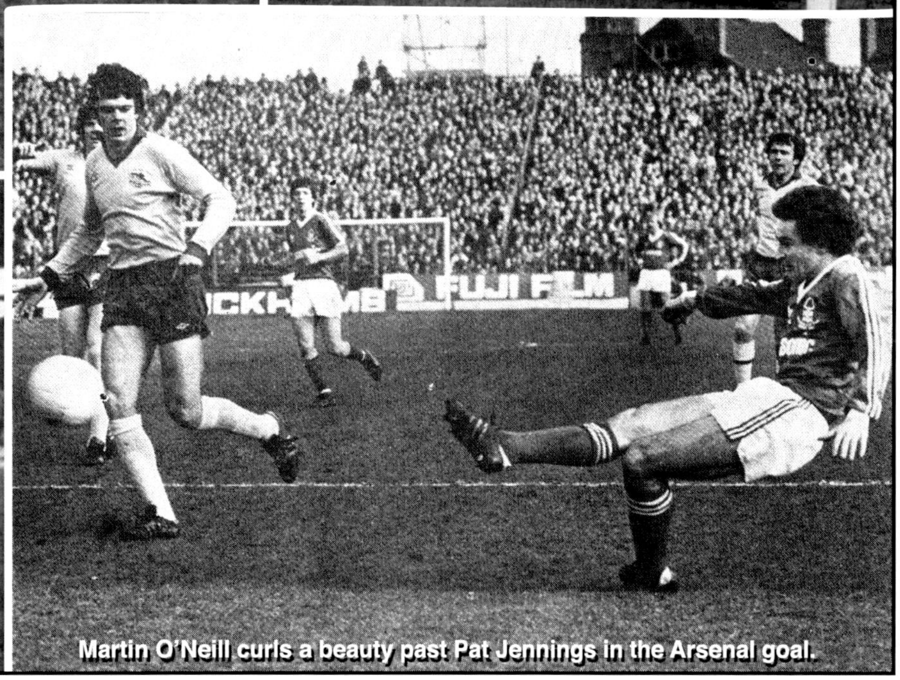

Martin O'Neill curls a beauty past Pat Jennings in the Arsenal goal.

ACTION FROM APRIL & MAY...

Francis beats ex Reds' keeper Chris Woods, to put Forest 1 - 0 up against Norwich.

Trevor Francis once more on target against Wolves.

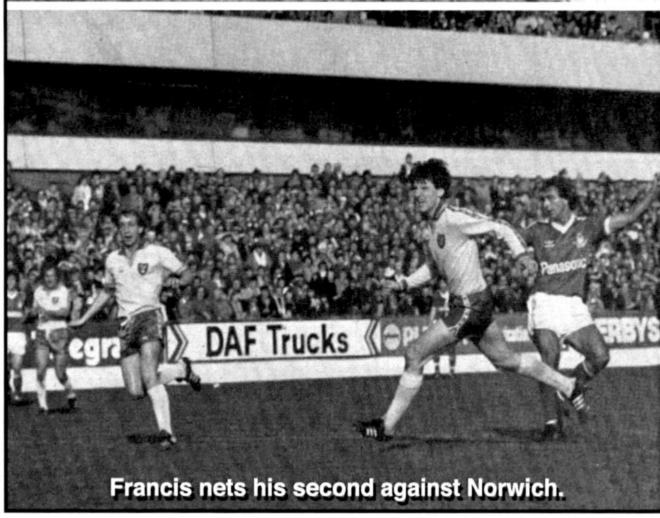

Francis nets his second against Norwich.

It looks like it's in, but in fact the ball hits the post.

Brian Clough presents Kenny Burns with his Player of the Year award.

Francis himself responded in the best possible fashion, by scoring both goals in a 2-1 win over Norwich, also notable because it saw the debut of Einar Aas, coming on as a second half substitute for Dave Needham. The Norwich goal was scored by their up and coming young striker, Justin Fashanu, who impressed the Forest management, particularly because he appeared to be unfazed by the presence of Kenny Burns.

John McGovern tells a story about Einar Aas and a training session down by the river: "If the manager thought that training was going a bit stale, he had these little games that he would introduce, using a variety of code words to let the players know what he expected. On one occasion, he shouted his codeword that indicated we had to sprint through the nettles, touch a tree and return as quickly as possible, with the last player doing press ups. Einar looked at me bemused, he had no idea what was going on. Run I said......It was just another day at Nottingham Forest."

The club's battle for a European place, was not helped by unnecessarily dropping points to their closest rivals during the run in. They had already lost to West Brom who were to finish above them in fourth place and they were then beaten by Southampton who finished sixth, before they could only draw at home to Liverpool who finished fifth. Just three extra points from these games would have seen them finish a highly creditable third and eligible for the UEFA Cup.

April 23rd, 1981 and a routine 1-0 win over Wolverhampton Wanderers, but it was significant because it was also the last public appearance of the European Cup, before it was returned to UEFA. It wouldn't be out of the country for long however, Liverpool would regain the trophy after beating Real Madrid in that season's final. Brian Clough and Nottingham Forest did their best to help the Spaniards though, meeting Real in a friendly game before the final, which would have undoubtedly been useful practice for them against similar English opposition.

The season ended with a 3-1 victory away at Selhurst Park over Malcolm Allison's already relegated Crystal Palace, before the curtain came down on the league campaign, and a low key 1-1 draw with Coventry City.

Ian Wallace had finished the season as top scorer with only thirteen goals, but with constantly changing attacking partners, this perhaps wasn't as disappointing as it looked. Trevor Francis was then awarded the manager's player of the year, whilst Kenny Burns picked up the supporters' award.

Jimmy Gordon after giving the matter a great deal of thought, had decided to retire. The club granted him a testimonial, with Notts County providing the opposition. The 5,000 crowd gave him a great send off, whilst Ron Fenton was announced as his replacement for first team trainer.

Peter Taylor once more came out with the fighting talk that the fans wanted to hear: "Nothing must come second to the re-shaping of the side, we have set standards, and when we fall beneath them, the people who pay to watch us have all the right in the world to moan and grumble."

Though, as we were soon to find out, this was to be a last throw of the dice by the assistant manager. A seismic change would rock the City Ground the following season.

FOREST

APPEARANCES TEAM LINE-UPS

Aug 16th, A, v Tottenham Hotspur, L, 0-2, AT 43,398, Shilton, Gunn, Gray, McGovern, Needham, Burns, Ponte, Bowyer, Birtles, Wallace, Robertson.

Aug 20th, H, v Birmingham City, W, 2-1, Scorers Ponte, Birtles, AT 26,561, Shilton, Anderson, Gray, McGovern, Needham, Burns, O'Neill, Ponte, Birtles, Wallace, Robertson. SUB Bowyer.

Aug 23rd, A, v Everton, D, 0-0, AT 25,981, Shilton, Anderson, Gray, McGovern, Needham, Burns, Ponte, Bowyer, Birtles, Wallace, Robertson.

Aug 27th, LC, H, v Peterborough United, W, 3-0, Scorers Gray, Birtles, Robertson, AT 16,117, Shilton, Anderson, Gray, O'Hare, Lloyd, Needham, O'Neill, Bowyer, Birtles, Wallace, Robertson.

Aug 30th, H, v Stoke City, W, 5-0, Scorers Birtles (20, Wallace (2), Robertson (P), AT 21,915, Shilton, Anderson, Gray, McGovern, Lloyd, Needham, O'Neill, Bowyer, Birtles, Wallace, Robertson.

Sept 3rd, LC, A, v Peterborough United, D, 1-1, Scorer Mills, AT 11,503, Shilton, Anderson, Gray, McGovern, Needham, Burns, Ponte, Bowyer, Birtles, Mills, Robertson.

Sept 6th, A, v Middlesbrough, D, 0-0, AT 17,119, Shilton, Anderson, Gray, McGovern, Needham, Burns, O'Neill, Bowyer, Birtles, Wallace, Robertson.

Sept 13th, H, v Manchester City, W, 3-2, Scorers Bowyer, Birtles, Wallace, AT 23,164, Shilton, Anderson, Gray, McGovern, Needham, Burns, O'Neill, Bowyer, Birtles, Wallace, Robertson.

Sept 17th, EC, A, v CSKA Sofia, L, 0-1, AT 65,000, Shilton, Anderson, Gray, McGovern, Lloyd, Needham, O'Neill, Bowyer, Birtles, Wallace, Robertson. SUB Ponte.

Sept 20th, H, v Leicester City, W, 5-0, Scorers Gray, Birtles (2), Robertson (P), Mills, AT 27,145, Shilton, Anderson, Gray, McGovern, Needham, Burns, O'Neill, Ponte, Birtles, Wallace, Robertson. SUB Mills.

Sept 23rd, LC, A, v Bury, W, 7-0, Scorers Anderson, Ponte (3), Birtles (2), Mills, AT 8,826, Shilton, Anderson, Gray, McGovern, Needham, Burns, O'Neill, Ponte, Birtles, Mills, Robertson.

Sept 27th, A, v Arsenal, L, 0-1, AT 37,582, Shilton, Anderson, Gray, McGovern, Needham, Burns, O'Neill, Ponte, Birtles, Mills, Robertson. SUB Bowyer.

Oct 1st, EC, H, v CSKA Sofia, L, 1-0, AT 25,813, Shilton, Anderson, Gray, McGovern, Needham, Burns, O'Neill, Bowyer, Birtles, Wallace, Robertson. SUB Lloyds.

Oct 4th, H, v Manchester United, L, 1-2, Scorer Wallace, AT 29,801, Shilton, Anderson, Gray, McGovern, Lloyd, Needham, O'Neill, Bowyer, Birtles, Wallace, Robertson. SUB Mills.

Oct 8th, A, v Sunderland, D, 2-2, Scorers Bowyer, Mills, AT 30,485, Shilton, Gunn, Gray, McGovern, Lloyd, Needham, O'Neill, Bowyer, Mills, Wallace, Robertson.

Oct 11th, H, v Brighton, W, 1-0, Scorer Wallace, AT 17,391, Shilton, Gunn, Gray, McGovern, Lloyd, Needham, O'Neill, Bowyer, Mills, Wallace, Robertson.

Oct 18th, H, v West Bromwich Albion, W, 2-1, Scorers Bowyer, Mills, AT 25,096, Shilton, Gunn, Gray, Ponte, Lloyd, Burns, O'Neill, Bowyer, Mills, Wallace, Robertson.

Oct 22nd, H, v Leeds United, W, 2-1, Scorers Burns, Wallace, AT 25,033, Shilton, Gunn, Gray, Ponte, Lloyd, Burns, O'Neill, Bowyer, Ward, Wallace, Robertson. SUB Mills.

Oct 25th, A, v Norwich City, D, 1-1, Scorer Robertson, AT 17,792, Sutton, Gunn, Gray, McGovern, Lloyd, Burns, O'Neill, Bowyer, Ward, Wallace, Robertson.

Oct 28th, LC, A, v Watford, L, 1-4, Scorer Wallace, AT 22,597, Sutton, Gunn, Gray, Ponte, Lloyd, Burns, O'Neill, Bowyer, Mills, Wallace, Robertson.

Nov 1st, H, v Southampton, W, 2-1, Scorers Ward, Robertson (P), AT 24,669, Shilton, Anderson, Gray, Ponte, Lloyd, Burns, O'Neill, Bowyer, Ward, Wallace, Robertson.

Nov 8th, A, v Liverpool, D, 0-0, AT 43,143, Shilton, Anderson, Gray, McGovern, Lloyd, Burns, O'Neill, Bowyer, Ward, Wallace, Robertson.

Nov 11th, A, v Birmingham City, L, 0-2, AT 22,433, Shilton, Gunn, Gray, McGovern, Lloyd, Burns, O'Neill, Bowyer, Ward, Wallace, Robertson.

Nov 15th, H, v Tottenham Hotspur, L, 0-3, AT 25,400, Shilton, Anderson, Gray, Bowyer, Lloyd, Burns, Mills, Ponte, Ward, Wallace, Robertson. SUB O'Neill.

Nov 22nd, H, v Ipswich Town, L, 1-2, Scorer Wallace, AT 24,423, Shilton, Anderson, Gray, McGovern, Lloyd, Burns, Mills, Bowyer, Ward, Wallace, Robertson.

Nov 25th, SC, H, v Valencia, W, 2-1, Scorer Bowyer (2), AT 12,246, Shilton, Anderson, Gray, McGovern, Lloyd, Burns, Mills, Bowyer, Ward, Wallace, Robertson. SUB Ponte.

Nov 29th, A, v Coventry City, D, 1-1, Scorer Wallace, AT 15,151, Shilton, Anderson, Gray, Gunn, Lloyd, Ponte, Mills, Bowyer, Ward, Wallace, Robertson. SUB Walsh.

Dec 6th, H, v Crystal Palace, W, 3-0, Scorers Gray (P) Ward, Walsh, AT 20,223, Shilton, Anderson, Gray, McGovern, Lloyd, Gunn, Mills, Bowyer, Ward, Wallace, Walsh. SUB O'Neill.

Dec 13th, A, v Leeds United, L, 0-1, AT 21,882, Shilton, Anderson, Gray, McGovern, Lloyd, Gunn, Mills, O'Neill, Ward, Wallace, Walsh. SUB Ponte.

Dec 17th, SC, A, v Valencia, L, 0-1,AT 29,083, Shilton, Anderson, Gunn, McGovern, Lloyd, Burns, O'Neill, Ponte, Francis, Wallace, Walsh.

Dec 20th, H, v Sunderland, W, 3-1, Scorers Ponte, Francis, Walsh, AT 23,151, Shilton, Anderson, Gray, McGovern, Lloyd, Gunn, O'Neill, Ponte, Francis, Wallace, Walsh.

Dec 26th, A, v Wolverhampton Wanderers, W, 4-1, Scorers Gray (P), Ponte..................... , AT 31,588, Shilton, Anderson, Gray, McGovern, Lloyd, Gunn, O'Neill, Ponte, Francis, Wallace, Walsh. SUB Mills.

1980 - 1981 DIVISION 1 TABLE

TEAMS	P	W	D	L	F	A	W	D	L	F	A	PTS
1 Aston Villa	42	16	3	2	40	13	10	5	6	32	27	60
2 Ipswich T	42	15	4	2	45	14	8	6	7	32	29	56
3 Arsenal	42	13	8	0	36	17	6	7	8	25	28	53
4 W.B.A	42	15	4	2	40	15	5	8	8	20	27	52
5 Liverpool FC	42	13	5	3	38	15	4	12	5	24	27	51
6 Southampton	42	15	4	2	47	22	5	6	10	29	34	50
7 Nottingham Forest	42	15	3	3	44	20	4	9	8	18	24	50
8 Manchester U	42	9	11	1	30	14	6	7	8	21	22	48
9 Leeds U	42	10	5	6	19	19	7	5	9	20	28	44
10 Tottenham H	42	9	9	3	44	31	5	6	10	26	37	43
11 Stoke C	42	8	9	4	31	23	4	9	8	20	37	42
12 Manchester C	42	10	7	4	35	25	4	4	13	21	34	39
13 Birmingham C	42	11	5	5	32	23	2	7	12	18	38	38
14 Middlesbrough	42	14	4	3	38	16	2	1	18	15	45	37
15 Everton	42	8	6	7	32	25	5	4	12	23	33	36
16 Coventry C	42	9	6	6	31	30	4	4	13	17	38	36
17 Sunderland	42	10	4	7	32	19	4	3	14	20	34	35
18 Wolverhampton W	42	11	2	8	26	20	2	7	12	17	35	35
19 Brighton & H.A	42	10	3	8	30	26	4	4	13	24	41	35
20 Norwich C	42	9	7	5	34	25	4	0	17	15	48	33
21 Leicester C	42	7	5	9	20	23	6	1	14	20	44	32
22 Crystal Palace	42	6	4	11	32	37	0	3	18	15	46	19

WHO? WHAT!

FACTFILE ★★★

RESULTS LEAGUE TABLE

Dec 27th, H, v Aston Villa, D, 2-2, Scorers O'Neill, Francis, AT 33,900, Shilton, Anderson, Gray, McGovern, Lloyd, Gunn, O'Neill, Ponte, Francis, Wallace, Robertson.

Jan 3rd, FAC, H, v Bolton Wanderers, D, 3-3, Scorers Ponte, Francis (2), AT 22,920, Shilton, Anderson, Gray, McGovern, Lloyd, Gunn, O'Neill, Ponte, Francis, Wallace, Robertson.

Jan 6th, FAC, A, v Bolton Wanderers, W, 1-0, Scorer Francis, AT 22,799, Shilton, Anderson, Gray, McGovern, Lloyd, Burns, O'Neill, Bowyer, Francis, Ward, Robertson.

Jan 10th, A, v Ipswich Town, L, 0-2, AT 25,697, Shilton, Anderson, Gray, McGovern, Needham, Burns, O'Neill, Bowyer, Francis, Ward, Robertson.

Jan 24th, FAC, H, v Manchester United, W, 1-0, Scorer Bailey (OG), AT 34,110, Shilton, Anderson, Gray, McGovern, Burns, Gunn, Ponte, Wallace, Francis, Walsh, Robertson.

Jan 31st, H, v Everton, W, 1-0, Scorer Burns, AT 25,631, Shilton, Anderson, Gray, McGovern, Burns, Gunn, Ponte, Wallace, Francis, Walsh, Robertson.

Feb 7th, A, v Manchester City, D, 1-1, Scorer Francis, AT 40,524, Shilton, Anderson, Gray, Gray.S, Burns, Gunn, Mills, Wallace, Francis, Walsh, Robertson.

Feb 11th, WC, N, v Nacional Montevideo, L, 0-1, AT 70,000, Shilton, Anderson, Gray, Gray.S, Lloyd, Burns, O'Neill, Ponte, Francis, Wallace, Robertson. SUB Ward.

Feb 14th, FAC, H, v Bristol City, W, 2-1, Scorers Wallace, Robertson (P), AT 26,742, Shilton, Anderson, Gray, Gray.S, Burns, Gunn, Mills, Wallace, Francis, Walsh, Robertson.

Feb 18th, A, v Stoke City, W, 2-1, Scorers Walsh****, AT 17,303, Shilton, Anderson, Gray, Gray.S, Burns, Gunn, Mills, Wallace, Francis, Walsh, Robertson. SUB O'Neill.

Feb 21st, H, v Arsenal, W, 3-1, Scorers Burns, O'Neill (2), AT 25,357, Shilton, Anderson, Gray, Gray.S, Burns, Gunn, Mills, Wallace, Francis, O'Neill, Robertson.

Feb 28th, A, v Leicester City, D, 1-1, Scorer Walsh, AT 26,608, Shilton, Anderson, Gray, Gray.S, Burns, Gunn, Mills, Wallace, Francis, Walsh, Robertson. SUB Ponte.

March 3rd, H, v Middlesbrough, W, 1-0, Scorer Burns, AT 19,690, Shilton, Anderson, Gray, Gray.S, Burns, Gunn, Mills, Wallace, Francis, Walsh, Robertson. SUB Ponte.

March 7th, FAC, H, v Ipswich Town, D, 3-3, Scorers Francis, Walsh, Robertson (P), AT 3,796, Shilton, Anderson, Gray, Gray.S, Burns, Gunn, Mills, Wallace, Francis, Walsh, Robertson. SUB Ponte.

March 10th, FAC, A, v Ipswich Town, L, 0-1, AT 31,060, Shilton, Gunn, Gray, Gray.S, Needham, Burns, Mills, Wallace, Francis, Walsh, Robertson. SUB Ponte, Ward.

March 14th, H, v Brighton, W, 4-1, Scorers Burns, Wallace, Mills, Robertson (P), AT 20,688, Shilton, Gunn, Gray, Gray.S, Needham, Burns, Ponte, Wallace, Mills, Walsh, Robertson. SUB Ward.

March 18th, A, v Manchester United, D, 1-1, Scorer Wallace, AT 38,205, Shilton, Gunn, Gray, Gray.S, Needham, Burns, Ponte, Wallace, Mills, Walsh, Robertson. SUB Ward.

March 21st, A, v West Bromwich Albion, L, 1-2, Scorer Mills, AT 19,532, Smelt, Gunn, Gray, Gray.S, Needham, Burns, Mills, Wallace, Francis, Walsh, Robertson. SUB Ponte.

March 28th, H, v Norwich City, W, 2-1, Scorer Francis (2), AT 22,353, Shilton, Anderson, Gray, Gray.S, Needham, Burns, Ponte, Wallace, Francis, Walsh, Robertson. SUB Aas.

April 4th, A, v Southampton, L, 0-2, AT 22,712, Shilton, Anderson, Gray, Gray.S, Aas, Burns, Mills, Wallace, Francis, Walsh, Robertson.

April 11th, H, v Liverpool, D, 0-0, AT 27,363, Shilton, Anderson, Gray, McGovern, Aas, Burns, Mills, Gray.S, Francis, Ward, Robertson.

April 18th, A, v Aston Villa, L, 0-2, AT 34,707, Shilton, Anderson, Gunn, McGovern, Needham, Aas, Mills, Ward, Francis, Gray.S, Robertson.

April 20th, H, v Wolverhampton Wanderers, W, 1-0, Scorer Francis, AT 19,711, Shilton, Anderson, Gray, McGovern, Aas, Gunn, Mills, Ward, Francis, Walsh, Robertson.

April 25th, A, v Crystal Palace, W, 3-1, Scorers Aas, Wallace, Gray.S, AT 13,352, Shilton, Anderson, Gunn, McGovern, Burns, Aas, Mills, Wallace, Francis, Gray.S, Robertson.

May 2nd, H, v Coventry City, D, 1-1, Scorer Robertson (P), AT 21,511, Shilton, Gunn, Gray, McGovern, Burns, Aas, Mills, Wallace, Francis, Gray.S, Robertson.

May 4th, CC, H, Mansfield Town, W, 2-1, Scorers Ward, Gray.S, AT 3,405, Shilton, Gunn, Gray, Needham, Aas, Walsh, Mills, Ward, Burns, Gray.S, Robertson.

Brian Clough, gives outgoing groundsman Mervyn Davies a kiss goodbye after 12 years service,

WHERE! WHEN! ★★★

SEASON 1981-82

Back Row L to R: Bryn Gunn, Dave Needham, Ian Wallace, Mark Proctor, Justin Fashanu, Peter Shilton, Viv Anderson.
Front Row L to R: Trevor Francis, Peter Ward, Colin Walsh John McGovern, Stuart Gray, John Robertson.

The country was about to enter a period of economic recession, unemployment climbed to over two and a half million and Margaret Thatcher was the most unpopular Prime Minister ever, according to a poll.

It wasn't all doom and gloom however, the country had celebrated the wedding of Prince Charles and Lady Diana Spencer and the BBC aired the first episode of 'Only Fools and Horses'.

The country may be suffering, but clubs still carried on spending money, on ever increasing transfer fees, seemingly oblivious to this fact. Attendances would soon plummet around the country, crowds at the City Ground would dip below 20,000, despite 13,000 season tickets being sold. Attendances of only 20,000 at Anfield and Highbury would be the norm, whilst at other so called giants as Newcastle and Chelsea, they could go as low as 10,000.

Brian Clough often criticised the fans of Nottingham Forest for not supporting the team in high numbers, but in reality for the size of the city and the fact that there was another professional club Notts County, joining them in the top division, they were good in comparison. Local rivals Derby, who the manager always brought up as an example of a football town, were down to less than 15,000 as their average gate.

One of the most significant changes in football was introduced for the coming season. Not a rule change as such, but the introduction of three points for a win, which it was hoped would encourage teams to attack more. Brian Clough was not so sure, but he was in a minority.

The best news for Forest supporters came when it was announced that Peter Shilton had settled his differences with the club and signed on for a further season. The position of Trevor Francis however was not so clear. He was linked with a variety of clubs and it certainly looked as if he was desperate to get away.

There were a couple of outgoings to report. Frank Gray left to rejoin Leeds United, whilst Raimondo Ponte joined Bastia. Ponte, after a promising start to his Forest career, had soon found himself frozen out, and it had not been a surprise to see him go.

The first big signing turned out to be Mark Proctor from Middlesbrough, for a fee in excess of £400,000, that fee being decided by tribunal because the two clubs could not agree a figure. He was a combative midfielder with an eye for goal, but the most surprised people at his signing were Alan Hill and Liam O'Kane, who had been trailing his colleague Craig Johnstone. As Alan puts it: "Peter Taylor often didn't take kindly to other people suggesting signings, he wanted to be the main man."

The next signing would turn out to be the most controversial of Brian Clough's managerial career, for a variety of reasons.

Justin Fashanu was a big bruising centre forward for Norwich City. Forest had tried to land the player the previous season as part of the deal that took Martin O'Neill to Carrow Road, but the player, a local lad, decided to stay and try and help them avoid relegation. To no avail though, City went down and Fashanu wanted to stay in the First Division. Manchester City were also interested, but Fashanu was fascinated by the chance to play for Brian Clough, who he thought could help him improve as a centre forward. At one stage it looked as if the deal would stall over the fee, but Taylor wanted him, so persuaded Clough to pay up. Fashanu said one of the other

Forest players get on their bike for pre-season training.

reasons he chose Forest, was to play alongside Trevor Francis.

Fashanu joined up with the Forest squad in Spain where they were playing a pre-season tournament. The player immediately set an unwanted record when he was sent off in only his second game against Real Zaragosa, having already been sent off for Norwich pre-season in Canada and also in Africa whilst guesting for a club there. Three sendings off, on three different continents, in one month. Kenny Burns added to the manager's anger by also getting sent off in the same tournament against Osasuna.

Adidas unveiled the team's new style shirt for the season, featuring white pinstripes on the body and sleeve. After some early negative comments, it became a classic amongst Reds' supporters. The club's commercial department also announced they had signed their first shirt sponsorship deal in the club's history with Panasonic, although initially, the FA would only allow the shirts to be used for FA Cup matches and not even then if the game was televised.

There were a couple of changes to the backroom staff to report, Ron Fenton of course had been promoted to assistant manager, but a couple of old faces had returned. Alan Hill came back to head up youth development and Frank Clark who had recently been sacked along with Ken Knighton at Sunderland was helping with the reserves.

Francis couldn't be accused of letting the uncertainty about his future affect his performances, after his two goals in the first game of the season gave Forest a 2-1 victory before 25,000 at the City Ground. The attendance no doubt boosted by another opportunity to see Kevin Keegan back in England for the visitors.

The departure of Francis wasn't delayed for much longer though, his next appearance at Old Trafford was his last, before he signed for their rivals Manchester City. City had decided to spend big money in an attempt to overtake United, but it was to end in abject failure less than eighteen months later, when the money ran out, wages weren't met and players had to be sold quickly to raise cash. Francis who had already suffered several injuries in his short career, lasted only a few months at Maine Road, before he missed the rest of the season.

Ian Wallace immediately took up the scoring mantle, firing three goals past Birmingham at St Andrews, the only problem was, Forest managed to concede four. Clough was particularly scathing about Kenny Burns, who the manager thought was reverting back to his old ways. Clough was also none too pleased with the performance of his new centre forward. The following week the match programme contained a letter.

'I have read a newspaper report that you (Mr Clough) blasted Justin's performance against Birmingham.
As Justin's auntie, I feel this was very harsh and I would like you to apologise to him'. Yours, Norga Untalim.

It seemed as if the manager had already made his mind up about the player. The striker's situation wasn't helped by a police visit to the City Ground looking for the player. Fashanu had a very casual attitude to where he should park, amassing over thirty unpaid fines in Norwich and Nottingham. The police told Clough that they were sorry but that they would have to arrest the player. Clough was said to have replied: "Don't tolerate it, put him in jail."

There was clearly unrest in the camp, and when the manager fell out with one of his favourites John Robertson, things were not looking good. For the game at Stoke City, Clough left out the player and sent word to Nottingham for Colin Walsh to dash over to the Potteries to take his place. He scored and Forest won. Robertson was restored to the first team the following weekend though. At that same game, John Lawson reports that a rumour had swept the press box at Stoke, that Garry Birtles had scored for Manchester United, but it turned out be just that, a rumour.

There was some success for Nottingham sport however. Nottinghamshire Cricket Club, led by Clive Rice and Richard Hadlee clinched the County Championship for the first time since 1929.

Mark Proctor.

FASHANU

EXCLUSIVE

Nottingham Forest's new £1 million striker launches the first of SHOOT'S new series of interviews with big name soccer personalities.

STAR SPOT

IT looked as though he'd be kicking-off the new season in the Second Division with Norwich. But suddenly, Brian Clough made one of his lightning-fast, no-nonsense moves. And in next-to-no-time Justin Fashanu was heading for Spain to pull on the Forest shirt for the first time in a summer tournament in Zaragoza, and to share a room with fellow million-pound superstar Trevor Francis. Two million pounds of talent in one room!

"Justin amazed me," recalls Trevor. "On the first morning he leapt out of bed and did 58 press-ups on the floor. I just sat there and applauded!"

SHOOT was quick off the mark too, and here he talks about his £1m transfer . . . his hopes . . . and his regrets.

' I think this move is a stepping-stone towards *anything* now, and I've joined a club capable of winning anything, just as long as we all want to work hard and to play good soccer. Other clubs were interested in me, and I had the chance to talk to other clubs, but I felt that Forest have the best chance of really going places.

I don't think people have a good look at the players we've got at Forest, but we've got class in every department in the side. We're going to be knocking on the door this season.

Having said that, I've got lots of regrets about leaving Norwich, and if we'd stayed in the First Division I'm sure I would have stayed and seen my contract out.

Personal

I mean, I've been with Norwich since I left school, and obviously they've been a very big part of my personal and professional life. I promise you it was a very emotional day when I had to go and say goodbye to people.

One of the great things I've discovered since I've been at Forest is that their style of football is almost exactly the same, so I haven't felt lost at all.

What's more, the lads have given me a great welcome, and I can't see that I'm going to have any problems with the boss either.

So far, I've enjoyed the training. Obviously I can only compare it with Norwich and England, but I've felt more relaxed at Forest. As Peter Taylor keeps saying, if a

Brian Clough and Peter Taylor are the men who can bring the best out of their latest big-money signing Justin Fashanu.

JUSTIN FASHANU says

'I'LL BE BRITAIN'S BEST STRIKER'

while. I'm in no hurry to buy a house, and I'll wait till the right accommodation comes along — at the right price!

You know, joining Forest *should* make me a better player. There are so many good players here that some of the talent should rub off on me.

What's more, I don't think I'll have to make any big changes in my style of play, because Norwich and Forest play such similar styles.

But maybe I'll have to stop doing one or two things which I recognise were perhaps detrimental to my game, and in this way I'm bound to improve.

Obviously I'll also be aiming to further my international career, because any footballer worth his salt wants more than anything to represent his country and I'm hoping that playing top football at Forest will be a stepping-stone towards a long international career.'

player is relaxed you have more chance of getting the best out of him.

I've been asking Trevor Francis plenty of questions about Forest — and he's told me a lot of things I haven't asked him, too!

Talking about Trevor, I think possibly *he's* had more pressure because of his £1 million pricetag than I will. After all, he was the first, but nowadays it's become almost normal, and I don't think it's going to affect me very much.'

In the meantime, Justin Fashanu's name has barely been out of the headlines. The endless transfer rumours, the signing, how he arrived at the airport without his passport, how a Spanish referee sent him off for a minor offence in his second game.

'Yes, things have really been hectic in the past weeks, because at Norwich I had to keep playing well without knowing if I was staying or not.

And the papers were saying that every match was my last! It definitely was off-putting, but I hope I did the right thing by Norwich — because I know the club did the right thing by me.

The most hectic moment was when Forest came in for me, because I knew at six o'clock, and four or five hours later I'd signed and was on my way to Spain.

As for forgetting my passport, well, these things only happen to me! I also found that my boots had mysteriously disappeared — maybe someone wanted some souvenirs! — and I had to travel with just one pair. Luckily the conditions in Spain were OK.

Perhaps I'll get more organised when I settle in Nottingham, though I'll be in an hotel for a

ABOVE: John Robertson's wing service will be crucial if Fashanu is to succeed at Forest. LEFT: Relaxing in Spain with new Forest team-mates Peter Shilton and Trevor Francis.

Francis in action against Southampton.

Action from the Albion game.

Ian Wallace nets from close range with the winner against Brighton.

Justin Fashanu soars...

Burns scores his final goal for the club against Brighton.

Wallace and Fashanu celebrate this goal against Birmingham.

EARLY SEASON ACTION FROM THE CITY GROUND

STUART
GRAY
Nottingham
Forest
Panasonic
adidas

"WHEN I step out on the park, I just don't want to lose. I hate losing. If we lose it annoys me, to say the least. It takes a lot out of me. That's why I get so keyed up at matches, and that's why I talk and shout a lot, trying to get everybody in the right place and doing their job. They might think I'm giving them stick, but it's for their sake as well as mine, because I really want to win that game. Maybe that's why I've always responded well to the boss, because he's not the best of losers either. He hates defeat as much as I do."

The words express the attitude of Kenny Burns, one of the most determined competitors in the British game. And the defeat-hating boss that he mentions is, of course, Brian Clough — the man who helped wild and wayward Burns to become the rock-solid tower of strength at the heart of a European Champion defence. SHOOT asked Kenny to look back briefly at the decisive moments in his career and here is what the Forest and Scotland star told us:

Clough's threat 'IF YOU DON'T YOU'RE

'I suppose certain moments have been decisive in my career, but you don't always realise at the time. I mean, I started playing at a primary school in Glasgow, then a group of friends formed a Boys' Club team that started to do well.

We won a lot of trophies in three or four years until we all began to go our different ways. I played a lot of youth football, and then came the important moment when I signed for Glasgow Rangers.

I didn't last long at Ibrox. It wasn't really a case of me leaving Rangers — they'd just had enough of me. They didn't reckon I was good enough anyway.

Nowadays I can look back and realise I was a tearaway who

In attack for Birmingham against Everton's Howard Kendall.

posed problems for the club. It was a kick in the teeth for me, but I was still determined to make the grade in football, so I just gritted my teeth and got on with the job.

Luckily I was given a chance at Birmingham, and I settled in quickly. Then moving to Nottingham was another real turning point.

Peter Taylor took a chance on signing me, because I think he'd only seen me play once for Scotland. What's more, I think I was playing in midfield. But he decided I could do a job at Forest, ahd that was that.

The funny thing is I never specialised in any one position until I was at Birmingham. I used to play midfield or up front.

we went out, we seemed to play well and win, and this gave a calmness and confidence that I'd never known before.

We had a remarkable run of 42 games without defeat, and I can't ever see that record getting beaten. That was unbelievable.

In my career, I suppose I've always been trying to prove a point. We did it in the League and suddenly we were in Europe. We had to win against some of the best teams on the Continent. And we did.

We beat teams like Ajax, Cologne and Hamburger SV and we were European Champions for two consecutive years.

It gave me confidence and pride in the football we were playing. I'm sure my team-mates felt the same — it gave us the conviction that we were playing football the *right* way.

We were enjoying the game and

to Burns

MAKE IT HERE FINISHED!'

Another funny thing was when I arrived at Birmingham I had to play in a trial game against their youth side, marking a player called Trevor Francis!

I did quite well, and they signed me! Anyway, it was Freddie Goodwin who just said to me one day "Do you fancy playing centre-half?" I said I didn't mind, and I had a try-out that Wednesday in the third team.

The following Saturday I made my debut in the first team at centre-half.

Up to that point I'd been mostly in midfield or up front. I remember playing alongside Trevor for one season, and we scored about 40 goals between us.

No exception

I think it is true that Cloughie has changed me. I am a different person these days. I think a lot of people are a bit wild when they're young, and I was no exception.

A lot of lads just tend to be like that. Luckily I was still young when I arrived in Nottingham — young enough to change my ways. I've matured here, I've really grown up and I'm a lot more level-headed.

The boss' system was basically very simple, but it worked. He just told me: "This is your last go. If you don't make it here, you're finished."

Also, I don't like paying fines! My temperament was hitting me in the pocket too, you know.

But let's be honest, apart from that, I came into a good team — which was also very important for me. And we got off to a great start.

We won the League and we played good football. Every time

Burns is desperate to make a return to the Scottish national side in time for next year's World Cup Finals (below). Beating Hamburger SV in the 1980 European Cup Final was the highlight of Kenny's career so far (right).

winning, so we felt proud of what we were doing.

As a result, I'm sure I'm a much better player now. There's no substitute for experience against top teams, and that's what I have been getting since I came to Nottingham.

Of all our European matches, maybe that Final against Hamburger SV in Madrid was my highlight because I had a good game all round. In the air, on the ground . . . I marked well. I felt I did well and it was great that it was one of those games when everybody was watching.

The happiest feeling I get from playing football is when we keep a clean sheet and we win. That's why I've been happy at Forest, because we've done that regularly. We started conceding silly goals last season and hence our disappointing campaign.

Another low point in my career was when I played for Scotland in the last World Cup. We failed to live up to expectations, as everybody knows. The worst part for me was being involved in some bad goals conceded. When we let in a soft goal it affects me badly. It's an insult. It's a feeling like grim death when we start to make mistakes in our own penalty-area.

I'd dearly like to get back in the Scotland side and represent my country in next year's World Cup.

I've missed a couple of games, but I like to think the boss knows what I can do and he can count on me to produce the goods.

If I didn't want to be in Spain next year, I'd be wasting my time playing football — it's a question of pride quite apart from all the financial and other aspects.

This could be a good season at Forest, too. I think we could achieve something in the League. I hope for his sake and for ours that things work out really well for Justin Fashanu — he could make a big difference to us once he's settled in.

Spoilt

Possibly all the success we've had here in recent years has spoilt us, but we're determined to win something.

For me, that's what football is all about, and I like to think I'm a winner. The League is our top target, with the Cup a bonus.

I don't anticipate having any troubles with referees — they're just an occupational hazard! No, seriously, I get on very well with most referees these days. They know I like talking and most of them just talk back — except one or two of the less experienced ones.

You know the bookmakers are still quoting us at 12-1 for the title? If I were you, I'd have a little flutter on Forest.❜

THRILLS GOALS AND NEAR MISSES

The Reds draw a blank against the Hammers.

Fashanu scores against Arsenal.

Peter Ward salutes Mark Proctor's goal against Wrexham.

More action from the Tranmere game.

Grobelaar just manages to turn this effort around the post.

Ian Wallace in action against Liverpool.

Jurgen Roeber scores against Tranmere.

Roeber's team mates join in the celebrations.

Jurgen Roeber.

Willie Young.

Two successive home wins against Sunderland and Brighton pushed Forest up to fourth place. Burns scored what turned out to be his last goal for the club in the Brighton game, but it appeared the rift between him and the management was now too wide. Using the pages of a weekly football magazine, Clough was strong in his choice of words. 'If you don't make it here, you're finished'. His final appearance came in a 3-2 victory over Birmingham in the League Cup. Kenny Burns moved to Leeds United for a fee of £400,000. It has to be said that Kenny's career was now on a downward trajectory, but his place in the history of Nottingham Forest was secure.

Justin Fashanu finally opened his scoring account with the equaliser away at Middlesbrough. According to his team mates he was a nice enough fellow, he joined in the dressing room banter, but it was often the little things that alienated fellow players. All the players were issued with club towels, and after a few months, these often were looking a bit tired, but Justin immediately started bringing his own. He had his own routines, he brought his own masseuse to the club and he often spoke to the players about diet and perhaps more pointedly he rarely socialised with them. His surprising lack of skill is highlighted by a story from Steve Hodge, who remembers that he was asked along with a couple of apprentices to stay behind after training for shooting practice. He recalls: "The simple shooting drills turned into a nightmare for him, and us apprentices showed far better technique than the one million pound player."

Steve Hodge was to get his first taste of first team action shortly after. Following on from the success of the previous season's game with Tampa Bay, Forest entertained Vancouver Whitecaps. The novelty had clearly worn off, only 6,500 attended, but to Steve that didn't matter. The game was played on a Sunday, and although he had played the previous day for the reserves, he was told to report to the ground and scored the opening goal in a 2-2 draw. Chris Fairclough and Calvin Plummer also started.

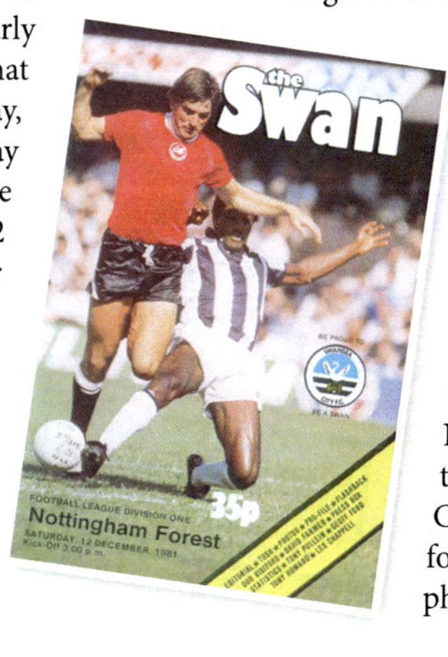

Birmingham City had a reputation for rough play at this time, they had a number of players seemingly out to live up to this notoriety. Full back Mark Dennis, centre forward Mick Harford and Kevin Broadhurst. So it wasn't altogether a surprise when the League Cup second leg tie spilled over and Broadhurst was sent off. He was joined by the normally mild mannered Ian Wallace who retaliated after a crude challenge.

November saw a positive goal rush from Fashanu as he scored in three successive games, including the winner at Blackburn in the League Cup. It proved to be a false dawn however, as he failed to find the target again that season. If only he could score as many goals as the disciplinary points he collected. For a player who came with a reputation for a physical approach, many of his bookings were for back chatting referees.

Forest were about to enter the transfer market once again. First in was Jurgen Roeber, who had made his name in Germany with Bayern Munich, but in fact joined from Chicago Sting for a fee of £250,000. Jurgen was a busy right sided midfielder, in the style of Martin O'Neill. The other signing was to be typical Clough one of the next couple of years, as Forest were forced more and more to cut their cloth accordingly. Willie Young, a tall no nonsense centre half joined from Arsenal after losing his place to David O'Leary. Young proved to be a capable replacement for Larry Lloyd, not only on the pitch but also in standing up to the manager. Willie tells a story of how Brian Clough was banging on to Fashanu about how many goals he had scored, Young shouted out: "Aye, but most of yours were in the f***ing Second Division."

On joining the club, Einar Aas had made an instantly favourable impression on supporters. He was very cultured and adept at bringing the ball out of defence, he was also captain of Norway, but the injury he picked up away at Sunderland turned out to be far more serious than anyone could have imagined at the time, and would lead to him quitting the game eighteen months later. He not only dislocated his knee when turning to chase a through ball, but x- rays showed that he had also broken a bone just below the knee.

Jurgen Roeber made a scoring debut against Tranmere Rovers in the League Cup, alongside Chris Fairclough, also making his first appearance, standing in for the cup tied Willie Young. Their reward for beating Rovers was to be an away tie at Tottenham Hotspur. Nottingham Forest had enjoyed far more success than any other club in this competition. Before Clough had arrived they had never got passed the fourth round, but the club's record since 1977 was phenomenal. Played 33, won 23, drawn 8, lost 2,

EVENING POST
NORTH
RED'S BOSS, BRIAN CLOUGH ADMITTED TO HOSPITAL.

for 83, against 28.

John McGovern was out of the team injured in November, when he received a request from Peter Taylor to go to his office. Clough was away at the time on one of his regular mid-season breaks. McGovern had no idea what was coming. Taylor said: "John, we have had a good run, but all good things come to an end."

When Clough returned from holiday he was fuming: " Who told you you were on the transfer list? That's my decision, you're going nowhere." Then Taylor told the player again that he was going. At that point Clough then said: "Don't listen to Taylor you're not going." Now McGovern really was confused about who to believe and the way that Clough had called his partner 'Taylor', rather than 'Pete' or 'my mate', revealed to the player that all was not well between the pair.

Forest ended 1981 in sixth place after a 2-1 win at Swansea, Willie Young scoring on his debut, but freezing weather led to multiple postponements and Forest wouldn't play another league game until the 9th of January.

The real story came off the pitch, when it was announced that Brian Clough had been rushed to hospital on the 29th of December with chest pains. The pressure not only of managing the club, but also the stress of his declining relationship with Peter Taylor, were contributing factors. This front page news was accompanied by another story, Justin Fashanu had driven his car into the side of a bus.

Calvin Plummer.

Taylor took charge of the team, and he most definitely would have wished that the FA Cup game at home to Wrexham had also fallen foul of the weather, as had the previous league fixtures. Originally planned to take place the day before on New Year's Day, it was put back 24 hours for the pitch to thaw out. Forest despite the fillip of a second minute Proctor goal, were terrible. Wrexham took full advantage and clinically clinched the game with three goals in eleven second half minutes. This was undoubtedly the worst result of the Clough and Taylor reign. It cannot be ignored, but these type of setbacks happened more often than not when Peter Taylor was left in charge.

A 2-1 win over Birmingham City did little to lift the gloom, the attendance for the second successive game was only 15,000. And when Tottenham knocked the Reds out of the League Cup, 1-0, the season was virtually over.

Desperate measures were needed, and it was to an old boy that Brian Clough turned. Ian Bowyer had been taken to Sunderland by Frank Clark for a fee of £250,000. Clark had now parted company with the Wearsiders, leaving Bowyer high and dry. He had not enjoyed the best of times at Roker Park, never really creating a rapport with the fans, who rarely saw the best of him, especially in a struggling side. Ian Bowyer had picked up a serious injury that sidelined him for six months, so when Clough turned up with an offer for him, both the club and Bowyer jumped at the opportunity, Ian returned for a ridiculously low fee of £50,000. Clough was never afraid to go back for players whose careers had faltered after moving away, Birtles, Hodge and Robertson would all make the return journey in years to come.

There was still no respite in the league either, Notts County visited the City Ground for the first time in the top flight for forty years, and left with a deserved 2-0 victory. Justin Fashanu who had been restored to the line-up after suspension, was particularly anonymous. He even felt it necessary to apologise to supporters for his performance through the pages of the Evening Post.

Brian Clough, back in the hot seat after being given the all clear and taking a short break, was convinced that Fashanu just couldn't play football, and blamed only one person for his signing. Talking to Duncan Hamilton of the Post he said: "The person who did buy him didn't do his job properly, we signed an idiot." Not only was the manager concerned about the player's ability, but also his off the pitch behaviour as well. There is no getting away from it, football has a problem with homophobia even to this day, so when the manager, who had eyes and ears everywhere, received reports that the player was a regular visitor to a gay club in Nottingham, called 'Part Two', it coloured his judgement further. Though the player was engaged, it didn't stop speculation about him from his team mates as well. On one occasion, John Robertson was egged on by team mates, to ask Fashanu if he was a 'poof'. "Give us a kiss and I'll tell you was the reply."

February turned out to be an even bigger disaster on the pitch; three defeats, two draws and a solitary victory, with only two goals scored, whilst another youngster, local lad Calvin Plummer, was thrown in at the deep end, a case of sink or swim, after all, a struggling team was not the perfect environment to make your debut.

Clough and Taylor by now, barely seemed to be talking to each other and when they did, it seemed like Taylor was looking for a way out. Clough told journalist friends that Taylor had said to him: "I think we've shot it." - "I told him, you speak for yourself." Clough added that he held his partner entirely responsible for the rubbish signings, and said that: "Maybe if he had left his office a bit more, they might not have been so bad". Then he himself, put McGovern, Wallace and Fashanu on the open to offers transfer list.

The lack of goals was to be a persistent problem right through until the end of the season, though it was fortunate that the defence was solid enough. Ian Wallace had found himself increasingly sidelined, whilst Ward was playing only the odd game here or there. A run of fourteen games only

Robertson misses from the penalty spot against Notts County.

Justin Fashanu can't evade this challenge against Notts County.

Ian Wallace nips in to score against Birmingham.

Ward coolly beats the Birmingham City keeper.

WINTER BLUES FOR FOREST

Colin Walsh lets fly against Middlesbrough.

Anderson in attacking mode against Boro'.

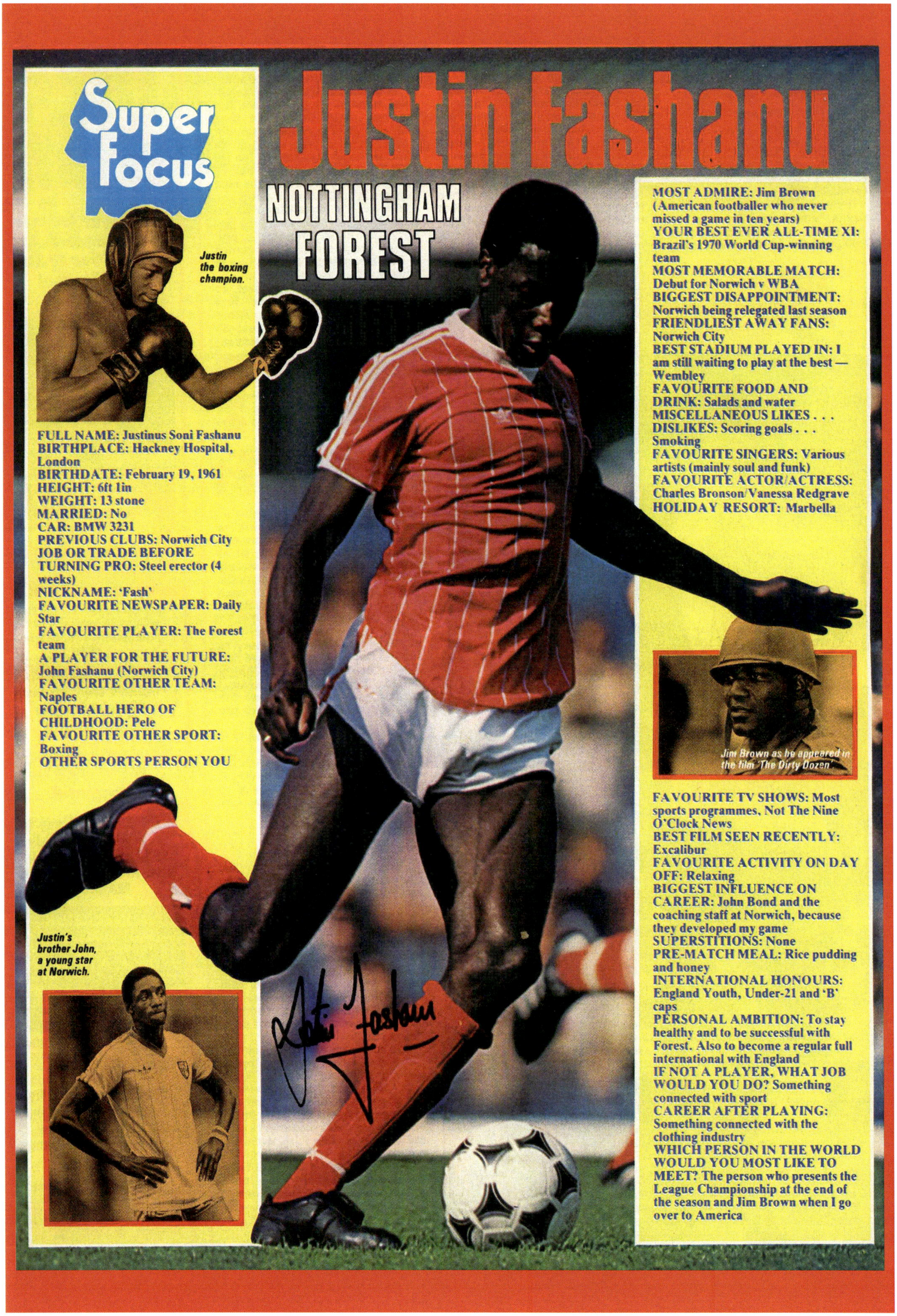

Justin Fashanu

Super Focus

NOTTINGHAM FOREST

Justin the boxing champion.

FULL NAME: Justinus Soni Fashanu
BIRTHPLACE: Hackney Hospital, London
BIRTHDATE: February 19, 1961
HEIGHT: 6ft 1in
WEIGHT: 13 stone
MARRIED: No
CAR: BMW 3231
PREVIOUS CLUBS: Norwich City
JOB OR TRADE BEFORE TURNING PRO: Steel erector (4 weeks)
NICKNAME: 'Fash'
FAVOURITE NEWSPAPER: Daily Star
FAVOURITE PLAYER: The Forest team
A PLAYER FOR THE FUTURE: John Fashanu (Norwich City)
FAVOURITE OTHER TEAM: Naples
FOOTBALL HERO OF CHILDHOOD: Pele
FAVOURITE OTHER SPORT: Boxing
OTHER SPORTS PERSON YOU
MOST ADMIRE: Jim Brown (American footballer who never missed a game in ten years)
YOUR BEST EVER ALL-TIME XI: Brazil's 1970 World Cup-winning team
MOST MEMORABLE MATCH: Debut for Norwich v WBA
BIGGEST DISAPPOINTMENT: Norwich being relegated last season
FRIENDLIEST AWAY FANS: Norwich City
BEST STADIUM PLAYED IN: I am still waiting to play at the best — Wembley
FAVOURITE FOOD AND DRINK: Salads and water
MISCELLANEOUS LIKES . . .
DISLIKES: Scoring goals . . . Smoking
FAVOURITE SINGERS: Various artists (mainly soul and funk)
FAVOURITE ACTOR/ACTRESS: Charles Bronson/Vanessa Redgrave
HOLIDAY RESORT: Marbella

Jim Brown as he appeared in the film 'The Dirty Dozen'

FAVOURITE TV SHOWS: Most sports programmes, Not The Nine O'Clock News
BEST FILM SEEN RECENTLY: Excalibur
FAVOURITE ACTIVITY ON DAY OFF: Relaxing
BIGGEST INFLUENCE ON CAREER: John Bond and the coaching staff at Norwich, because they developed my game
SUPERSTITIONS: None
PRE-MATCH MEAL: Rice pudding and honey
INTERNATIONAL HONOURS: England Youth, Under-21 and 'B' caps
PERSONAL AMBITION: To stay healthy and to be successful with Forest. Also to become a regular full international with England
IF NOT A PLAYER, WHAT JOB WOULD YOU DO? Something connected with sport
CAREER AFTER PLAYING: Something connected with the clothing industry
WHICH PERSON IN THE WORLD WOULD YOU MOST LIKE TO MEET? The person who presents the League Championship at the end of the season and Jim Brown when I go over to America

Justin's brother John, a young star at Norwich.

Justin Fashanu

Ian Wallace leaps, but glances the ball wide against Manchester City.

Goalmouth action from the encounter with Ipswich Town.

Peter Ward scores from the penalty spot against Manchester City.

Action from the Aston Villa game.

Desperate defending from Everton.

Action from the Ipswich game.

The Reds' draw a blank against Wolves.

Plummer and Everton keeper Neville Southall.

ACTION FROM FIVE GAMES

Calvin Plummer opens his scoring account with this close range effort against Ipswich.

THE CURTAIN COMES DOWN ON ANOTHER SEASON

Willie Young with the County Cup.

Davenport scores his first goal against Tottenham Hotspur.

Viv Anderson in full flight against Man Utd.

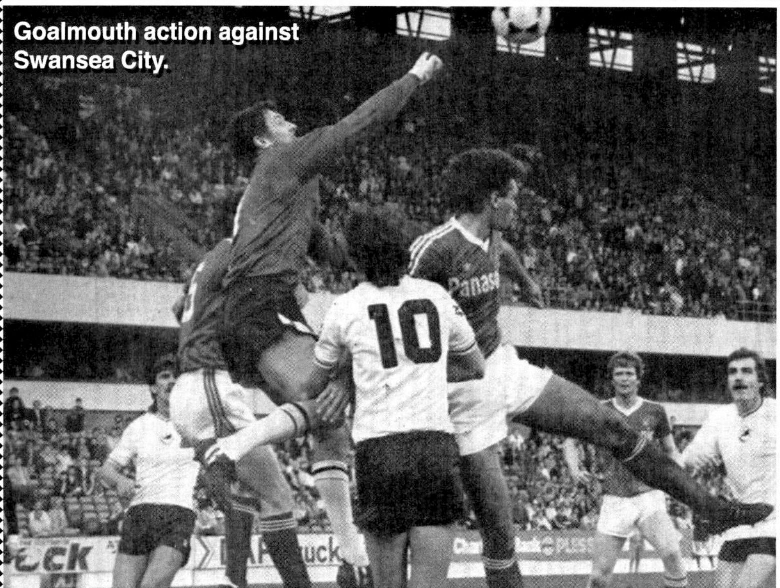
Goalmouth action against Swansea City.

Ian Wallace with a header.

JOHN
McGOVERN
Nottingham
Forest

EVENING POST

TAYLOR BOMBSHELL, I'M QUITTING.

Brian Clough pictured with Colin Walsh (left) and Gary Mills (right) after the pair had signed new contracts.

returned a total of eight goals and 15 points, relegation form in all honesty.

Jurgen Roeber was given an extended run in the number seven shirt. He could never be faulted for lack of effort, but if it was hoped that he might bring some 'continental' craft to the side, it didn't happen. He just looked like an inferior Martin O'Neill, but no player was helped by the constantly changing line-up that was attempting to arrest the slump in Forest's fortunes. How far the team and their standards had fallen, was brought home by a comment from Andy Gray after Wolves had departed Nottingham with all the points after a 1-0 win. "Teams used to be scared of coming here, not anymore!" Gray said.

At the same time as the first team couldn't score a goal, the reserves literally couldn't stop. They scored an amazing 33 goals in only 6 games. One player was particularly catching the eye, his name was Peter Davenport. Similar in appearance to Garry Birtles, he had trod the same path, also joining Forest from non league football. Cammell Laird received a nominal fee for the player. He had originally been on the books of Everton as a youngster, but been released from the club aged sixteen. The Forest players nicknamed him Birkenhead, as he was so homesick and returned to Merseyside as often as he could.

Results continued to be disappointing, defeat at Arsenal, 2-0, described as 'inept' by the manager, followed by a 2-1 defeat at Everton. Both of these games were particularly noticeable for the poor attendances they attracted, 21,000 at Highbury, but an incredibly low 15,000 at Goodison Park. Perhaps Forest fans were not as fickle as they were portrayed.

Peter Taylor then dropped his bombshell: "That's it, I've had it," and with that, the partnership was over. Brian Clough was acutely aware that Taylor had had health problems himself over previous years, including a heart attack and didn't try to persuade him to stay. He did say that he would speak to the club on his behalf about getting him some cash and a few other things. Perhaps he along with a lot of other people thought he might have acted in haste, after a poor season, and after some time away to re-charge his batteries, Peter Taylor would be back.

Davenport was finally given his opportunity, making his debut on his home territory at Anfield against Liverpool, a dissappointing 2-0 defeat. He did well enough to keep his place for the next two games, although both were lost, to Manchester United and Swansea. However, it was in the next game, where he wore the number ten shirt rather than number nine, that he was to break his duck, scoring along with Stuart Gray in a win over Tottenham Hotspur. That fixture also provided a memory for Steve Hodge that he recalls to this day: "The manager spoke to me and invited me to sit on the bench next to him during the game," saying, "come and learn your trade."

Steve hadn't been totally confident about his future, after all he had seen various team mates make their league debuts, including Chris Fairclough, who were younger than him, whilst he himself had made just a couple of appearances and they were only against Vancouver and Grantham. His main concern was that his contract was due to expire at the end of the season and there was no guarantee that he would be offered a new one.

The following week, Steve travelled with the team to Suffolk for the final game of the season at Ipswich Town. Although he had an inkling that he might be involved in some way, he was still the skivvy on the Friday coach journey to Portman Road.

This game looked like it could be the final showdown between the manager and Justin Fashanu. The player had been chosen to play, despite having a gashed leg, but at the last minute, he cried off saying he couldn't turn out. The row was loud, Clough thought that the player wasn't really bothered and could have played. The upshot of this was, that despite not really being a forward, Steve Hodge made his debut. Clough read the team out and said: "Young Hodge, you're playing centre forward." Peter Davenport was to be his partner upfront.

Ipswich Town were still competing with Aston Villa for the title and they were really up for the game, but Forest, showing an energy and desire that had been sadly lacking for much of the season, matched them and proceeded to win 3-1, Davenport scoring a splendid hat-trick, captured by the Match of the Day cameras. Steve Hodge obeyed orders and ran around a lot, and didn't feel out of place As he was substituted in the 85th minute after creating Davenport's third goal, the manager hugged him and lifted him off his feet with a: "Well done son."

As the team prepared to leave Portman Road, there was an incident that showed what could happen if you got on the wrong side of the manager. The players were seated on the coach when the manager insisted that the doors were closed on Justin Fashanu who was continuing to talk to people outside the ground. "Tell him to walk home," the manager shouted. However, surprisingly he was later persuaded to let the player get on board.

The good news for Steve Hodge was that he was called into the manager's office the following week and offered the new contract that he'd hoped for. It might have only be for one year, but there was also a pay rise to £90 per week and his confidence was further boosted when the manager said he hoped Steve

Peter Shilton receives his Player of the Year trophy.

would be playing forty games the next season.

This was always likely to be a season of change, however the speed with which the team was broken up could be seen in hindsight as too hasty. How much of this was influenced by the managerial pair drifting apart we can only guess, but a partnership that had been so strong, had rapidly descended into antipathy. The increasing lack of trust that the manager had in Taylor's judgement on player recruitments was evident by conversations he had with several people, and it was fair to ask, when was the last signing that had been an unequivocal success? It had probably been Trevor Francis and that signing hadn't exactly been a shot in the dark.

For a club that would always have to be careful with its finances, the signings of Fashanu, Ward, Wallace, Ponte and Proctor had cost over £3 million pounds and for what return? If young talent such as Colin Walsh, Stuart Gray and Peter Davenport hadn't emerged, the club would have been in serious trouble. Another anecdote from the manager provides further insight. Clough said: "Geoffrey McPherson, who in truth I regarded as a bumbling amateur, came up to me and said that he had been recommended that the club look at a young player at Chester called Ian Rush. So I mentioned this to Taylor who said, 'Yeah, we know about him, not good enough', so I said, perhaps best to go and have another look. He said, 'okay', although I don't know whether he actually ever did."

Twelfth place with only fifteen wins and forty goals scored was not of the standard expected from a Clough and Taylor team and the situation would be uncertain the following season as the manager was heading back into uncharted territory without his best mate. Many pundits expected, and perhaps hoped that Brian Clough was heading for a fall. This was to be the hardest challenge of his managerial career so far. He not only had to manage the team, but also the finances of the club, as football slumped in the consciousness of spectators due, not only to the worsening recession, but also an increasing hooligan problem that was to lead to a series of tragic events, that would blacken the name of the sport.

★★★ FOREST

APPEARANCES TEAM LINE-UPS

Aug 29th, H, v Southampton, W, 2-1, Scorers Francis (2), AT 25,234, Shilton, Anderson, Gray .S, McGovern, Burns, Aas, Francis, Ward, Fashanu, Proctor, Robertson.

Aug 31st, A, v Manchester United, D, 0-0, AT 51,496, Shilton, Anderson, Gray .S, McGovern, Burns, Aas, Francis, Ward, Fashanu, Proctor, Robertson.

Sept 5th, A, v Birmingham City, L, 3-4, Scorers Wallace (3), AT 19,035, Shilton, Anderson, Gray .S, McGovern, Burns, Aas, Mills, Wallace, Fashanu, Proctor, Robertson. SUB Gunn.

Sept 12th, H, v West Bromwich Albion, D, 0-0, AT 22,618, Shilton, Anderson, Gray .S, McGovern, Burns, Aas, Proctor, Wallace, Fashanu, Mills, Robertson. SUB Walsh.

Sept 19th, A, v Stoke City, W, 2-1, Scorers Mills, Walsh, AT 15,569, Shilton, Anderson, Gray .S, McGovern, Burns, Aas, Mills, Wallace, Fashanu, Proctor, Walsh.

Sept 23rd, H, v Sunderland, W, 2-0, Scorers Wallace, Proctor, AT 21,133, Shilton, Anderson, Gray .S, McGovern, Aas, Gunn, Mills, Wallace, Fashanu, Proctor, Robertson.

Sept 26th, H, v Brighton, W, 2-1, Scorers Burns, Wallace, AT 19,220, Shilton, Anderson, Gray .S, McGovern, Burns, Aas, Mills, Wallace, Fashanu, Proctor, Robertson.

Oct 3rd, A, v Tottenham Hotspur, L, 0-3, AT 34,870, Shilton, Anderson, Gray .S, McGovern, Burns, Gunn, Mills, Wallace, Fashanu, Proctor, Robertson. SUB Walsh.

Oct 6th, LC, A v Birmingham City, W, 3-2, Scorers Proctor, Wallace (2), AT 14,330, Shilton, Anderson, Gray .S, Aas, Burns, Gunn, Proctor, Wallace, Fashanu, Walsh, Robertson. SUB Mills.

Oct 10th, A, v Middlesbrough, D, 1-1, Scorer Fashanu, AT 15,043, Shilton, Anderson, Gray .S, Mills, Aas, Gunn, Proctor, Wallace, Fashanu, Walsh, Robertson. SUB McGovern.

Oct 17th, H, v Coventry City, W, 2-1, Scorers Wallace (2), AT 20,101, Shilton, Anderson, Gunn, McGovern, Needham, Aas, Gray .S, Wallace, Fashanu, Proctor, Robertson. SUB Walsh.

Oct 24th, A, v Manchester City, D, 0-0, AT 34,881, Shilton, Anderson, Gunn, McGovern, Needham, Aas, Proctor, Wallace, Fashanu, Gray .S, Robertson. SUB Walsh.

Oct 28th, LC, H, v Birmingham City, W, 2-1, Scorers Needham Robertson, AT 16,316, Shilton, Anderson, Gunn, McGovern, Needham, Aas, Gray .S, Wallace, Fashanu, Proctor, Robertson. SUB Walsh.

Oct 31st, H, v Leeds United, W, 2-1, Scorers Ward, Robertson (P), AT 25,272, Shilton, Anderson, Gunn, McGovern, Needham, Aas, Gray .S, Ward, Fashanu, Proctor, Robertson.

Nov 7th, H, v West Ham, D, 0-0, AT 26,327, Shilton, Anderson, Gunn, McGovern, Needham, Aas, Gray .S, Wallace, Fashanu, Proctor, Robertson. SUB Walsh.

Nov 11th, A, v Blackburn Rovers, W, 1-0, Scorer Fashanu, AT 14,752, Shilton, Anderson, Gunn, McGovern, Needham, Aas, Gray .S, Ward, Fashanu, Proctor, Robertson.

Nov 21st, H, v Arsenal, L, 1-2, Scorer Fashanu, AT 20,912, Shilton, Anderson, Gunn, McGovern, Needham, Aas, Gray .S, Ward, Fashanu, Proctor, Robertson. SUB Walsh.

Nov 25th, A, v Sunderland, W, 3-2, Scorers Needham, Walsh, Fashanu, AT 17,419, Shilton, Anderson, Gunn, Gray .S, Needham, Aas, Walsh, Ward, Fashanu, Proctor, Robertson. SUB Mills.

Nov 28th, A, v Aston Villa, L, 1-3, Scorer Walsh, AT 26,847, Shilton, Anderson, Gray .S, McGovern, Needham, Gunn, Mills, Ward, Fashanu, Walsh, Robertson. SUB Proctor.

Dec 2nd, LC, H, v Tranmere Rovers, W, 2-0, Scorers Roeber, Wallace, AT 12,244, Shilton, Anderson, Gray .S, Proctor, Fairclough, Gunn, Roeber, Wallace, Fashanu, Walsh, Robertson. SUB Mills.

Dec 5th, H, v Liverpool, L, 0-2, AT 24,521, Shilton, Mills, Gray .S, Proctor, Anderson, Gunn, Roeber, Wallace, Fashanu, Walsh, Robertson.

Dec 12th, A, v Swansea City, W, 2-1, Scorers Young, Robertson (P), AT 17,559, Shilton, Anderson, Gunn, Needham, Young, Gray .S, Roeber, Wallace, Fashanu, Proctor, Robertson.

Jan 2nd, FAC, H, v Wrexham, L, 1-3, Scorer Proctor, AT 15,649, Shilton, Anderson, Gunn, Needham, Young, Walsh, Roeber, Wallace, Ward, Proctor, Robertson. SUB McGovern.

Jan 9th, H, v Birmingham City, W, 2-1, Scorers Wallace, Ward, AT 15,906, Shilton, Anderson, Gray .S, Gunn, Young, Walsh, McGovern, Wallace, Ward, Proctor, Robertson. SUB Bowyer.

Jan 18th, LC, A, v Tottenham Hotspur, L, 0-1, AT 31,192, Shilton, Proctor, Gray .S, Gunn, Needham, Roeber, McGovern, Wallace, Ward, Mills, Robertson.

Jan 23rd, H, v Notts County, L, 0-2, AT 26,158, Shilton, Gunn, Gray .S, McGovern, Needham, Young, Proctor, Wallace, Fashanu, Bowyer, Robertson. SUB Roeber.

Jan 30th, H, v Stoke City, D, 0-0, AT 16,219, Shilton, Anderson, Bowyer, Gunn, Young, McGovern, Roeber, Wallace, Fashanu, Proctor, Robertson.

Feb 6th, A, v West Bromwich Albion, L, 1-2, Scorer Ward, AT 15,006, Shilton, Anderson, Gray .S, Gunn, Young, McGovern, Roeber, Wallace, Fashanu, Bowyer, Robertson. SUB Ward.

Feb 13th, A, v Southampton, L, 0-2, AT 21,350, Shilton, Anderson, Gunn, Needham, Young, Bowyer, Mills, Roeber, Fashanu, Ward, Robertson. SUB Gray .S.

Feb 16th, A, v Wolverhampton Wanderers, D, 0-0, AT 11,195, Shilton, Anderson, Gunn, Gray .S, Young, Needham, Mills, Wallace, Ward, Bowyer, Robertson.

Feb 20th, A, v Brighton, W, 1-0, Scorer Ward, AT 17,175, Shilton, Anderson, Gunn, Gray .S, Young, Needham, Mills, Plummer, Ward, Bowyer, Robertson.

Feb 27th, H, v Middlesbrough, D, 1-1, Scorer Gray .S, AT 16,464, Shilton, Anderson, Gray .S, McGovern, Young, Gunn, Mills, Plummer,

1981 - 1982 DIVISION 1 TABLE

TEAMS	P	W	D	L	F	A	W	D	L	F43	A	PTS
1 Liverpool FC	42	14	3	4	39	14	12	6	3	41	18	87
2 Ipswich T	42	17	1	3	47	25	9	4	8	28	28	83
3 Manchetser U	42	12	6	3	27	9	10	6	5	32	20	78
4 Tottenham H	42	12	4	5	41	26	8	7	6	26	22	71
5 Arsenal	42	13	5	3	27	15	7	6	8	21	22	71
6 Swansea C	42	13	3	5	34	16	8	3	10	24	35	69
7 Southampton	42	15	2	4	49	30	4	7	10	23	37	66
8 Everton	42	11	7	3	33	21	6	6	9	23	29	64
9 West Ham U	42	9	10	2	42	29	5	6	10	24	28	58
10 Manchester C	42	9	7	5	32	23	6	6	9	17	27	58
11 Aston Vila	42	9	6	6	28	24	6	6	9	27	29	57
12 Nottingham F	42	7	7	7	19	20	8	5	8	23	28	57
13 Brighton & H.A	42	8	7	6	30	24	5	6	10	13	28	52
14 Coventry C	42	9	4	8	31	24	4	7	10	25	38	50
15 Notts Co	42	8	5	8	32	33	5	3	13	29	36	47
16 Birmingham C	42	8	6	7	29	25	2	8	11	24	36	44
17 W.B.A	42	6	6	9	24	25	5	5	11	22	32	44
18 Stoke C	42	9	2	10	27	28	3	6	12	17	35	44
19 Sunderland	42	6	5	10	19	26	5	6	10	19	32	44
20 Leeds U	42	6	11	4	23	20	4	1	16	16	41	42
21 Wolverhampton W	42	8	5	8	19	20	2	5	14	13	43	40
22 Middlebrough	42	5	9	7	20	24	3	6	12	14	28	39

★★★★ WHO? WHAT!

FACTFILE ★ ★ ★

RESULTS LEAGUE TABLE

Ward, Bowyer, Walsh. SUB Wallace.

March 9th, A, v Coventry City, W, 1-0, Scorer Roeber, AT 9,677, Shilton, Anderson, Bowyer, McGovern, Young, Gunn, Roeber, Wallace, Ward, Proctor, Gray .S.

March 13th, H, v Manchester City, D, 1-1, Scorer Ward (P), AT 20,927, Shilton, Anderson, Bowyer, McGovern, Young, Gunn, Roeber, Wallace, Ward, Proctor, Gray .S. SUB Fashanu.

March 17th, H, v Ipswich Town, D, 1-1, Scorer Plummer, AT 16,686, Shilton, Anderson, Bowyer, McGovern, Young, Gunn, Plummer, Wallace, Ward, Proctor, Roeber.

March 20th, A, v Leeds United, D, 1-1, Scorer Roeber, AT 18,036, Shilton, Anderson, Bowyer, McGovern, Young, Gunn, Roeber, Wallace, Fashanu, Proctor, Plummer.

March 27th, A, v West Ham, W, 1-0, Scorer Wallace, AT 24,633, Shilton, Anderson, Bowyer, McGovern, Young, Gunn, Roeber, Wallace, Fashanu, Proctor, Robertson.

April 3rd, H, v Everton, L, 0-1, AT 17,323, Shilton, Gunn, Bowyer, McGovern, Young, Gray .S, Roeber, Wallace, Fashanu, Proctor, Robertson. SUB Plummer.

April 10th, H, v Wolverhampton Wanderers, L, 0-1, AT 15,691, Shilton, Kendal, Bowyer, Gunn, Young, Gray .S, Roeber, Wallace, Fashanu, Proctor, Robertson. SUB Plummer.

April 12th, A, v Notts County, W, 2-1, Scorers Bowyer, Plummer, AT 19,304, Shilton, Anderson, Gray .S, Gunn, Young, Bowyer, Roeber, Plummer, Fashanu, Proctor, Robertson.

April 17th, A, v Arsenal, L, 0-2, AT 21,986, Shilton, Anderson, Gray .S, Gunn, Young, Bowyer, Roeber, Plummer, Fashanu, Proctor, Robertson. SUB McGovern.

April 20th, A, v Everton, L, 1-2, Scorer Roeber, AT 15,463, Shilton, Anderson, Gunn, Needham, Young, Bowyer, Roeber, Plummer, Fashanu, Proctor, Robertson. SUB McGovern.

April 24th, H, v Aston Villa, D, 1-1, Scorer Needham, AT 18,213, Shilton, Anderson, Gunn, Needham, Young, Bowyer, Roeber, Proctor, Fashanu, Wallace, Robertson. SUB McGovern.

May 1st, A, v Liverpool, L, 0-2, AT 34,321, Shilton, Anderson, Gunn, Needham, Young, Bowyer, Roeber, Proctor, Davenport, Wallace, Robertson. SUB McGovern.

May 5th, H, v Manchester United, L, 0-1, AT 18,449, Shilton, Anderson, Gunn, Needham, Young, Bowyer, Roeber, Proctor, Davenport, Wallace, Robertson. SUB Walsh.

May 8th, H, v Swansea City, L, 0-2, AT 15,037, Shilton, Anderson, Gunn, Needham, Young, Bowyer, Roeber, Proctor, Davenport, Wallace, Robertson. SUB Walsh.

May 12th H, v Tottenham Hotspur, W, 2-0, Scorers Gray .S, Davenport, AT 15,273, Shilton, Anderson, Bowyer, Gunn, Young, Gray .S, Proctor, Roeber, Fashanu, Davenport, Robertson.

May 15th, A, v Ipswich Town, W, 3-1, Scorer Davenport (3), AT 19,974, Shilton, Anderson, Bowyer, Gunn, Young, Gray .S, Roeber, McGovern, Hodge, Davenport, Robertson. SUB Proctor.

May 18th, CC, H, v Notts County, W, 7-1, Scorers Gray .S (2), Proctor (2), Wallace, Davenport, Robertson, AT 3,970, Shilton, Anderson, Bowyer, Fairclough, Young, Gray .S, Proctor, Roeber, Wallace, Davenport, Robertson. SUB Walsh, Hodge.

NOTTINGHAM FOREST FOOTBALL CLUB 1981/82

Back Row (left to right) : Peter Ward, Gary Mills, Mark Proctor, Colin Walsh.

Middle Row : Ron Fenton (Coach), Stuart Gray, David Needham, Lee Smelt, Peter Shilton, Einar-Jan Aas, Kenny Burns.

Front Row : Ian Wallace, John Robertson, John McGovern, Trevor Francis, Viv Anderson, Bryn Gunn.

WHERE! WHEN! ★ ★ ★

SEASON 1982-83

Back Row L to R: John Sheridan (Physio), Calvin Plummer, Peter Davenport, Bryn Gunn, Mark Proctor, Colin Todd, Ian Wallace
Middle Row L to R: Liam O'Kane (Coach), Chris Fairclough, Einar Aas, Steve Sutton, Hans van Breukelen, Willie Young, Viv Anderson, Garry Birtles, Ron Fenton (Asst. Manager)
Front Row L to R: Colin Walsh, Stuart Gray, Ian Bowyer, Brian Clough (Manager), John Robertson, Steve Hodge

There were lots of comings and goings in the build up to the new season. The major news was that Peter Shilton had finally got his wish, with a move away, to Southampton who paid out £350,000 for the keeper. The influence and role that this player had on the history of Nottingham Forest can never be over estimated. It is hard to understand now, that at the time of his signing in September 1977, many fans thought it unnecessary, and the club should have stuck with John Middleton. Peter Taylor knew the worth of a keeper though, reckoning Shilton could be worth at least fifteen points a season. He was worth even more than that. He helped to organise the defence, never afraid to bawl out Lloyd or Burns, every goal conceded was an affront to his ability. Even in his thirties, there was no obvious decline in his abilities and in fact he was to continue playing for another fourteen years, amassing over 1,000 league appearances.

How do you replace a colossus? Steve Sutton was given the unenviable task initially, whilst Alan Hill searched for a his successor.

The break up of the 1980 squad was almost complete, Dave Needham moved to America and joined the Toronto Blizzard whilst skipper John McGovern, whose career had been so entwined with Brian Clough, since signing for Hartlepool as a sixteen year old, moved into management with Bolton Wanderers.

Let John explain the events: "Many people thought that I was the manager's 'blue eyed boy', but our relationship was strictly professional, he was good for me and I hope that I was good for him. When it came to a parting of the ways it was quite matter of fact, 'Bolton want you as player manager, I think it would be good experience for you'. As an aside, he said that he would try and sort out a bit of extra money. This became a conflict, before he told me the chairman said I could have £5,000. At the end there was no sentiment, no handshake from Brian or Peter, just a professional relationship."

Further outgoings from the previous season were Jurgen Roeber who returned to Germany, joining Bayer Leverkusen and Peter Ward who initially went to the Seattle Sounders before rejoining Brighton.

To replace Einar Aas, the manager turned once again to one of his ex players. Colin Todd had been one of his favourites at Derby, a player who exuded class. He was signed from Birmingham City for only £65,000 and formed an experienced partnership with Willie Young, although there were high hopes that Chris Fairclough would make a strong push for a regular first team spot. But there can have been no finer teachers than this pair to advance his career.

Pre-season began in Malaysia before another four team tournament in Spain. Brian Clough must have wondered what he was letting himself in for with these Spanish adventures, this time Forest had three players sent off. Fashanu, who had been given one final chance to make an impression, Willie Young and more surprisingly John Robertson who was sent off for 'glaring' at the referee as the players left the pitch at half time. The player only found out when Liam O'Kane came into the dressing room to pass the news on.

Justin Fashanu was given ample opportunity to rehabilitate himself during this pre-season. He started seven out of eight games, but still couldn't score a goal. When Clough received a call out of the blue from Southampton manager Lawrie McMenemy asking to take the player on loan, it was a case of

The players are pictured with the impressive Huelva trophy.

The manager welcomes new signing Colin Todd.

taxi for Fashanu, the manager couldn't get him out of the door quick enough.

The Sunday People newspaper had ran a story about the player a few months previously, all but accusing the player of being gay. Fashanu had responded by not only denying it, but also launching a law suit against the paper for defamation of character. Despite all this innuendo against the player, there was almost no baiting of Fashanu from the terraces. It was if no-one could believe that a footballer who played in such a physical style might be gay.

At national level, there was another rule change. The introduction of a maximum number of four steps allowed for goalkeepers whilst they had the ball in their hands. The Football Association also announced another clampdown on rough play, plus a crackdown on gamesmanship such as time wasting etc.

As the opening game against West Ham United approached, Brian Clough announced that Ian Bowyer would be the club's new skipper, a move that was popular with players and fans alike. In a last ditch attempt to solve the keeper connundrum, an approach was made to Queens Park Rangers to re-sign Chris Woods, but both club and player turned down the deal.

In his column for the Sun newspaper, ex-player turned pundit, Jimmy Greaves predicted a season of worry for the Reds, promising a sizeable donation to charity if he was wrong. It was a strange looking line up for the opener at Upton Park. Sutton in goal, Bowyer left back and Calvin Plummer at centre forward. Davenport missed the game through injury, but Steve Hodge retained his place, in his more favoured midfield role. Forest left with the points after a promising 2-1 victory. The undoubted highlight was the goal from Colin Walsh, after a powerful run through the Hammers' defence led to him rounding keeper Phil Parkes, before firing into an empty net. Forest immediately fell foul of the referees' clampdown in the first home game of the season against Manchester United, Colin Todd reaching above his head caught a through ball. He was sent off for ungentlemanly conduct. Forest held out until the 70th minute before conceding three goals.

Garry Birtles watched the game from the directors' box. He was ready to end an unhappy spell at Old Trafford and return to the club where he had made his name. No-one can say for certain why things didn't click for the player in Manchester. Garry himself thinks that it wasn't as bad as many critics made out. He was a regular choice for most of his period there, but a centre forward tends to be judged on his scoring record and it has to be said that the player's goals total fell far short of what himself would have expected.

Brian Clough said that the club couldn't really afford the player, but claimed that the number of season tickets sold had persuaded him.

Birtles wasn't the only new face to start the next game at home to Brighton. Forest had turned to the continent to solve their goalkeeping problem. Steve Sutton may have been disappointed not to be given the chance to claim the jersey, but when a keeper of the quality of Hans van Breukelen, FC Utrechts' Dutch international comes available, you sign him. Alan Hill, the ex Forest goalkeeper had been following the player, and reported back that he was certain to adapt to English football. He cost £165,000. Less than half the fee, that had been received for Peter Shilton, but along with the outlay of £275,000 on Birtles, this represented a hefty outlay for the club.

Forest thrashed Brighton 4-0, but the attendance was only 13,709, a worryingly low figure for so early in the season. Birtles injured an ankle and would miss the next couple of games.

It has to be said that on the majority of visits made to Anfield during this era, they tended to be constructed around a defensive approach. Maybe it was because of a more youthful outlook, but this season, the game was an exact opposite. Taking the game to Liverpool, a first goal for Hodge, one of two, and another from Davenport gave Forest a 3-2 lead until the 82nd minute.

It took a hugely deflected shot from Souness off the unfortunate Fairclough, to level, but Liverpool didn't deserve the late winner from Ian Rush. To those who claim that the scouse fans are the best, an attendance of only 27,000 might make them re-consider.

Steve Hodge felt like he'd arrived that night. In truth he had taken the step up in his stride, and going toe to toe with Souness and co. merely confirmed it. As Steve says: "It was great to be accepted, to be invited to continue the tradition of going to McKays café after training meant a lot to me."

Forest were unfortunate to concede another four goals in the next game at Aston Villa. Yet again they fell foul of the professional foul rule when Bowyer was sent off. They stayed in the game until late in the second half, when they were effectively down to nine men after Davenport went off with a

1. Colin Walsh advances on Hammers' keeper Phil Parkes.

2. Colin sends the keeper the wrong way.

SUNS AND GOA

Mark Proctor.

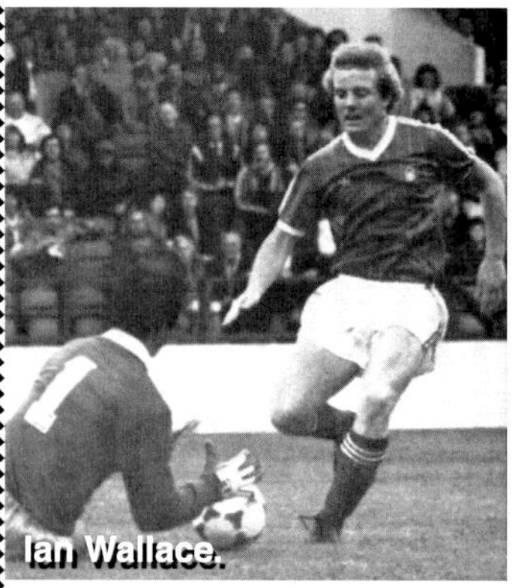

Ian Wallace.

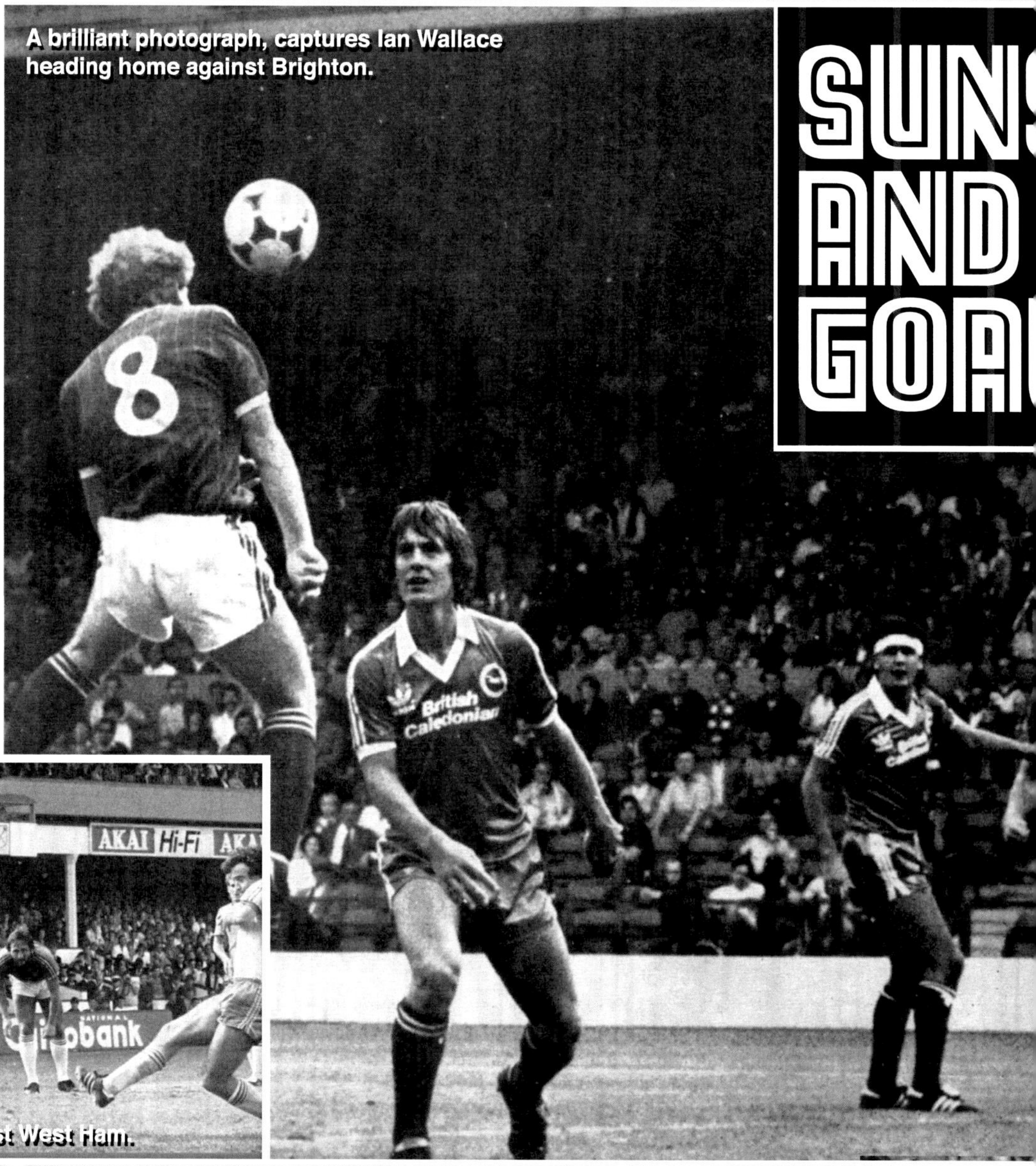

A brilliant photograph, captures Ian Wallace heading home against Brighton.

Robbo with the winner against West Ham.

Garry Birtles...

...bursts through...

3. An open goal awaits.

4. The ball is on its way in to the net for our opening goal.

It's celebration time.

Diminutive Ian Wallace leaps.

Walsh slides in this goal against Brighton.

Proctor fires wide.

Robertson from the spot against Brighton.

...and the Watford keeper...

...is beaten.

CLOUGH v ROBERTSON... Who has the greater willpower? The manager challenges Robbo, I will give up drinking, if you stop smoking.

ligament injury after they had already used their substitute.

The manager made no secret of the high standards that he expected from his players and supporters, so when he saw a pitch invader during the home game with Watford, he decided to deal with the matter himself. That the pitch invader was fully dressed as a clown made no difference to him, and the newspapers next day were full of photographs of Cloughie marching the offender off. Underneath the make up was Mick Scarrott, who was well known to Reds fans.

Van Breukelen admitted that he found that English game very different to what he was used to. He was blamed for Villa's second goal scored by Peter Withe. Hans said: "I have to improve with the way that I deal with crosses, I am working hard with Alan Hill on this aspect of my game."

Birtles returned from his minor injury against Watford and scored the first goal of his second spell in a 2-0 win. Van Breuklen might be struggling with some aspects of the English game, but he endeared himself to supporters by saving a penalty from Luther Blissett that would have equalled the scores.

The keeper's lack of confidence was again exposed when they conceded four more in the next away game at Tottenham, twelve goals in three successive away games.

Interesting news off the pitch. Brian Clough challenged John Robertson to stop smoking, whilst he would stop drinking. They both probably lasted about five minutes after the photographer had got his picture.

In a small article, the club listed a number of new apprentices joining the club, one being Desmond Walker from Hackney, who was to have a major impact at the club.

Birtles was back on the scoresheet with the winner against Stoke, his return to the club had also rejuvenated his strike partner Ian Wallace, who was even given the captaincy in the absence of Ian Bowyer.

After a bye in the first round, Forest began their Milk Cup campaign (formerly known as the League Cup) with an exhilarating 6-1 demolition of West Brom. The only pity was that there were less than 12,000 there to witness it. Wallace, Robertson, Hodge and Birtles were the scorers, Birtles scoring for the fourth successive game, and his barren spell at Old Trafford was beginning to seem like a bad dream.

As is the way with football, Forest travelled to the Hawthorns for a league game three days later and fell to a 2-1 defeat. Yet another sending off, Steve Hodge this time for an innocuous foul, while Cyrille Regis wasn't even booked for elbowing Colin Todd who required stitches. Even Forest were now complaining about the inconsistency of the over zealous referees' crackdown, and as a result, clubs demanded an urgent meeting with the referees' association to sort things out.

The following week, Viv Anderson injured himself while on England duty. This left Forest short of defenders, so Clough was forced into the market. Not really wanting to pay out, he looked for someone he could bring in initially on loan, because Anderson wasn't considered likely to be out for too long. Kenny Swain takes up the story: "I had been part of the Aston Villa team that had won the European Cup only four months before, but had found myself being made the scapegoat for the team's poor performances. I was playing for the reserves, when our manager Tony Barton said that there was a manager waiting upstairs to see me, Brian Clough. I had never really fancied playing for him, but of course I was flattered that he was interested. After

'Stop clowning about'.

introducing himself to my wife with a kiss, we sat down with the Villa secretary and I agreed to join Forest, initially on a months loan. As the manager said, 'You can have a look at us', and his parting words were, 'you know what we're about, see you on Friday'. The minute I walked into the club I felt at home, John Robertson was the first player I met and he

COLIN WALSH
Nottingham Forest

VIV ANDERSON
Nottingham Forest

JOHN ROBERTSON
Nottingham Forest

GARRY BIRTLES
Forest

GOAL AND ACTION

Wallace with this fantastic overhead kick scores against West Brom.

Steve Hodge bursts through the Ipswich defence.

Scramble in the Ipswich box.

Robertson beats Ipswich keeper Cooper.

Kenny Swain fires a cross over.

Garry Birtles in action at Roker Park.

Birtles completes the scoring against Albion.

Hans van Breukelen cycling his way back to fitness.

introduced me to the rest of the team. I think I played my best football at Forest, and it was certainly one of the happiest times of my career."

Forest produced perhaps their best performance of the season when they beat Arsenal 3-0, Proctor, Wallace and Birtles on the score sheet. There was yet another debutant, twenty one year old Steve Wigley. Steve was a slim, lightly built right winger, who joined the club for a fee of only £2,000 from non league Curzon Ashton.

Justin Fashanu who had scored three goals in nine appearances for Southampton and regained his place in the England under 21's returned to the City Ground, determined to fight for his place. Lawrie McMenemy the Saints' manager had asked him to stay longer, but the player was adamant. Fashanu even managed to earn a place on the subs bench for the away game at Luton, before the relationship broke down completely and the story continued on the front pages of the newspapers and on national television.

The player had been told to turn up for a Milk Cup tie, despite him not being picked. When the player failed to show up for the game and for what was perceived as a general lack of discipline, the manager used this as an excuse to suspend the player for fourteen days and ban him from the ground and the training facilities.

Having taken advice from the PFA, the player defied the ban and turned up at the training ground to find that the first team were not there. He then turned up for a second time and Clough ordered him to leave. The police were then called and led a visibly distressed Fashanu away.

When Fashanu presented his case to a League Commission several weeks later, he won, as Forest were unable to prove that the player had behaved in the way that he had been accused of. But there was no way back for the player now, and he began using his contacts in the local media to try and engineer a move to Notts County.

In the meantime, back to matters on the pitch, which by now were going surprisingly well. They followed up the thrashing of West Brom in the Milk Cup, by going one better in the next round, by hammering Watford 7-3, five different scorers, including two from Mark Proctor, who finally looked as if he was settling down. And in the league, an unbeaten run of seven games pushed them up to third place in the table, Garry Birtles and Ian Wallace were both continuing their fine run of form.

This run of good form was to be overshadowed by a blockbuster announcement. When Peter Taylor had walked away from football back in April, many had predicted that he would be back in the game after a period of re-charging his batteries. What they didn't expect to happen, was that he would return down the A52 with Derby County.

Danny Wilson (centre) is welcomed to the City Ground by Peter Davenport and Chris Fairclough.

Many people think that the breakdown of the relationship between Clough and Taylor started here, but in fact, although Clough was initially angry that Taylor hadn't offered to return to Forest, he was supportive of his old friend. A story from Viv Anderson backs this up:

"Whilst I was coming back from injury, the manager said that he wanted myself and Mark Proctor to go on loan to Derby and help out his old mate who was struggling at the bottom of Division Two. I said no, I don't want to go, but he was persistent and said that he would take us there, we could listen to what Peter Taylor had to say, and if we still didn't want to go we could tell him ourselves. Brian Clough could be persuasive, so the upshot was that Mark and I went all the way over to Peter's house and told him we weren't going. At

Super Focus

MARK PROCTOR

Forest

TERRY COOPER

BOBBY MURDOCH

FULL NAME: Mark Gerard Proctor
BIRTHPLACE: Middlesbrough
BIRTHDATE: January 30, 1961
HEIGHT: 5ft 10ins
WEIGHT: 11st 6lbs
MARRIED: No
CAR: Toyota Celica
PREVIOUS CLUB: Middlesbrough
JOB OR TRADE BEFORE TURNING PRO: None
NICKNAME: 'Proc'
FAVOURITE NEWSPAPER: Daily Mirror
FAVOURITE PLAYER: Tottenham's Glenn Hoddle
A PLAYER FOR THE FUTURE: My nephew Justin Forster
FAVOURITE OTHER TEAM: Middlesbrough
FOOTBALL HERO OF CHILDHOOD: Georgie Best
FAVOURITE OTHER SPORT: Badminton
OTHER SPORTS PERSON YOU MOST ADMIRE: Muhammad Ali
YOUR BEST EVER ALL-TIME XI: Shilton, Vogts, Cooper, Gerson, Beckenbauer, Moore, Maradona, Ball, Pele, Best, Cruyff.
MOST MEMORABLE MATCH: My debut for Middlesbrough
BIGGEST DISAPPOINTMENT: None just yet
FRIENDLIEST AWAY FANS: Millwall
BEST STADIUM PLAYED IN: Old Trafford
FAVOURITE FOOD AND DRINK: Fruit and Guinness
MISCELLANEOUS LIKES . . .
DISLIKES: Winning, playing well . . . Injuries, travelling, smoking
FAVOURITE SINGERS: UB40, Ry Cooder, Ramsey Lewis
FAVOURITE ACTOR/ACTRESS: Charles Bronson/Bo Derek
FAVOURITE HOLIDAY RESORT: Ibiza
FAVOURITE TV SHOW: Match of the Day
BEST FILM SEEN RECENTLY: 'Coma'
FAVOURITE ACTIVITY ON DAY OFF: Going home to Middlesbrough
BIGGEST INFLUENCE ON CAREER: My family, Bobby Murdoch, John Neal, Brian Clough, Paddy Hopkins (PE teacher)
SUPERSTITIONS: None
PRE-MATCH MEAL: Boiled fish (Dover sole)
INTERNATIONAL HONOURS: England Youth and Under-21 caps
PERSONAL AMBITION: To be healthy, happy and successful
IF NOT A PLAYER, WHAT JOB WOULD YOU DO? A tradesman
CAREER AFTER PLAYING: Hopefully I'll have my own business by then
WHICH PERSON IN THE WORLD WOULD YOU MOST LIKE TO MEET? The Pope

Birtles leaps to score against Manchester City.

Steve Hodge battles with McDonald of Manchester City.

WINTER FUN AT THE CITY GROUND

Willie Young times his jump to perfection as he heads home against Coventry City.

The centre half celebrates with joy as the ball enters the net.

Hodge turns away after another goal against Coventry.

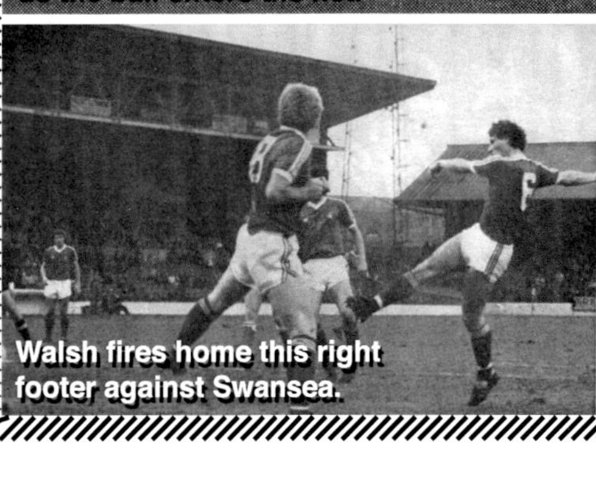

Walsh fires home this right footer against Swansea.

Wallace is on the spot against Brentford.

Reds HOT Shots

PETER DAVENPORT

CHRIS FAIRCLOUGH

BRYN GUNN

STEVE SUTTON

STEVE WIGLEY

KENNY SWAIN

DANNY WILSON

PAUL HART

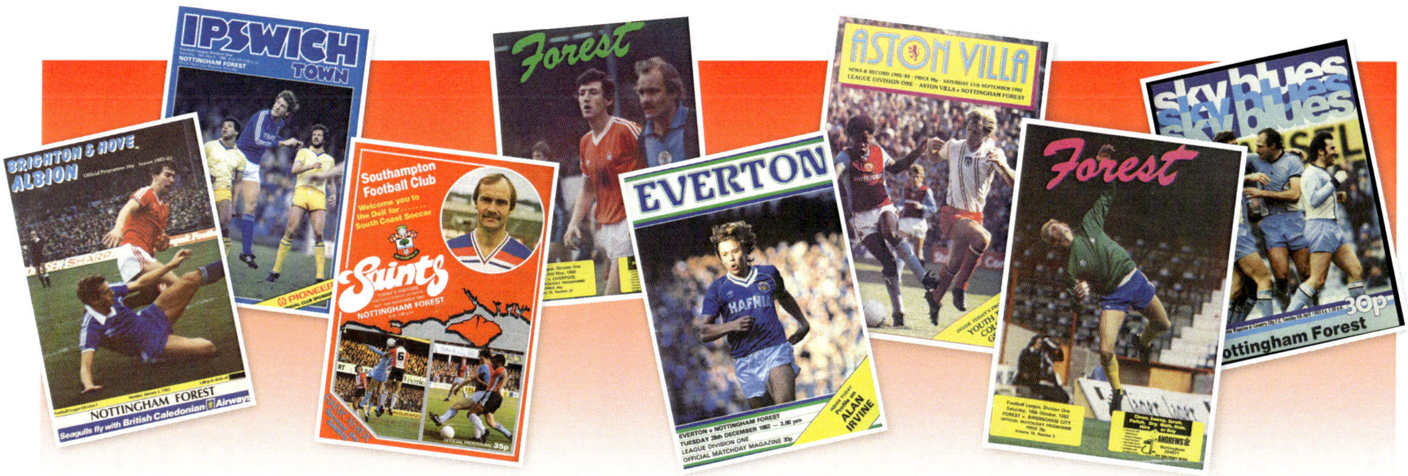

this, the manager went mad and said you can make your own way home. It was clear that he was trying to help him."

Hans van Breukelen was getting fed up at being the butt of Ian Wallace's jokes, especially the one's about the size of his nose and decided to get his own back. After training one day, he asked the flame haired striker if he would crack two eggs on his head for £10? "Of course", said Wallace. Van Breukelen duly gave him the first egg, which Wallace cracked on his forehead, the yolk running down his face. "Where's the second egg?" he asked. "You've got to be joking," the keeper replied, as the room full of players exploded with laughter.

Kenny Swain

As negotiations between Notts County and Forest over the transfer of Fashanu continued, the player sat in the stands as his new club beat the Reds 3-2 at Meadow Lane. It must have been awkward for him as both sets of fans ridiculed the player. There was a set back for Forest even before the game started, Hans van Breukelen injured himself in an innocuous domestic incident, missing the game and a large part of the season, not returning until March. Steve Sutton was given the chance to replace him.

Fashanu's move was completed for a cut price fee of only £150,000. Rarely can a player's value have fallen so sharply in such a short space of time. There was still time for one final barb from Clough as he explained why the club was prepared to accept such a loss: "The fee is still substantial for a commodity that has little appeal to others, and is not wanted here."

Putting the Notts defeat behind them, they duly won the next three games to go second as the year ended, including a 1-0 win at Norwich, where Steve Hodge scored after only twenty two seconds.

After this game, with a break in the pre Christmas fixture list, a squad of Forest players left for Italy, to compete in a prestigious indoor 5 a side competition against amongst others, AC Milan and Ajax, who had Marco van Basten and Frank Rjkaard in their ranks. Steve Hodge remembers the surreal instruction by the manager, to mark Johan Cryuff.

With Forest riding so high in the league, Jimmy Greaves was man enough to come out and say that he had got it all wrong, and settled his bet early. If he had left it another week, he would have seen Forest hit a mighty slump that threatened to de-rail the season.

Football as we all know, has a particular way of throwing up the unexpected expected. So it wasn't entirely a surprise when Derby County and Nottingham Forest were drawn out of the hat to meet each other in the Third Round of the FA Cup at the Baseball Ground. To the media, this was manna from heaven. Clough versus Taylor. The struggling Rams against the high flying Reds.

Steve Hodge remembers that this was a game Cloughie was desperate to win. Forest were missing Colin Todd and Viv Anderson, but Peter Davenport returned to the first team squad as substitute. Derby had Gary Mills on the left wing, who although still technically a Forest player was on loan from Seattle Sounders, where he was on loan from Forest.

Derby also had Archie Gemmill in their line up. If there was one player that ever wanted to put one over on Brian Clough, it was Archie. His perceived injustice at the way that he was excluded from the 1979 European Cup final team, still burned brightly.

In truth he had not really found his form since returning to the club, but on this day, he turned the clock back, and almost single handedly drove the Rams on to a 2-0 victory, scoring the first goal, on a deliberately heavily watered mud bath of a pitch. Forest were now embroiled in a run of fixtures that was to return only one win from thirteen games, plus there was the added disappointment of being knocked out of the Milk Cup, 4-0 at Old Trafford.

When they returned to Manchester for the league encounter, there were a couple of noteworthy occurrences. Anderson was by now fit enough to return to the team, but the manager kept faith with Kenny Swain. This meant a great deal to the player, after the disappointment of his treatment by Aston Villa. The manager also had a quiet word with him and said that if he returned for a third month on loan, he would do his best to make the move permanent.

Swain agreed, but it wasn't all plain sailing to make it happen. Villa initially asked for a fee of over £100,000, whilst Clough was only willing to go to £20,000. At one point, the player returned to Villa Park, disgusted at the behaviour of Villa hierarchy, before realising that he was so happy at the City Ground, and money wasn't everything. With a little common

Wallace with the winner against West Ham.

A glancing header from Steve Hodge.

Birtles fails to connect with this cros

A debut goal for Danny Wilson against Aston Villa.

Joy for Hodge on this occasion, as he beats the Saints' keeper Shilton.

Wilson jumps for joy.

Fairclough foiled again by the ex Forest legend.

er Shilton keeps out this effort from Steve Hodge.

Davenport drills home against Liverpool.

Swain from inside the box against Notts County.

HAPPINESS IS A NOTTINGHAM FOREST GOAL

Wallace and Davenport.

Wallace beats Kilcline to this cross.

Its Willie Young!

Another attack against Southampton.

Pedro Richards fails to block this effort from Robertson.

ROBERTSON... ANDERSON... PROCTOR...

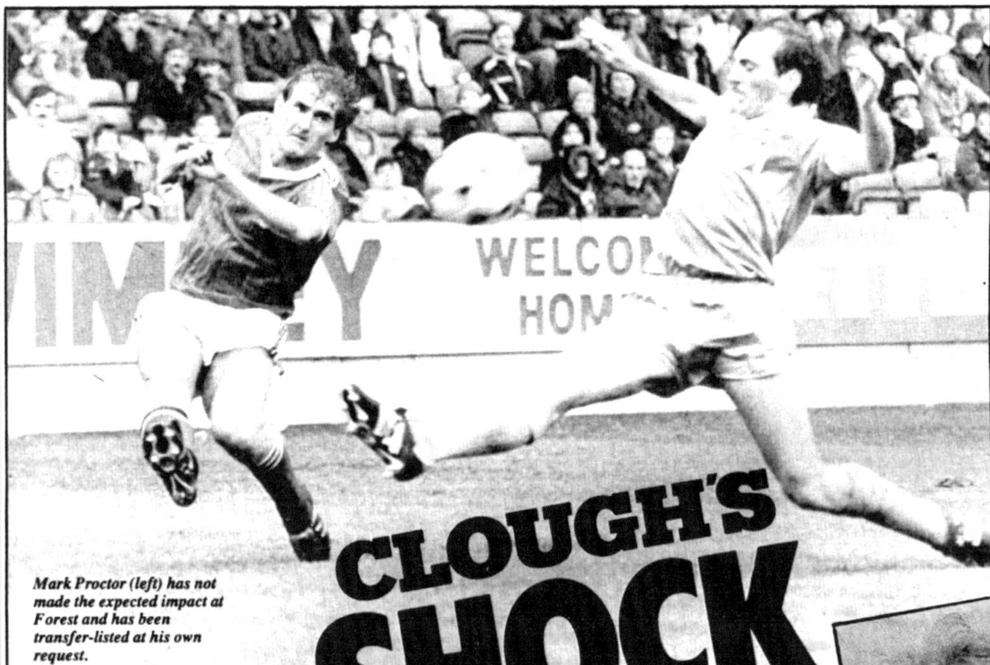

Mark Proctor (left) has not made the expected impact at Forest and has been transfer-listed at his own request.

CLOUGH'S SHOCK CLEAR-OUT!

John Robertson

Viv Anderson

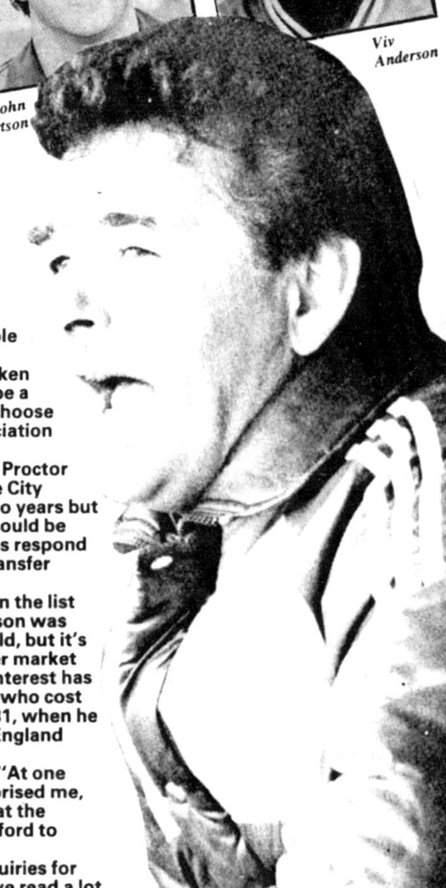

THE face of Nottingham Forest football has altered dramatically since their halcyon European Cup days, when their players were household names across the Continent.

But as Forest brace themselves for a final push for a place in Europe next season, there could be more cosmetic changes in the make-up of Brian Clough's side.

And the major areas of doubt currently surround two of the players who figured so significantly in transforming Forest from the mediocrity of the Second Division to the heights of Munich and Madrid.

John Robertson and Viv Anderson, the only two players with unbroken service under Clough's management at the City Ground, have their futures shrouded in uncertainty.

In the case of Robertson, his contract expires at the end of the season and despite gentle pressure to cement his links to the club, he is keeping his options wide open until the summer.

As for Anderson, he recently returned to full fitness from a dislocated knee but finds his path to his familiar number two spot blocked following the signing of Kenny Swain from Aston Villa. He is now on the transfer list at his own request.

And although Clough steadfastly insists that he does not want to lose the 26-year-old England defender, he concedes that Anderson's career is at something of a crossroads.

"At the time that Viv was injured in England training, I was left in a situation where I had to do without him for a lengthy period... and that was no good to me," says Clough.

"I was so concerned about it, I came straight back from Scotland, where I had gone to watch an international and an Under-21 game, in order to sign Kenny Swain.

"In the time that Viv was out, Kenny did a magnificent job for me.

"Had I not gone ahead with the permanent transfer of Kenny it would have been bad management on my part. But now that Viv is fit again, I do admit that it leaves a certain matter to be resolved."

Bargaining

While Clough muses over that issue, he will no doubt face a bargaining session with Robertson when the time eventually comes in the summer for talks over a new contract.

Robertson, currently recovering from a cartilage operation, has had such an influence on Forest's style of play over the last five or six years that it would be difficult to imagine the machinery functioning effectively without him.

Clough has made overtures to re-sign the 30-year-old Scotland winger but so far his attempts have been unsuccessful.

It is almost unthinkable for a Forest side to be without Robertson's silken talents but there must be a possibility that he will choose to end his 15-year association with the club.

By comparison, Mark Proctor has been resident at the City Ground for less than two years but it appears that his link could be terminated if other clubs respond to the granting of his transfer request.

Proctor asked to go on the list the day that Danny Wilson was bought from Chesterfield, but it's indicative of the transfer market that so little apparent interest has been shown in a player who cost £450,000 in August, 1981, when he was established as an England Under-21 regular.

As Clough reflected: "At one time it would have surprised me, but the way football is at the moment nobody can afford to make much of a move.

"I had a couple of inquiries for Mark but although I have read a lot about managers going to ring me, I can only assume that they couldn't find the telephone number.

"It's a buyer's market all right, but you've got to have the money to make use of it."

Clough scraped enough together in January to buy Wilson from Chesterfield while Forest youngsters Steve Kendall and Calvin Plummer made the trip to Saltergate. And he could move again.

With injury sadly ending the career of Norwegian international Einar Aas and Colin Todd facing injury problems, it's a fair bet that Forest's next target will be a central defender.

As the Forest manager stressed: "I wouldn't swop our three strikers for any other club's three, and with the signing of Wilson we're quite well off in midfield.

"There are still areas at the back where things have got to be put right but I'm quite happy with us... very happy in fact."

sense and compromise, a deal was done.

For the game at Old Trafford, John Robertson was given the number seven shirt, while Colin Walsh was handed the number eleven. Robbo will admit that even with his ability, he couldn't ignore the march of time. The appearance of a younger rival and the delay in a new contract offer left him feeling vulnerable. The situation wasn't helped when he damaged a cartilage during the game, and Clough cruelly taunted him with: "Bad timing young man." It was also around this time that he was 'tapped' up by Peter Taylor.

With Robertson out, Clough once more added to his squad. £250,000 was spent on bringing the Chesterfield midfielder, Danny Wilson to the club. He was given the poisoned chalice of the number seven shirt. Meanwhile, Mark Proctor, who at one point of the season looked to be producing his best form, was allowed to return to the North East and join Sunderland on loan.

Wilson marked his debut with a goal, but it was returning old boy, Peter Withe who stole the show, with a brace, as Villa left with the points.

There was sad news to report from Norway, as Einar Aas admitted defeat in his attempt to overcome his injury, and announced his retirement from the game.

Scoring goals had become a real problem, only four in thirteen games. Without the craft of John Robertson, they were finding it increasingly difficult to break teams down, and the partnership of Wallace and Birtles, that contributed so much earlier in the season had stalled. It was not helped by the back problems that Birtles was enduring. A particularly heavy challenge by Mick Buckley of Sunderland, caused the initial injury. He was eventually forced to have an operation to rectify the problem. Forest were lucky that they had a ready made replacement in Peter Davenport.

Steve Hodge Player of the Year.

Stuart Gray who had made such a promising start to his career, left to join Bolton, initially on loan. The player whose early development had been blighted by injury, had once more succumbed and found himself out of the picture at the City Ground.

By the time that Forest lost 2-1 to Southampton, they had slumped to tenth place, but as quickly as the poor run had started, it was to end, and they began a surge back up the table that was to culminate in a spot in The UEFA Cup.

By now Hans van Breukelen had cycled his way back to fitness, Anderson had regained the right back spot and Kenny Swain in the manager's own words had the chance to: "Become the second best right footed left back that I've had at the club, behind Frank Clark." But most importantly, Davenport hit a hot streak.

Out of the remaining nine fixtures, seven ended in victory, the other two were draws. Beginning with a 2-0 home victory over Everton, featuring Ian Bowyer's first goal of the season, they then travelled to Coventry, where a last minute winner gave them the points. It was around this time that they changed their routine for away games, and as it is with footballers, who tend to be a superstitious lot, they kept it going as they went unbeaten.

As with many clubs, Forest were feeling the pinch. Rather than stop for a pre-match meal, they decided on taking soup and sandwiches with them to eat on the coach. Steve Hodge recalls fondly the sight of 'elite' footballers tucking in to this basic fayre, but it worked. Often these little things, 'all in it together', foster closer camaraderie.

John Robertson had by now returned to the team, and the switching of roles with Colin Walsh, from centre midfield to left wing throughout the game, regularly confused the opposition.

Forest even managed to regain some pride when they beat Notts County. Mark Proctor who had been unhappy at being forced to return from Sunderland, scored the winning goal, but it was to be his final league appearance for the club. The other goal from Swain was unusual, because it came from an indirect free kick inside the penalty area.

The manager had his own idiosyncrasy's, that he repeated over the years with different groups of players. Steve Hodge recalls a couple of them: "On one occasion we were returning to Nottingham after a 3-1 victory at Watford. The manager instructed Albert the bus driver to make a detour past East Midlands airport. As we went past he said, 'not long now until we are all there going on our holidays', and he instructed the players to wave at the airport. What people must have thought of a group of men waving from their bus at an airport, heaven knows." Brian Clough loved winning football matches, he was once quoted as saying 'he would kick his grandma if it was necessary to get three points'. Steve remembers an incident in the dressing room after a game during the run in to the end of the season: "After the Liverpool game, a hard fought 1-0 win, someone came in and read out the other results, after they had finished Cloughie shouted, 'hang on, there's only one result today lads, Nottingham Forest won', although I might have missed out a swear word."

For Forest to qualify for Europe, they had to go to Swansea on the last day of the season and win. They not only did this, but the result was never in doubt as they produced their most polished and professional performance of the season to win 3-0. The soup and sandwiches consumed in a layby outside Swansea never tasted so good.

Brian Clough had prospered whilst his old partner had floundered. He had changed the team, reduced the wage bill and found success on his own.

Fifth place, only two points off second spot. The emergence of young talent continued, Steve Hodge was voted player of the year, whilst Walsh, Fairclough, Davenport and Wigley continued their development. The manager even had time to make a quick new signing, Willie Young was released and Paul Hart was signed from Leeds in time to join the squad for the end of season trip to Canada.

One player missing from that trip was John Robertson and he was to unfortunately play his part in the acrimonious argument that led to Brian Clough and Peter Taylor falling out, a breakdown in a relationship that was never repaired before Peter's death, years later.

FOREST

APPEARANCES TEAM LINE-UPS

Aug 28th, A, v West Ham, W, 2-1, Scorers Walsh, Robertson(P), AT 24,796, Sutton, Anderson, Bowyer, Proctor, Young, Todd, Hodge, Wallace, Plummer, Walsh, Robertson. SUB Gunn

Sept 1st, H, v Manchester United, L, 0-3, AT 23,956, Sutton, Anderson, Bowyer, Proctor, Young, Todd, Hodge, Wallace, Plummer, Walsh, Robertson. SUB Gunn.

Sept 4th, H, v Brighton, W, 4-0, Scorers Wallace (2), Walsh, Robertson (P), AT 13,709, Van Breukelen, Anderson, Bowyer, Proctor, Young, Todd, Plummer, Wallace, Birtles, Walsh, Robertson. SUB Hodge.

Sept 7th, A, v Liverpool, L, 3-4, Scorers Hodge (2), Davenport, AT 27,145, Van Breukelen, Anderson, Bowyer, Proctor, Fairclough, Todd, Hodge, Wallace, Davenport, Walsh, Robertson.

Sept 11th, A, v Aston Villa, L, 1-4, Scorer Robertson (P), AT 21,224, Van Breukelen, Anderson, Bowyer, Todd, Young, Fairclough, Hodge, Wallace, Davenport, Walsh, Robertson. SUB Proctor.

Sept 18th, H, v Watford, W, 2-0, Scorers Walsh, Birtles, AT 16,550, Van Breukelen, Anderson, Gunn, Fairclough, Young, Bowyer, Proctor, Hodge, Birtles, Wallace, Walsh.

Sept 25th, A v Tottenham Hotspur, L 1-4, Scorer Birtles, AT 30,662, Van Breukelen, Anderson, Gunn, Fairclough, Young, Gray .S, Proctor, Hodge, Birtles, Wallace, Walsh. SUB Ward.

Oct 2nd, H, v Stoke City, W, 1-0, Scorer Birtles, AT 17,222, Van Breukelen, Anderson, Gunn, Proctor, Fairclough, Todd, Hodge, Wallace, Birtles, Walsh, Robertson. SUB Ward.

Oct 6th, LC, H, v West Bromwich Albion, W, 6-1, Scorers Hodge, Wallace (2), Birtles, Robertson (2P), AT 11,969, Van Breukelen, Anderson, Gunn, Proctor, Fairclough, Todd, Hodge, Wallace, Birtles, Walsh, Robertson. SUB Bowyer.

Oct 9th, A, v West Bromwich Albion, L, 1-2, Scorer Wallace, AT 13,657, Van Breukelen, Anderson, Gunn, Bowyer, Fairclough, Todd, Hodge, Wallace, Birtles, Walsh, Robertson. SUB Proctor.

Oct 16th, H, v Birmingham City, D, 1-1, Scorer Hodge, AT 14,528, Van Breukelen, Swain, Gunn, Proctor, Fairclough, Todd, Hodge, Wallace, Birtles, Walsh, Robertson. SUB Bowyer.

Oct 23rd, H, v Arsenal, W, 3-0, Scorers Proctor, Wallace, Birtles, AT 17,248, Van Breukelen, Swain, Gunn, Todd, Fairclough, Bowyer, Proctor, Wallace, Birtles, Walsh, Robertson. SUB Wigley.

Oct 27th LC, A, v West Bromwich Albion, L, 1-3, Scorer Birtles, AT 6,536, Van Breukelen, Swain, Gunn, Todd, Fairclough, Bowyer, Proctor, Wallace, Birtles, Wigley, Robertson. SUB Plummer.

Oct 30th, A, v Luton Town, W, 2-0, Scorers Gunn, Wallace, AT 12,648, Van Breukelen, Swain, Gunn, Todd, Young, Bowyer, Proctor, Wallace, Birtles, Hodge, Robertson.

Nov 6th, H, v Ipswich Town, W, 2-1, Scorers Robertson (P), (OG), AT 17,669, Van Breukelen, Swain, Gunn, Todd, Young, Bowyer, Proctor, Wallace, Birtles, Hodge, Robertson.

Nov 10th, LC, H, v Watford, W, 7-3, Scorers Young, Bowyer, Proctor (2), Wallace, Birtles (2), AT 14,973, Van Breukelen, Swain, Gunn, Todd, Young, Bowyer, Proctor, Wallace, Birtles, Hodge, Robertson. SUB Walsh.

Nov 13th, A, v Southampton, D, 1-1, Scorer Wallace, AT 18,178, Van Breukelen, Swain, Bowyer, Gunn, Young, Walsh, Proctor, Wallace, Birtles, Hodge, Robertson. SUB Fairclough.

Nov 20th, A, v Sunderland, W, 1-0, Scorer Wallace, AT 14,716, Van Breukelen, Swain, Bowyer, Gunn, Young, Walsh, Proctor, Wallace, Birtles, Hodge, Robertson. SUB Fairclough.

Nov 27th, H, v Manchester City, W, 3-0, Scorers Young, Birtles (2), AT 18,845, Van Breukelen, Swain, Gunn, Todd, Young, Bowyer, Proctor, Wallace, Birtles, Hodge, Robertson.

Dec 1st, LC, H, v Brentford, W, 2-0, Scorers Wallace, Robertson (P), AT 16,479, Van Breukelen, Swain, Gunn, Todd, Young, Bowyer, Proctor, Wallace, Birtles, Hodge, Robertson. SUB Walsh.

Dec 4th, A, v Notts County, L, 2-3, Scorers Young, Wallace, AT 23,552, Sutton, Swain, Gunn, Todd, Young, Bowyer, Proctor, Wallace, Birtles, Hodge, Robertson. SUB Walsh.

Dec 11th, H, v Swansea City, W, 2-1, Scorers Walsh, Proctor, AT 14,585, Sutton, Swain, Bowyer, Gunn, Young, Walsh, Proctor, Wallace, Birtles, Hodge, Robertson.

Dec 18th, A, v Norwich City, W, 1-0, Scorer Hodge, AT 13,334, Sutton, Swain, Bowyer, Gunn, Young, Walsh, Proctor, Wallace, Birtles, Hodge, Robertson.

Dec 27th, H, v Coventry City, W, 4-2, Scorers Young, Proctor, Birtles, Robertson (P), AT 24,487, Sutton, Swain, Gunn, Todd, Young, Bowyer, Proctor, Wallace, Birtles, Hodge, Robertson. SUB Walsh.

Dec 28th, A, v Everton, L, 1-3, Scorer Hodge, AT 25,160, Sutton, Swain, Gunn, Todd, Young, Bowyer, Proctor, Wallace, Birtles, Hodge, Robertson. SUB Walsh.

Jan 1st, H, v Sunderland, D, 0-0, AT 20, 382, Sutton, Swain, Gunn, Todd, Young, Bowyer, Proctor, Wallace, Birtles, Hodge, Robertson. SUB Walsh.

Jan 3rd, A v Brighton, D, 1-1, Scorer Young, AT 10,389, Sutton, Swain, Gunn, Todd, Young, Bowyer, Proctor, Wallace, Davenport, Hodge, Walsh.

Jan 8th, FAC, A, v Derby County, L, 0-2, AT 28,494, Sutton, Swain, Bowyer, Gunn, Young, Walsh, Proctor, Wallace, Birtles, Hodge, Robertson. SUB Davenport.

Jan 15th, H, v West Ham, W, 1-0, Scorer Wallace, AT 17,031, Sutton, Swain, Gunn, Todd, Young, Bowyer, Proctor, Wallace, Birtles, Hodge, Robertson.

Jan 19th, LC, A, v Manchester United, L, 0-4, AT 44,413, Sutton, Swain, Gunn, Todd, Young, Bowyer, Proctor, Wallace, Davenport, Hodge, Robertson. SUB Gray .S.

Jan 22nd, A, v Manchester United, L, 0-2, AT

1982 - 1983 DIVISION 1 TABLE

TEAMS	P	W	D	L	F	A	W	D	L	F	A	PTS
1 Liverpool FC	42	16	4	1	55	16	8	6	7	32	21	82
2 Watford	42	16	2	3	49	20	6	3	12	25	37	71
3 Manchester U	42	14	7	0	39	10	5	6	10	17	28	70
4 Tottenham H	42	15	4	2	50	15	5	5	11	15	35	69
5 Nottingham F	42	12	5	4	34	18	8	4	9	28	32	69
6 Aston Villa	42	17	2	2	47	15	4	3	14	15	35	68
7 Everton	42	13	6	2	43	19	5	4	12	23	29	64
8 West Ham U	42	13	3	5	41	23	7	1	13	27	39	64
9 Ipswich T	42	11	3	7	39	23	4	10	7	25	27	58
10 Arsenal	42	11	6	4	36	19	5	4	12	22	37	58
11 W.B.A	42	11	5	5	35	20	4	7	10	16	29	57
12 Southampton	42	11	5	5	36	22	4	7	10	18	36	57
13 Stoke C	42	13	4	4	34	21	3	5	13	19	43	57
14 Norwich C	42	10	6	5	30	18	4	6	11	22	40	54
15 Notts Co	42	12	4	5	37	25	3	3	15	18	46	52
16 Sunderland	42	7	10	4	30	22	5	4	12	18	39	50
17 Birmingham C	42	9	7	5	29	24	3	7	11	11	31	50
18 Luton T	42	7	7	7	34	33	5	6	10	31	51	49
19 Coventry C	42	10	5	6	29	17	3	4	14	19	42	48
20 Manchester C	42	9	5	7	26	23	4	3	14	21	47	47
21 Swansea C	42	10	4	7	32	29	0	7	14	19	40	41
22 Brighton & H.A	42	8	7	6	25	22	1	6	14	13	46	40

WHO? WHAT!

FACTFILE

RESULTS LEAGUE TABLE

38,615, Sutton, Swain, Gray .S, Gunn, Young, Bowyer, Robertson, Wallace, Davenport, Hodge, Walsh. SUB Fairclough.

Feb 5th, H, v Aston Villa, L, 1-2, Scorer Wilson, AT 16,352, Sutton, Swain, Gunn, Todd, Young, Bowyer, Wilson, Wallace, Birtles, Proctor, Walsh.

Feb 19th, H, v West Bromwich Albion, D, 0-0, AT 14,507, Sutton, Swain, Gunn, Anderson, Young, Bowyer, Proctor, Wallace, Birtles, Hodge, Walsh. SUB Wilson.

Feb 26th, A, v Birmingham City, D, 1-1, Scorer Davenport, AT 12,987, Sutton, Anderson, Swain, Todd, Young, Bowyer, Wilson, Wallace, Birtles, Hodge, Walsh. SUB Davenport.

March 5th, A, v Arsenal, D, 0-0, AT 21,698, Sutton, Anderson, Swain, Todd, Young, Bowyer, Wilson, Wallace, Birtles, Hodge, Walsh. SUB Davenport.

March 12th, H, v Luton Town, L, 0-1, AT, 14,387, Sutton, Anderson, Swain, Todd, Young, Bowyer, Wilson, Wallace, Birtles, Hodge, Walsh. SUB Davenport.

March 16th, A, v Stoke City, L, 0-1, AT 10,880, Sutton, Anderson, Swain, Gunn, Young, Bowyer, Wilson, Wallace, Birtles, Hodge, Walsh. SUB Robertson.

March 19th, A, v Ipswich Town, L, 0-2, AT 17,530, Van Breukelen, Anderson, Swain, Gunn, Fairclough, Bowyer, Wilson, Hodge, Davenport, Walsh, Robertson. SUB Smalley.

March 26th, H, v Southampton, L, 1-2, Scorer Hodge, AT 13,461, Van Breukelen, Anderson, Bowyer, Gunn, Fairclough, Walsh, Wilson, Wallace, Davenport, Hodge, Robertson. SUB Wigley.

April 2nd, H, v Everton, W, 2-0, Scorers Bowyer, Hodge, AT 14,815, Van Breukelen, Anderson, Swain, Todd, Fairclough, Bowyer, Wilson, Wallace, Davenport, Hodge, Robertson. SUB Wigley.

April 5th, A, v Coventry City, W, 2-1, Scorers Wallace, Robertson (P), AT 9,760, Van Breukelen, Anderson, Swain, Fairclough, Young, Bowyer, Wilson, Wallace, Davenport, Hodge, Robertson. SUB Walsh.

April 9th, H, v Tottenham Hotspur, D, 2-2, Scorers Bowyer, Davenport, AT 18,265, Van Breukelen, Anderson, Swain, Gunn, Young, Bowyer, Walsh, Wallace, Davenport, Hodge, Robertson.

April 16th, A, v Watford, W, 3-1, Scorers Bowyer, Davenport, Hodge, AT 17,537, Van Breukelen, Anderson, Swain, Gunn, Young, Bowyer, Walsh, Wallace, Davenport, Hodge, Robertson.

April 23rd, H, v Notts County, W, 2-1, Scorers Swain, Proctor, AT 25,554, Van Breukelen, Anderson, Swain, Gunn, Young, Bowyer, Proctor, Wallace, Davenport, Walsh, Robertson.

April 30th, A, v Manchester City, W, 2-1, Scorers Wallace, Davenport, AT 23,563, Van Breukelen, Anderson, Swain, Gunn, Young, Bowyer, Hodge, Wallace, Davenport, Walsh, Robertson.

May 2nd, H, v Liverpool, W, 1-0, Scorer Davenport, AT 25,017, Van Breukelen, Anderson, Swain, Gunn, Young, Bowyer, Hodge, Wallace, Davenport, Walsh, Robertson.

May 7th, H, v Norwich City, D, 2-2, Scorers Bowyer, Walsh, AT 16,308, Van Breukelen, Anderson, Swain, Gunn, Young, Bowyer, Hodge, Wallace, Davenport, Walsh, Robertson.

May 14th, A, v Swansea City, W, 3-0, Scorers Anderson, Wallace (2), AT 9,226, Van Breukelen, Anderson, Swain, Gunn, Young, Bowyer, Hodge, Wallace, Davenport, Walsh, Robertson. SUB Wigley.

May 18th, CC, H, v Notts County, W, 4-3, Scorers Anderson, Hodge, Davenport, Robertson, AT 5,141, Van Breukelen, Anderson, Swain, Gunn, Young, Wilson, Hodge, Wigley, Davenport, Walsh, Robertson. SUB Proctor.

Kerry Levers the new 'Miss Nottingham Forest' pictured alongside Chris Fairclough.

Nottingham Forest Youth Team

Back Row: John Sheridan (coach), Gary Fleming, Paul Raynor, Jim McKechnie, Adrian Shaw, Ian Chaplin, Ricky Gachagan, Russell Turley, Paul White (assistant secretary), Mick Raynor (Colts coach).

Front Row: Ronnie Sinclair, David Longhurst, Mark Smalley, David Campbell, Kevin Fawsitt, Shaun Finney.

WHERE! WHEN!

SEASON 1983-84

Back Row L to R: Bryn Gunn, Peter Davenport, Mark Smalley,
Colin Todd, Ian Wallace, Danny Wilson
Middle Row L to R: Ron Fenton (Asst. Manager), Chris Fairclough, Viv Anderson,
Steve Sutton, Hans van Breukelen, Paul Hart, Willie Young, Brian Clough (Manager).
Front Row L to R: Garry Birtles, Ken Swain, Ian Bowyer, Steve Wigley,
Colin Walsh, Steve Hodge.

Brian Clough couldn't have been happier. A successful season now meant that once more the club would be competing in Europe, and he had a group of players that he knew would only improve. However, his mood was about to nosedive.

Plans had long been in place for the manager, along with Alan Hill to undertake a charity walk in the Peak District, to raise money to buy wheelchairs for a Derby hospital. Two days into the walk, Brian Clough was to receive the news that not only turned his football world upside down, but also fractured the relationship with his pal Peter Taylor, that had survived many ups and downs over the thirty years that they had know each other. At the hotel where they were staying after the day's trek, Alan Hill was pre-warned, he had already spoken to his wife, so he knew what was coming. Brian then phoned his wife Barbara for a chat, only to be told that John Robertson had signed for Derby. Taylor had known that the player was due to become a free agent at the end of the season and had moved in. Why Taylor thought that Derby needed a subtle ball player in the lower reaches of the Second Division isn't clear, but you can't help thinking that it was just done to get one over his erstwhile partner.

Back in the hotel where they were staying, Clough returned to the bar with Alan Hill, ordered a bottle of whisky and said: "That bastard, I'll never speak to him again," and to the best of our knowledge, never did, except for a few words on the telephone just before he died. It wasn't that the player had joined Taylor, it was the underhand manner in which it had been done, which rankled most. Clough said: "If Taylor had just picked up the phone and said, 'by the way, I'm going to sign John Robertson', the row need never have happened."

John Robertson recalls the move from his point of view: "It was the worst decision that I ever made in football, and virtually signalled the end of my career. All that I can say in my defence was that I was feeling vulnerable, I had just turned thirty and younger players were coming through. But I should never have handled it like I did. I remember the day I went to see Peter about clarifying details of the move, Sally my then wife said, 'don't sign anything, just listen to what he has to say and come back'. She went ballistic when I came back and told her I had signed. I had just committed football suicide." Derby weren't best pleased either when they were ordered by a tribunal to pay £135,00 for the player, money they could ill afford, that impacted on their abilities to strengthen other areas of their squad.

Robertson also felt the backlash, he was barred from the City Ground for eighteen months before Clough held out the olive branch and invited the player to watch a game, but this was only after Taylor had left Derby.

Mark Proctor finally got the move that he wanted back to Sunderland, whilst Stuart Gray was allowed to join Barnsley for a cut price £40,000, although he quickly moved on to Aston Villa and then Southampton, enjoying a decent career in the top flight, before going in to coaching.

These outgoings meant that Forest would enter the new season with only twenty professionals and eleven apprentices. Forest had lined up eight pre-season games, but initially they were based at the Dutch National training centre, making use of the superb facilities.

One of the pre-season matches was against Barcelona, where Brian Clough introduced himself to the legendary Maradona in inimitable style: "Have you ever had your balls cupped son?"

EVENING POST

Shock NEWS! as John Robertson walks out on Brian Clough....

Brian Clough and Alan Hill prepare for their sponsored walk, unaware of the trouble ahead.

before doing just that.

Forest allowed Leo Ehlen, a Dutch midfielder from Roda Kerkrade to train with them, he even played a couple of trial matches against Real Zaragoza and Groningen, but the club decided against signing him.

Forest began their campaign with a 1-0 home defeat to Southampton, before their lowest opening days crowd since promotion, only 14,690. A handsome victory would have been theirs, but for Peter Shilton who was simply unbeatable in the Saints' goal, but they bounced back immediately, inflicting Manchester United's first home defeat for sixteen months. Anderson and Davenport with the goals in a 2-1 victory. This was the club's fifth successive win on the road, the best sequence since 1906.

The difficult start to the season continued at Anfield. The end of season table would show that the Reds had met three of the top four teams in the first two weeks of the season. Despite van Breukelen saving a Phil Neal penalty, an 84th minute Ian Rush shot, gave the home side the points.

Van Breukelen then saved a disputed Gary Shaw penalty at Villa Park, but the referee ruled that he had moved and ordered a retake, that the same player scored.

Forest had the boost of a 3-2 win over Queens Park Rangers before they began their UEFA Cup campaign with a home tie against Vorwaerts Frankfurt from East Germany. In a low key start to the competition, Forest secured a two goal home advantage in front of less than 15,000 spectators. Hodge and Wallace scored the goals, and they then completed the job a couple of weeks later when Bowyer scored the only goal in Germany.

It was definitely a case of mixed emotions for Colin Walsh after the next game, a 3-2 win at Norwich. Walsh scored a hat trick, but received a severe kick to the head when scoring the third goal. He was carried off the pitch unconscious and went straight to hospital. Club Physio Tony Verity accompanied the player, meaning that the crowd were treated to the sight of Brian Clough taking over the 'sponge' duties. Subsequent to this, club secretary Ken Smales took the media to task over the reporting of the Walsh injury. Their premature reports that the player had suffered a broken neck, caused unnecessary alarm for the player's family.

It would be fair to say that Kenny Swain loved his time at Forest. He took to the unorthodox methods of the manager, the social life of the players and the relaxed way that they approached games. When the player had made the move to Nottingham, he had asked the manager whether he wanted him to move over from Solihull where he was living. The boss had said: "Don't uproot the kids." So it was usual when the team were playing in the south of the country, for the player to meet up with the team bus at the Crick Hotel, situated where the M1 meets the M6.

On one particular occasion, the day of the first televised league game at Tottenham, Kenny thought he would be early for the meeting, but a traffic jam meant that he ended up running late. With his wife driving their car, they were minutes away from the rendezvous, when he saw the team bus ahead of them speeding away down the hard shoulder. He told his wife to: "Follow that bus," and for the next half an hour, they were in pursuit. At one point, as the traffic stopped, Kenny saw his opportunity, grabbed his bag and legged it after the bus. As he almost caught up, the bus pulled away and he desperately made his way back to his car. Giving up on catching the bus, he telephoned White Hart Lane with a message for the manager and arranged for a relative from London, to meet him and take him to the ground.

After arriving, the player found the manager and tried to explain what he had gone through. Clough stood there, a quizzical look on his face: "That wasn't you running up the hard shoulder was it? I see now. Actually the lads were shouting down from the back seat, 'hey boss, Swainey's coming up the hard shoulder', but I simply asked how many we had on board. Thirteen was the head count, so I said f**k it, we've got enough."

Brian Clough was a football purist, and although he was friends with managers such as Graham Taylor, he deplored their rudimentary style of football. The problem was, it was often successful against the Reds, who struggled with the physicality and the aerial bombardment it encompassed. They were to come across a side who were a perfect example of this, when they met Wimbledon in the Milk Cup. Under Dave Bassett, they were climbing the leagues, bullying sides along the way.

WELCOME BACK TO THE NEW SEASON

No way through for Wallace against Southampton.

Acrobatics from Davenport against QPR.

Ian Bower bursting through on goal.

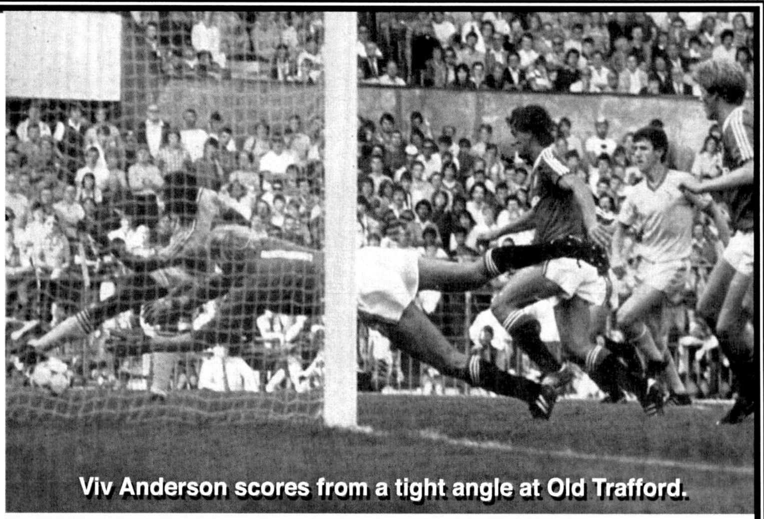
Viv Anderson scores from a tight angle at Old Trafford.

An own goal from QPR defender Hazel.

Hodge deftly lifts the ball over the Rangers' keeper.

Paul Hart on a rare venture forward against Manchester United.

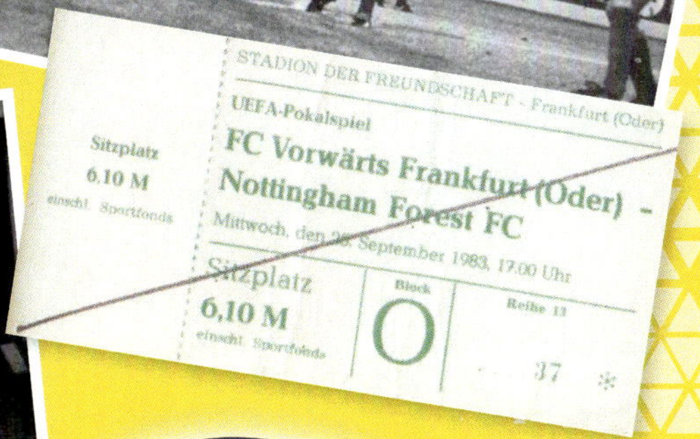
STADION DER FREUNDSCHAFT - Frankfurt (Oder)
UEFA-Pokalspiel
FC Vorwärts Frankfurt (Oder) - Nottingham Forest FC
Mittwoch, den 28. September 1983, 17.00 Uhr
Sitzplatz
6,10 M
einschl. Sportfonds
Block
O
Reihe 13
37

FRANKFURT

FIRST ROUND - FIRST LEG - 14TH SEPTEMBER 1983
FOREST 2 VORWARTS 0

FIRST ROUND - SECOND LEG - 28TH SEPTEMBER 1983
VORWARTS 0 FOREST 1

1983

IT'S A STROLL FOR THE REDS

FOCUS HANS VAN BREUKELEN

Nottingham Forest

FULL NAME: Johannes Franciscus van Breukelen
BIRTHPLACE AND BIRTHDATE: Utrecht in the Netherlands on October 4, 1956.
HEIGHT AND WEIGHT: 6ft 2ins. 13st 7lbs.
MARRIED: Yes, to Karen. We don't have any children, but we do have a Giant Schnauzer dog called Pepper!
HOME: We're now happily settled in a detached house on the outskirts of Nottingham.
CAR: Fiat Strada.

FAVOURITE OTHER SPORTS PERSON: England cricketer Ian Botham. Whenever he is under pressure he always seems to produce the best results possible.

PREVIOUS CLUBS: I started in Holland with my local amateur side B.V.C. before joining Utrecht, from whom Forest signed me in the summer of 1982.
NICKNAME: The boss always calls me 'The Daft Dutchman' because he reckons I'm crazy. The rest of the team call me 'Herman' because of the time I suffered an abcess in my mouth. My face swelled out and they all reckoned I looked like Herman Munster!
FAVOURITE CURRENT PLAYER: I don't have any particular favourites at the moment.
BOYHOOD HERO: The former PSV Eindhoven and Holland goalkeeper Jan van Beveren.
TEAM YOU SUPPORTED AS A BOY: F.C. Utrecht.
SUPERSTITIONS: I never shave a few days before a match.
MOST MEMORABLE MATCH: In the first-leg of Utrecht's First Round UEFA Cup tie away to SV Hamburg. We won 1-0. Unfortunately, we were beaten 6-3 in the return leg in Holland!
BIGGEST DISAPPOINTMENT: Losing the 1981-82 Dutch F.A. Cup Final against AZ67 Alkmaar.
INTERNATIONAL HONOURS: Seven Dutch Under-21 caps and 11 full caps.
CLUB HONOURS: Three times qualified for Europe with Utrecht, Cup Final with Utrecht, qualified for the UEFA Cup last season with Nottingham Forest.
FAVOURITE OTHER SPORTS: Tennis, basketball and baseball.
HOBBIES: Reading, listening to music and walking with my dog Pepper.
FAVOURITE SHOWBUSINESS STARS: My favourite actor is Jack Nicholson and my favourite actress Louis de Funes. I also like the woman who plays Mrs Slocombe in Are You Being Served — is it Molly Sugden? I enjoy watching Kenny Everett and Tommy Cooper on TV as well as all sports programmes. Musically, I prefer easy listening. Fleetwood Mac are the group I listen to most.
BIGGEST INFLUENCE ON CAREER: The trainers at my previous clubs B.V.C. and Utrecht, who brought me through from my apprenticeship into the Dutch national team. And also Brian Clough, because he has given me a chance in the First Division and has 'changed' me into a kind of 'English' goalkeeper.
AMBITIONS FOR 1983-84: To win something with Forest. The lads deserve it, because there is a great team atmosphere at the City Ground.
LONG-TERM AMBITIONS: To settle down and establish myself as a good First Division goalie. I also want to play in a World Cup Final with Holland.

SHOOT!

Davenport scores the clincher against County.

Steve Hodge dives full length.

Bowyer might be out numbered, but he squeezes the ball home against County.

THINGS JUST GET BETTER AND BETTER

Avromovic the Notts keeper can't keep out Ian Wallace.

Davenport fires off against Ipswich.

Walsh beats the keeper and the post.

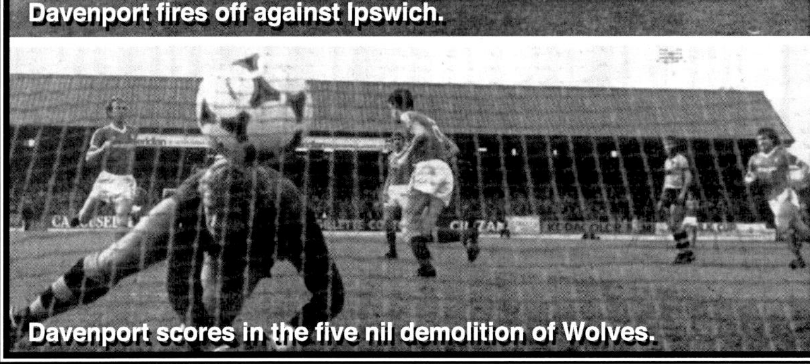

Davenport scores in the five nil demolition of Wolves.

More action from the Ipswich encounter.

Ian Bowyer exchanges penants before the game.

Celebrations in the dressing room, after the win in Holland.

Walsh turns away after scoring.

EINDOVEN

SECOND ROUND - FIRST LEG - 19TH OCTOBER 1983
PSV 1 FOREST 2

SECOND ROUND - SECOND LEG - 2ND NOVEMBER 1983
FOREST 1 PSV 0

1983

The defence stands firm.

The PSV defence can't handle Peter Davenport.

Ice cool Colin Walsh scores the winner after 89 minutes.

WALSH KEEPS HIS COOL...

Pictured left to right: Alan Hill, Colin Barrett (new Commercial Manager), Brian Clough and Billy Gray (new Groundsman).

Forest went to Plough Lane and barely got a kick, the only consolation was that they only lost 2-0. But even this proved too much as Wimbledon held out for a 1-1 draw in Nottingham, to go through 3-1 on aggregate.

In response to this, Clough went out and brought in another ball playing flair player in Franz Thijssen, who had made his reputation at Ipswich, but as was common at that time, joined on loan from Vancouver Whitecaps. The way that the league seasons fell across the two continents, led many players to lead a dual existence, playing twelve months of the year. At the same time, yet another right sided player bit the dust, as Danny Wilson left to join Brighton.

The stage was set. Justin Fashanu was to return to the City Ground with Notts County, and show Brian Clough what he was missing. That's not quite how it turned out. Forest won 3-1 and Fashanu was sent off after an hour, to the jeers and catcalls of the crowd. Notts actually finished the game with nine men, after David Hunt was also sent off for scything through Steve Hodge who had taken the ball to the corner flag to kill time. Brian Clough commented: "If I could have got to the corner flag quick enough, I would have kicked him myself."

The European campaign continued with a lively encounter against PSV Eindhoven. The proximity meant that the Reds were backed by a large following, including a contingent from van Breukelen's old club, Utrecht. Another impressive performance led to a 2-1 victory, courtesy of Peter Davenport and a last minute penalty from Colin Walsh, who was to keep his nerve despite the Dutch number eleven Thoresen, moving the ball off the spot and refusing to leave the area.

Forest completed the job two weeks later, Peter Davenport scoring the only goal, but the PSV coach Jan Reker was not complimentary, accusing Forest of employing negative tactics. This was a criticism that was often levelled at a Clough team, he liked to counter attack, but a team with two wingers and ball artists like Thijssen, certainly didn't deserve that label. Steve Sutton who had been standing in for van Breukelen, unluckily sustained a minor leg break away at Arsenal.

Forest then demolished Wolves 5-0 to continue their push up the table, Andy Gray played for the visitors, before joining Everton and facing the Reds again the following weekend. Only 15,000 at Goodison Park played against a backdrop of protests demanding the sacking of manager Howard Kendall. This manager then went on to win the FA Cup, the League Championship and a European trophy over the next thirty months!

Time was now running out on the career of Colin Todd, as he succumbed to regular injuries, the latest a torn hamstring. Chris Fairclough had always performed well when called upon, and now would be given an extended run in the first team. He responded admirably, and he couldn't have had a better tutor than Paul Hart to learn alongside.

The Forest squad was so thin, that players almost had to take it in turns to make up the numbers for reserve fixtures, most players thought that it was better than training, but the line up often wouldn't have looked out of place for a first team game. And with Brian Clough insisting that every match was played properly, results were good and contributed to the reserves usually being near the top of the table.

The next fixture was huge. A 'Battle of Britain'. England versus Scotland. European Champions Nottingham Forest against European Champions Celtic in the UEFA Cup.

Viv Anderson who had been with the manager for all of his time at the club could sense the difference: "The manager was flying, in his element. It felt like he'd got his mojo back."

The game at the City Ground was to be a full house, including officially 8,000 Celtic followers, but in fact many more. They turned up days early, but apart from a few skirmishes there was very little trouble. The major problem was to be the weather, a cold snap meant that half the pitch was ice bound. Kenny Swain remembers travelling to the game, certain it wouldn't be on, but the referee gave the go ahead.

Steve Hodge recalls the pre-match instructions from Brian Clough: "All I want tonight is a clean sheet, we've got 180 minutes to win this."

The game itself was a tight affair, which Celtic slightly shaded. There was a moment in the first half however when it looked as if the referee would be given no option but to abandon the game. Celtic fans were crammed in behind the Bridgford End, and some supporters climbed up the floodlight pylons to get a better view. Then suddenly one fan fell and needed treatment. A gate in the fencing at the front of the terracing was opened to allow medical staff in, but a surge in the crowd meant that spectators spilled forward through the gap, onto the pitch causing many to lose their footing and a crush developed. The game was stopped to allow the police to regain control of the situation, this wasn't crowd trouble, so it was possible to calm things. The referee gave an ultimatum that he would abandon the game in five minutes, unless he was able to restart the match. Luckily he was able to do so.

Cloughie got his clean sheet in a 0-0 draw, but for Kenny Swain, he recalls lying in the bath listening to the celebrations coming from the Celtic dressing room. They were convinced that they had done enough, he recalls: "After the Celtic game, the lads were a little disappointed, but not Clough. Never, ever

IAN
WALLACE
Nottingham
Forest

COLIN WALSH
Nottingham Forest

STEVE HODGE
Nottingham Forest

GARRY BIRTLES
Nottingham Forest

Peter Davenport keeps his balance.

Bonner claims this cross.

Bonner is once more called in to action.

Fans spill on to the City Ground pitch.

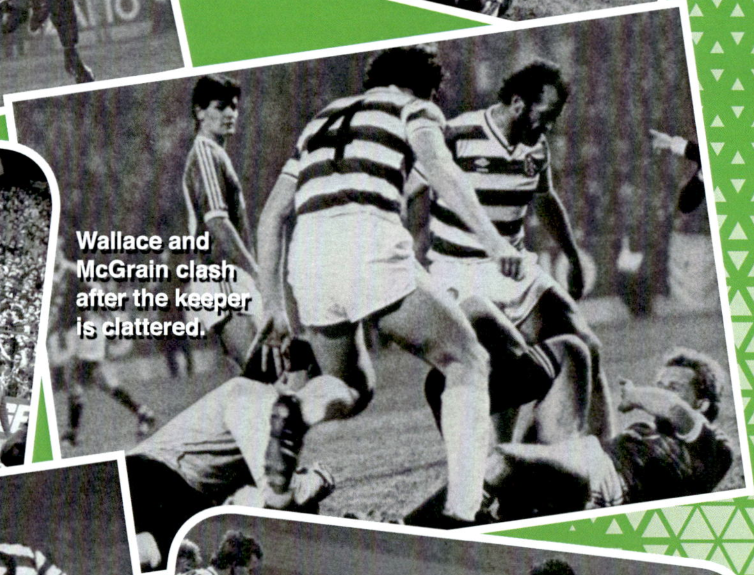
Wallace and McGrain clash after the keeper is clattered.

Davenport tricks his way past the Celtic defence.

Paul Hart challenging.

Hodge flicks the ball...

Hodge and Fairclough stand firm.

SMASH AND Hodge,

TOO little and too late— that's got to be the epitaph for Celtic as their Europe hopes died for yet another season.

They simply melted away in the rain as Brian Clough's Nottingham Forest made it three victories in a row in away ties in the UEFA Cup.

That statistic sums up how hard Forest are to beat away from home and Celtic's Battle of Britain victory dreams crumbled in a shock second-half.

A winning Under-21 international combination of England's Steve Hodge and Scotland's Colin Walsh were the starlets who sent Forest marching on to the quarter-finals of the competition.

HODGE PLUNGED THE DAGGER INTO CELTIC'S CHANCES IN 54 MINUTES.

FLICKED

He was the Forest fans' Player of the Year choice last season and he must have won the votes already for this year's award.

Celtic never recovered from that body blow and in 74 minutes Colin Walsh—a

CELTIC 1
MacLeod (80 mins).
FOREST 2
Hodge (54), Walsh (74).
Agg: 1-2 Attendance—66,938

RODGER BAILLIE

way down the right touchline, eluding a series of desperate tackles.

Striker Peter Davenport, who won the Man of the Match award, flicked on the winger's cross.

Gary Birtles brilliantly dummied the ball and Hodge strode in to shoot past the bewildered Pat Bonner.

AT THE SECOND, Davenport superbly survived a tackle by Tom McAdam on the touchline, shrugged off a desperate

...then turns away in delight as the ball enters the Celtic net.

Garry Birtles.

Wigley tracks back.

Brian Clough joins in the post match celebrations.

ONWARDS AND UPWARDS

Walsh fires a cracker to give Forest the lead against Leicester City.

Hodge challenges for a high ball against the Hammers.

No way past the Southampton defence on this occasion.

Anderson fires between the legs of the Norwich keeper.

Walsh on target against West Ham.

Steve Hodge turns away after scoring against Norwich.

Shilton versus Davenport in the F.A. Cup.

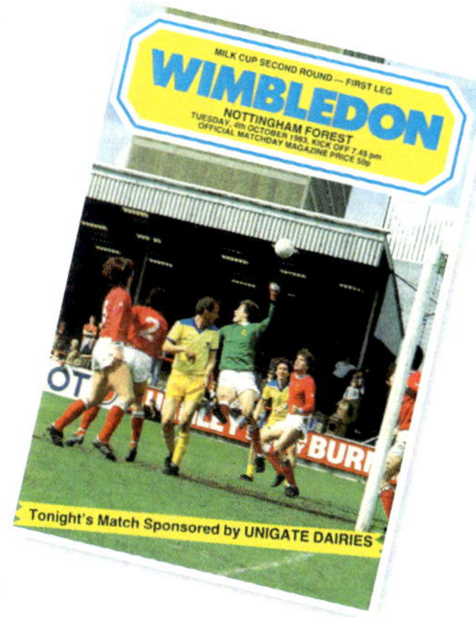

did he convey, by body language or words any sign of resignation."

The return leg in Glasgow further enhanced the mythology surrounding the manager. On the flight up to Glasgow, the champagne was passed around, then on the bus taking the team to the hotel, the manager ordered a detour to a rough looking bar, that turned out to be run by Celtic manager David Hay's brother. A few more drinks: "Stick them on Davie's tab," Clough said and they were off. Staying at a hotel out of Glasgow on the coast, the manager went through his usual routine of making sure that the players were relaxed, and not feeling the pressure of a game that all Britain was talking about. Fish and chips, a pint and sleep were the order of the day. Fellow guests at the hotel were convinced that Forest were going to get a hiding.

Kenny Swain had seen nothing like it. He and van Breukelen had even been encouraged to bring their wives along. Over sixty thousand fans awaited them at Parkhead, including a couple of thousand from Nottingham. In typical fashion, the players wandered over to an area of the ground known as The Jungle, to show that they weren't afraid, in fact the opposite. Ian Bowyer says that he could just 'tell' by the atmosphere in the dressing room that every player was 'up for it'.

Forest began with lots of attacking intent, taking the game to their hosts. They were unlucky not to go in at half time leading, but they quickly rectified this when Steve Hodge turned in a cross, arriving late in the box after a strong run by Steve Wigley down the right touchline. It was nothing more than they deserved, when they silenced the crowd with a second from Colin Walsh. Celtic did pull a goal back through Murdo Macleod, but Forest held on to record a famous victory, leaving the pitch to the sounds of not only their own jubilant fans, but also the sporting applause of the Celtic followers.

European competition could now be put on hold for three months and the team could concentrate on the league, but they were immediately brought back down to earth, losing 3-2 to Watford including a couple from their 6'6" striker George Reilly, who also managed to break the nose of Paul Hart along the way.

It was announced that Hans van Breukelen would be leaving the club at the end of the season. The manager of the Dutch national team had told the player that he wouldn't be considered unless he returned home.

Paul Hart was in the wars the following week as well, fracturing his cheek bone during a 3-0 home win against West Ham. He decided to get his nose done at the same time. This was the tenth successive game that the Hammers had failed to score at the City Ground.

There were a couple more victories over Birmingham and Coventry, before 1983 ended with a disappointing 1-0 defeat at home to Liverpool. But despite this they were still handily placed in fifth.

Steve Hodge remembers that Cloughie always seemed to have his favourites, although it might have been more a case of recognising that players reacted in different ways. As Steve comments: "He could bring you up, or he could bring you down, but he definitely had his own way of putting his point across. During one half time he said to me, 'Harry get forward, or f**k off. Or after the game, 'not bad for a player who can't play'. Whilst with Peter Davenport it would be, 'what day suits you for training? Friday, Ok, see you Friday'. Davenport was handled with kid gloves by the manager." The player suffered badly with homesickness, but Clough realised what he brought to the team, so he cut him a lot of slack.

They might have returned to winning ways at Luton, but

Viv Anderson on the attack.

Paul Hart with the only goal of the game.

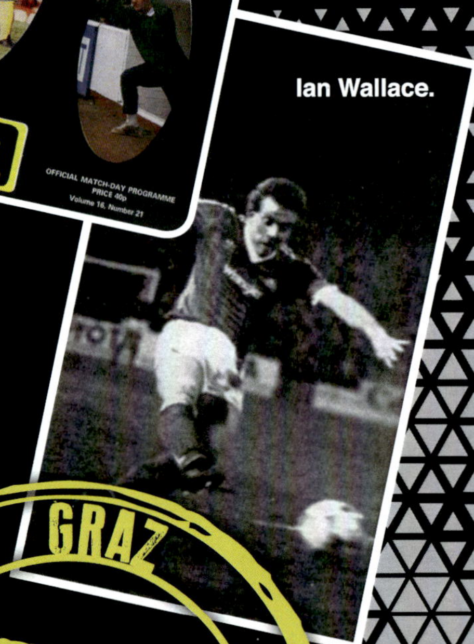
Ian Wallace.

Garry Birtles just fails to add a second goal.

GRAZ

FOURTH ROUND - FIRST LEG -7 MARCH 1984
FOREST 1 STRUM GRAZ 0
FOURTH ROUND - SECOND LEG - 21ST MARCH 1984
STRUM GRAZ 1 FOREST 1

1984

REDS ALMOST PAY THE PENALTY

Brain Clough acknowledges the travelling Reds' supporters.

Ian Bowyer rallies the troops.

Alan Hill has words with Van Breukelen before extra time.

Colin Walsh displays nerves of steel with this winner, only five minutes from the end of extra time.

'STEVIE WONDER'

STEVE WIGLEY was a local government officer playing football for a hobby when he first came to the attention of Brian Clough a couple of years ago.

Wigley, who was playing for Curzon in the Cheshire League, was offered a professional contract after a week's trial at the City Ground and he says: "I jumped at the chance."

Now he's Clough's replacement for Scottish winger John Robertson in the Forest team. And at 21, he looks a terrific prospect.

He can play on either wing and like team-mate Garry Birtles, who also came from non-League football, has the element of freshness on his side.

Not that experienced First Division defenders are naive enough to be suckered by the moves that used to dazzle Curzon's opponents. Wigley says: "The players in the First Division are obviously of a lot higher standard and they don't fall for the same tricks.

"You can't get away with quite as much, especially around the edge of the penalty box. But I'm having a good go.

"A few clubs had shown interest in me as a schoolboy but there was no follow up from any of them when I left school. So I had to go and find a career and for a while I lost my enthusiasm for football.

"I got a lot of it back playing for Curzon and in the back of my mind, I still hoped I might get a chance to play professionally. But if you haven't signed for someone by the time you're 18, you tend to think you've missed out.

"Everton and Manchester City also came to look at me while I was at Curzon but once Forest offered me terms I didn't have any doubts."

Circumstances

He would have found it difficult to sign for Manchester City under any circumstances. He's a Manchester lad from Ashton-under-Lyne who has always been strictly a 'Red'.

He says: "I used to watch United as a kid and I always liked the players who took people on. At first, it was George Best but later on I loved watching Steve Coppell.

"One of the sad things for me this season was that I didn't get a chance to play at Old Trafford. I was sub that day and never got called on. As you can imagine, I was itching to get a run out there."

Wigley, who cost Forest an ex-gratia payment of £2,000 to Curzon, is in his third season at Forest. He played one Milk Cup tie last season and started becoming a regular sub towards the back end.

This term, he's been given his head by Clough and says: "He has encouraged me to go out and play exactly the way I did in the reserves and at Curzon. I've even got the freedom to switch wings if things aren't going so well on the right. That's my basic position.

"I know people say that I've replaced 'Robbo' but I don't look at it like that. I knew there was a position available for a winger and I wanted the chance to fill it."

Wigley appreciates the professional life probably more than his team-mates. He says: "It's a lovely life when you compare it to working nine to five. The other lads probably take it for granted but when you've got something to compare it with, you realise how lucky you are."

Wigley carried on with his business studies night school course in his first year at Forest so that he'd always have something to fall back on. But the way things are going, he shouldn't have too many worries.

the season's FA Cup adventure was over before it began, after home defeat to Southampton in the third round. All three goals coming in the last fifteen minutes, Steve Moran's 86th minute winner came just two minutes after it looked like Paul Hart had earned a replay.

There was a return of two old favourites off the pitch to report. Billy Gray, who had been a member of the victorious 1959 FA Cup team, joined as the club's new groundsman. Billy had enjoyed success as a manager after finishing his playing career, but he had retired from the game disillusioned by the direction it was going. He had been working at the Boots Sports Ground, but jumped at the chance to come home. Billy was a real stickler about his pitch, even the manager got a tongue lashing if he caught him interfering in his job.

The other returner was Colin Barrett, who joined the club's commercial department, to help run the new lottery.

Franz Thijssen had struggled to make an impression so far, but to give the player his due, he buckled down and fought his way back into contention. He scored on his comeback, a 3-0 win over Norwich and then played his part in a six pointer at the Dell against Southampton, another win 1-0, on a waterlogged pitch, not really suited to his skills.

After beating West Brom 5-0 at the Hawthorns, the team were up to the dizzy heights of second. A couple of prudent signings could have lead to a sustained challenge for the title, but the only 'new' face that appeared was Gary Mills, returning after a broken leg.

The London press again seemed to have it in for the manager, after a 1-0 win at Queens Park Rangers, they accused the manager of being negative, this despite the fact that Forest were the division's top scorers and on this particular day they were playing on the home sides controversial artificial pitch. Forest were backed by their biggest away following of the season and trouble flared as they took over areas reserved for home spectators.

After Forest had surprisingly lost at home to Arsenal, they were due to fly out the next day to the Middle East for yet another friendly to raise cash for the club.

To some players this wasn't a chance to visit distant shores, but a real bind. On this occasion, Garry Birtles had it on him. He was moaning about the trip from the moment they set off. Eventually Clough cracked and told the coach driver to pull into the next services, where he ordered the player off: "What am I supposed to do?" asked the player. "That's your problem," replied the manager, and they resumed the journey.

Brian Clough was not the best air traveller, but he was prepared to put up with it, usually fortified by a couple of drinks. On this occasion, he couldn't settle. Firstly after boarding the aircraft, he was upset by the behaviour of unruly children and then when the plane aborted take off half way down the runway, he'd had enough: "We're getting off," he told the purser. "You can't," came the reply. "Yes we can," he said and with that, the steps were brought and Clough marched his players back through customs and out of the airport. The only problem being as far as the manager was concerned, that Birtles would have got home before them.

Bonuses always seemed to be a matter of contention between the players and management. Once again, there had been no provision made for a run in the UEFA Cup. Matters came to a head in the build up to the fourth round tie with Sturm Graz. A delegation that included senior players like Hans van Breukelen, Kenny Swain and Ian Bowyer, approached the manager. That they wanted to share in the financial success seemed only fair. Van Breukelen suggested £10,000: "Between the squad?" Clough asked. "No, each." Clough said he would give them £3,000, on the proviso that they didn't lose the next game at Wolves, 'our bread and butter' as he called it.

Ian Bowyer pictured with the Anderlecht skipper and referee, Emilio Guruceta Muro at the coin toss for the controversial UEFA Cup clash.

The players agreed, after all they had already beaten them 5-0 earlier in the season and they were heading for relegation. You can guess what happened. On a mud bath of a pitch, Forest were cruising to a goalless draw, the home side barely mustering an attack, until the 90th minute, when Paul Hart turned a hopeful cross from Danny Crainie past van Breukelen for the only goal of the game. In the dressing room the players were gutted, the manager jubilant.

Four days later against Sturm Graz, from Austria, Paul Hart this time scored in the right net, with a towering header, to give the Reds a slender advantage to take into the second leg. Viv Anderson sustained a dislocated elbow after an innocuous looking fall, although he would return in time for the second game.

The start of a glorious Nottingham Forest career would begin with the next fixture against Everton. Des Walker was plucked from the reserves to make his debut at right back, but it was not a winning start though, the Merseysiders leaving with a share of the points.

Forest were given a severe examination during the return tie in Austria. The referee gave a highly dubious penalty to the home side which took the game to extra time, before seemingly evening things up when he also gave Forest a questionable penalty, when Hodge was lightly bundled over. Colin Walsh took the penalty, holding his nerve with only five minutes remaining. Forest were now once more in the semi-finals of a major European competition.

Forest were due to play Manchester United on their return, whilst the country was suffering from an unusually dry spell. So it was decided to water the pitch to help the fast zippy style passing game they employed. Twenty fours before the game, the heavens opened and it rained for twelve solid hours and after the referee's mid-day inspection, the waterlogged pitch was considered unplayable and the game postponed, only for the skies to immediately clear.

Forest warmed up for their date with Anderlecht by disposing of West Brom 3-1, with the minimum of effort,

Hodge with the first goal.

BRUSSELS
SEMI FINAL - FIRST LEG - 11TH APRIL 1984
FOREST 2 ANDERLECHT 0
SEMI FINAL - SECOND LEG - 25TH APRIL 1984
ANDERLECHT 3 FOREST 0
1984

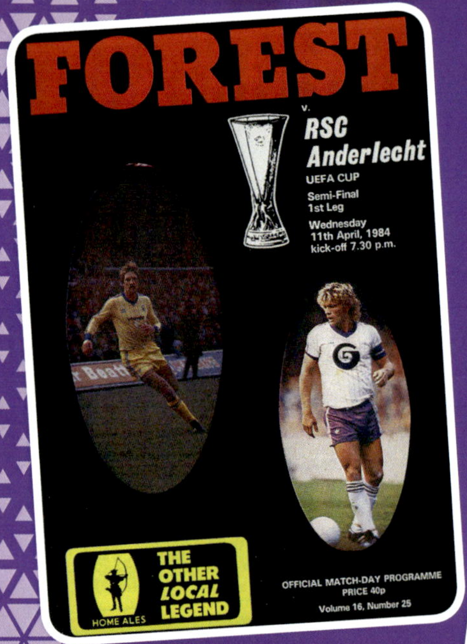

Hodge dives to score the second.

Hodge turns away after scoring the first goal.

Same goal different angle.

Paul Hart rises and heads home in the last minute.

Ian Bowyer watches the ball enter the net.

Then turns around in amazement as the referee disallows the goal.

REFEREE DENIES THE REDS...

GOALS GOALS AND MORE GOALS

Action from the Birmingham game.

Ian Wallace in action against Tottenham.

Colin Walsh receives the congratulations after scoring.

STEVE HODGE

Swain, Walsh and Bowyer.

The ever reliable Colin Walsh from the penalty spot against West Brom.

Steve Hodge with the first goal against Tottenham.

More action from the Spurs game.

Walsh with his goal.

Gary Mills back in action once more.

Action from the Albion game.

Davenport lashes home his second goal against Birmingham.

Shoot!
ARSENAL
+Swansea team groups
FREE INSIDE
Team tabs for the English and Scottish Second Divisions for our League Ladders.
SUPER SCOOP
BRIAN CLOUGH
SIGNS FOR SHOOT!
+Dundee United's PAUL STURROCK
BRITAIN'S EURO CAMPAIGN
BRYAN ROBSON KENNY DALGLISH CHARLIE NICHOLAS
GARY SHAW MURDO MacLEOD CLIVE ALLEN DOUG ROUGVIE

although there was a minor scare when Davenport left the field after picking up a knock. With Birtles sidelined once more, they could ill afford to lose him as well. Local boy Dave Riley from Keyworth, made his debut as his replacement.

Things couldn't have turned out much better for the first leg at home to Belgium side Anderlecht, apart from the attendance of only 22,000. Although it took until the 84th minute for Steve Hodge to break the deadlock with a far post header, it only took a further two minutes for Steve to score what he describes as one of his favourite goals, a full length twisting, diving header at the Trent End. Anderlecht who were the holders of the trophy possessed some fine players including, Enzo Scifo, Morten Olsen, van den Berg and Frankie Vercauteraen and were lucky to escape with only a two goal deficit. They had been comprehensively outplayed after Brian Clough paid them a massive compliment when he altered his own tactics and switched to a five man midfield to counter them.

Before the second leg Forest hammered Birmingham 5-1, with a side containing no less than seven players that had come through the club's own youth system. Great credit must be paid to Liam O'Kane and Alan Hill, who through their dedication and coaching, made this happen. The money saved on transfer fees during these harsh economic times was incalculable.

Forest set off for Belgium in fine fettle, though Brian Clough would always be wary about continental referees, dating back to the time he took his Derby team to Turin to face Juventus and was robbed by a corrupt official. Even this season, he had seen some strange decisions, but the events of this night and what was subsequently revealed was to leave the foulest of tastes.

In all honesty, Forest didn't play well on that evening. The manager admitting later that he had got the team selection wrong, picking two wingers and then expecting them to drop back. Hans van Breukelen had been a doubt right up until kick off with a finger injury, but he was in inspirational form as Forest strove to keep the voilet attackers at bay. Wave after wave towards the Forest goal, all repulsed except for an eighteenth minute effort from Scifo. The Reds' goal led a charmed life.

After half time, Forest came more into the game, even creating a couple of opportunities, until that is, referee Carlos Guruceta took a hand. As Swain tracked Brylle into the box, the Anderlecht player fell theatrically to the floor, penalty 2-2, and as Swain says: "I was nowhere near him." Up until the second half, Steve Hodge hadn't noticed anything really unusual about the referees performance: "He was a little officious maybe, didn't like you questioning him, but in the second half, it all changed. Every decision seemed to go the home sides way." Forest just couldn't get a foot hold in the game, every time they had possession, the referee seemed to blow for an offence. Perhaps up until half-time, Guruceta Muro thought that Anderlecht could handle things themselves, but as time ticked by, he had been forced to interfere.

Garry Birtles came on to replace Steve Hodge who had been booked, in an attempt to add more firepower, but it was to be Anderlecht who scored what they thought was the decisive goal in the 88th minute, when Vandenbergh fired home. However the game wasn't over, Forest could still go through on away goals if they could just score. They won a corner kick on the left, Walsh swung the ball in towards the penalty spot, Hart leapt and from his header the ball smacked into the back of the net. The Anderlecht players slumped to the floor, no sign of any complaints, when they suddenly realised that the goal had been disallowed. Paul Hart remembers that night as if it was yesterday: "I headed it as clean as a whistle, the ball flew past Ian Bowyer and into the net and that would have been us into the final." Paul turned to Bowyer: "Were you offside? Did you push someone?"-"Don't be silly." Garry Birtles gives his view of the incident: "Colin Walsh put over the corner and it was more or less a free header, there was no contact with the defender whatsoever. What is going on here?" This was not incompetence but corruption.

In what Paul Hart though was an attempt to quell trouble, Brian Clough quickly made his way onto the pitch to shake the referees hand, but Forest fans knew that they had been cheated and the atmosphere within the stadium quickly turned ugly. Back in the changing room, Clough sat quietly by himself, he knew that he had been done, but he put on a stoic face and refused to berate the official, in public at least. For many players however, they had been robbed of the highlight of their career, it wasn't about the money, it was the glory. Paul Hart once more: "I had never worn a medal as a player, so it was sickening, how can you put a price on a European medal."

Steve Hodge recalls an incident on the journey home, that perfectly encapsulates just how the manager was feeling: "I was sitting at the airport with the manager as he was explaining why he had subbed me, he thought I might get myself sent off, when an older female fan came up with a big smile and said, 'Brian, don't worry about it, there's always next season'. The manager smiled, but when she'd gone he turned to me and said, 'Harry, they haven't got a f***ing clue have they? They'll never know how much it hurts'. He was right."

The truth emerged years later. Using criminal intermediaries, the Anderlecht chairman had bribed the referee Guruceta Muro with £18,000, to ensure the result. By the time that this all came out, the main protagonists had all died. Anderlecht were banned from European football for one year, but Nottingham Forest and their players got nothing.

Muro even had previous with Belgian football. A couple of years earlier he had sent off two Napoli players and awarded Standard Liege a penalty in the same competition.

It is to the players' credit that they finished the season strongly, losing only one of the final five games, including handing anti football Watford a 5-1 lesson, before ending the season on a real high, with one of their best performances of the campaign, beating Manchester United 2-0, including a highly satisfying goal for Garry Birtles. The other scorer was Viv Anderson, in what was to turn out to be his last competitive appearance for the club, although he wasn't daft enough to miss out on the end of season tour to Australia.

Also making the trip was a young Scottish full back Jim McInally, signed from Celtic as a possible replacement for Anderson who was keeping his options open.

All in all the season had to be considered a success. Third place, only six points off being crowned champions, and with it qualification for the UEFA Cup again, plus they were the divisions' top goalscorers with 76 goals. And in addition, a magnificent run in Europe, that was only curtailed by a couple of dodgy decisions. More importantly though, the young effervescent side only promised further improvement.

Aug 27th, H, v Southampton, L, 0-1, AT 14,690, Van Breukelen, Anderson, Swain, Todd, Hart, Bowyer, Walsh, Wallace, Birtles, Hodge, Davenport. SUB Wigley.

Aug 29th, A, v Manchester United, W, 2-1, Scorers Anderson, Davenport, AT 43,005, Van Breukelen, Anderson, Swain, Todd, Hart, Bowyer, Walsh, Wallace, Birtles, Hodge, Davenport.

Sept 3rd, A, v Liverpool, L, 0-1, AT 31,376, Van Breukelen, Anderson, Swain, Todd, Hart, Bowyer, Walsh, Wallace, Birtles, Hodge, Davenport.

Sept 7th, H, v Aston Villa, D, 2-2, Scorers Birtles, Davenport, AT 16,379, Van Breukelen, Anderson, Swain, Todd, Hart, Bowyer, Walsh, Wallace, Birtles, Hodge, Davenport.

Sept 10th, H, v Queens Park Rangers, W, 3-2, Scorers Hodge, Davenport, (OG), AT 14,607, Van Breukelen, Anderson, Swain, Todd, Hart, Bowyer, Walsh, Wallace, Birtles, Hodge, Davenport. SUB Wigley.

Sept 14th, UEFA, H, v Vorwaerts, W, 2-0, Scorers Wallace, Hodge, AT 14,994, Van Breukelen, Anderson, Swain, Todd, Fairclough, Bowyer, Walsh, Wallace, Davenport, Hodge, Wigley. SUB Gunn.

Sept 17th, A, v Norwich City, W, 3-2, Scorer Walsh (3), AT 15,017, Van Breukelen, Anderson, Swain, Todd, Fairclough, Bowyer, Walsh, Wallace, Davenport, Hodge, Wigley. SUB Smalley.

Sept 24th, H, v Luton Town, W, 1-0, Scorer Wallace, AT 16,296, Van Breukelen, Anderson, Swain, Todd, Hart, Bowyer, Wigley, Wallace, Birtles, Hodge, Walsh.

Sept 28th, UEFA, A, v Vorwaerts, W, 1-0, Scorer Bowyer, AT 18,000, Van Breukelen, Anderson, Swain, Todd, Hart, Bowyer, Wigley, Wallace, Birtles, Hodge, Walsh. SUB Wilson, Gunn.

Oct 2nd, A, v Tottenham Hotspur, L, 1-2, Scorer Walsh, AT 30,596, Van Breukelen, Anderson, Swain, Todd, Hart, Bowyer, Wigley, Wallace, Birtles, Hodge, Walsh.

Oct 4th, LC, A, v Wimbledon, L, 0-2, AT 7,554, Van Breukelen, Anderson, Swain, Todd, Hart, Bowyer, Wigley, Davenport, Birtles, Hodge, Walsh.

Oct 16th, H, v Notts County, W, 3-1, Scorers Bowyer, Wallace, Davenport, AT 26,657, Van Breukelen, Anderson, Swain, Todd, Hart, Bowyer, Wigley, Wallace, Davenport, Thijssen, Hodge.

Oct 19th, UEFA, A, v PSV Eindhoven, W, 2-1, Scorers Davenport, Walsh (P), AT 26,000, Van Breukelen, Anderson, Swain, Todd, Hart, Bowyer, Wigley, Wallace, Davenport, Walsh, Hodge. SUB Fairclough.

Oct 22nd, A, v Arsenal, L, 1-4, Scorer Davenport (P), AT 22,874, Van Breukelen, Anderson, Swain, Todd, Hart, Bowyer, Wigley, Wallace, Davenport, Thijssen, Hodge.

Oct 26th, LC, H, v Wimbledon, D, 1-1, Scorer Wallace, AT 13,718, Sutton, Anderson, Swain, Todd, Hart, Bowyer, Wigley, Wallace, Davenport, Thijssen, Hodge. SUB Walsh.

Oct 29th, H, v Sunderland, D, 1-1, Scorer Thijssen, AT 13,968, Sutton, Anderson, Swain, Todd, Hart, Bowyer, Wigley, Wallace, Davenport, Thijssen, Hodge.

Nov 2nd, UEFA, H, v PSV Eindhoven, W, 1-0, Scorer Davenport, AT 16, 934, Sutton, Anderson, Swain, Todd, Hart, Bowyer, Wigley, Wallace, Davenport, Walsh, Hodge. SUB Birtles.

Nov 5th, H, v Wolverhampton Wanderers, W, 5-0, Scorers Davenport (P), Birtles, Hodge (2), Walsh, AT 13,885, Sutton, Anderson, Swain, Todd, Fairclough, Bowyer, Wigley, Davenport, Birtles, Thijssen, Hodge. SUB Walsh.

Nov 12th, A, v Everton, L, 0-1, AT 17,546, Sutton, Anderson, Swain, Todd, Fairclough, Bowyer, Wigley, Davenport, Birtles, Thijssen, Hodge. SUB Walsh.

Nov 19th, H, v Ipswich Town, W, 2-1, Scorers Swain, Birtles, AT 14,979, Sutton, Anderson, Swain, Fairclough, Hart, Bowyer, Wigley, Davenport, Birtles, Thijssen, Hodge. SUB Walsh.

Nov 23rd, UEFA, H, v Celtic, D, 0-0, AT 34,084, Sutton, Anderson, Swain, Fairclough, Hart, Bowyer, Wigley, Davenport, Birtles, Hodge, Walsh. SUB Wallace.

Nov 26th, A, v Stoke City, D, 1-1, Scorer Walsh (P), AT 11,655, Sutton, Anderson, Swain, Fairclough, Hart, Bowyer, Hodge, Thijssen, Birtles, Davenport, Walsh.

Dec 4th, H, v Leicester City, W, 3-2, Scorers Bowyer, Thijssen, Walsh, AT 23,247, Sutton, Anderson, Swain, Fairclough, Hart, Bowyer, Wigley, Thijssen, Birtles, Davenport, Walsh.

Dec 7th, UEFA, A, v Celtic, W, 2-1, Scorers Walsh, Hodge, AT 66,938, Van Breukelen, Anderson, Swain, Fairclough, Hart, Bowyer, Wigley, Davenport, Birtles, Walsh, Hodge.

Dec 10th, A, v Watford, L, 2-3, Scorers Birtles (2), AT 14,017, Van Breukelen, Anderson, Swain, Fairclough, Hart, Bowyer, Wigley, Davenport, Birtles, Walsh, Hodge.

Dec 17th, H, v West Ham, W, 3-0, Scorers Birtles, Walsh, (P), Hodge, AT 14, 544, Van Breukelen, Anderson, Swain, Fairclough, Hart, Bowyer, Wigley, Davenport, Birtles, Walsh, Hodge. SUB Wallace.

Dec 26th, A, v Birmingham City, W, 2-1, Scorers Birtles, Hodge, AT 14, 482, Van Breukelen, Anderson, Swain, Fairclough, Gunn, Bowyer, Wigley, Davenport, Birtles, Walsh, Hodge.

Dec 28th, H, v Coventry City, W, 3-0, Scorers Birtles (2), Davenport, AT 22,169, Van Breukelen, Anderson, Swain, Fairclough, Gunn, Bowyer, Wigley, Davenport, Birtles, Walsh, Hodge. SUB Wallace.

Dec 31st, H, v Liverpool, L, 0-1, AT 29,692, Van Breukelen, Anderson, Swain, Fairclough, Hart, Bowyer, Wigley, Davenport, Birtles, Walsh, Hodge. SUB Wallace.

Jan 2nd, A, v Luton Town, W, 3-2, Scorers Hodge, Birtles, Davenport, AT 12,126, Van Breukelen, Anderson, Swain, Fairclough, Hart, Bowyer, Wigley, Hodge, Birtles, Davenport, Walsh. SUB Wallace.

1983 - 1984 DIVISION 1 TABLE

TEAMS	P	W	D	L	F	A	W	D	L	F	A	PTS
1 Liverpool FC	42	14	5	2	50	12	8	9	4	23	20	80
2 Southampton	42	15	4	2	44	17	7	7	7	22	21	77
3 Nottingham F	42	14	4	3	47	17	8	4	9	29	28	74
4 Manchester U	42	14	3	4	43	18	6	11	4	28	23	74
5 Q.P.R	42	14	4	3	37	12	8	3	10	30	25	73
6 Arsenal	42	10	5	6	41	29	8	4	9	33	31	63
7 Everton	42	9	9	3	21	12	7	5	9	23	30	62
8 Tottenham H	42	11	4	6	31	24	6	6	9	33	41	61
9 West Ham U	42	10	4	7	39	24	7	5	9	21	31	60
10 Aston Villa	42	14	3	4	34	22	3	6	12	25	39	60
11 Watford	42	9	7	5	36	31	7	2	12	32	46	57
12 Ipswich T	42	11	4	6	34	23	4	4	13	21	34	53
13 Sunderland	42	8	9	4	26	18	5	4	12	16	35	52
14 Norwich C	42	9	8	4	34	20	3	7	11	14	29	51
15 Leicester C	42	11	5	5	40	30	2	7	12	25	38	51
16 Luton T	42	7	5	9	30	33	7	4	10	23	33	51
17 W.B.A	42	10	4	7	30	25	4	5	12	18	37	51
18 Stoke C	42	11	4	6	30	23	2	7	12	14	40	50
19 Coventry C	42	8	5	8	33	33	5	6	10	24	44	50
20 Birmingham C	42	7	7	7	19	18	5	5	11	20	32	48
21 Notts Co	42	6	7	8	31	36	4	4	13	19	36	41
22 Wolverhampton W	42	4	8	9	15	28	2	3	16	12	52	29

FACTFILE

RESULTS LEAGUE TABLE

Jan 7th, FAC, H, v Southampton, L, 1-2, Scorer Hart, AT 19,271, Van Breukelen, Anderson, Swain, Fairclough, Hart, Bowyer, Wigley, Hodge, Birtles, Davenport, Walsh. SUB Wallace.

Jan 21st, H, v Norwich City, W, 3-0, Scorers Anderson, Thijssen, Hodge, AT 13,993, Van Breukelen, Anderson, Swain, Fairclough, Hart, Bowyer, Thijssen, Wallace, Birtles, Hodge, Walsh. SUB Wigley.

Jan 23rd, A, v Southampton, W, 1-0, Scorer Birtles, AT 17,426, Van Breukelen, Anderson, Swain, Fairclough, Hart, Bowyer, Thijssen, Wallace, Birtles, Hodge, Walsh. SUB Wigley.

Feb 4th, H, v Tottenham Hotspur, D, 2-2, Scorers Hodge, Wash (P), AT 21,428, Van Breukelen, Anderson, Swain, Fairclough, Hart, Bowyer, Thijssen, Wallace, Birtles, Hodge, Walsh. SUB Davenport.

Feb 8th, A, v West Bromwich Albion, W, 5-0, Scorers Anderson, Bowyer, Birtles, Walsh (P), (OG), AT 11,020, Van Breukelen, Anderson, Swain, Fairclough, Hart, Bowyer, Thijssen, Wallace, Birtles, Hodge, Walsh. SUB Wigley.

Feb 11th, A, v Queens Park Rangers, W, 1-0, Scorer Birtles, AT 16,692, Van Breukelen, Anderson, Swain, Fairclough, Hart, Bowyer, Thijssen, Wallace, Birtles, Hodge, Walsh.

Feb 18th, A, v Sunderland, D, 1-1, Scorer Anderson, AT 15,958, Van Breukelen, Anderson, Swain, Fairclough, Hart, Bowyer, Thijssen, Wallace, Birtles, Hodge, Walsh. SUB Wigley.

Feb 25th, H, v Arsenal, L, 0-1, AT 20,045, Van Breukelen, Anderson, Swain, Fairclough, Hart, Bowyer, Thijssen, Wallace, Birtles, Hodge, Walsh. SUB Wigley.

March 3rd, A, v Wolverhampton Wanders, L, 0-1, AT 10,476, Van Breukelen, Anderson, Swain, Fairclough, Hart, Bowyer, Thijssen, Wallace, Birtles, Hodge, Walsh. SUB Wigley.

March 7th, UEFA, H, v Sturm Graz, W, 1-0, Scorer Hart, AT 19,450, Van Breukelen, Anderson, Swain, Fairclough, Hart, Bowyer, Wigley, Wallace, Birtles, Hodge, Walsh. SUB Davenport, Gunn.

March 14th, H, v Everton, W, 1-0, Scorer Hodge, AT 13,647, Van Breukelen, Walker, Swain, Fairclough, Hart, Bowyer, Wigley, Davenport, Birtles, Hodge, Walsh. SUB Wallace.

March 17th, A, v Aston Villa, L, 0-1, AT 16,270, Van Breukelen, Walker, Swain, Fairclough, Hart, Bowyer, Wigley, Davenport, Birtles, Hodge, Walsh.

March 21st, UEFA, A, Sturm Graz, D, 1-1, Scorer Walsh (P), AT 22,000, Van Breukelen, Anderson, Swain, Fairclough, Hart, Bowyer, Thijssen, Davenport, Birtles, Hodge, Walsh.

March 31st, A, v Notts County, D, 0-0, AT 18,357, Van Breukelen, Anderson, Swain, Fairclough, Hart, Bowyer, Wallace, Davenport, Birtles, Hodge, Walsh. SUB Walker.

April 7th, H, v West Bromwich Albion, W, 3-1, Scorers Anderson, Bowyer, Walsh (P), AT 15,245, Van Breukelen, Anderson, Swain, Fairclough, Hart, Bowyer, Wigley, Mills, Davenport, Hodge, Walsh. SUB Riley.

April 11th, UEFA, H, v Anderlecht, W, 2-0, Scorer Hodge (2), AT 22,681, Van Breukelen, Anderson, Swain, Fairclough, Hart, Bowyer, Wigley, Mills, Davenport, Hodge, Walsh.

April 14th, A, v Ipswich Town, D, 2-2, Scorers Wigley, Davenport, AT 15,421, Van Breukelen, Anderson, Swain, Walker, Hart, Bowyer, Wigley, Mills, Davenport, Hodge, Walsh.

April 17th, A, v Coventry City, L, 1-2, Scorer Walsh, AT 9,818, Van Breukelen, Anderson, Swain, Fairclough, Hart, Bowyer, Wigley, Mills, Davenport, Hodge, Walsh.

April 21st, H, v Birmingham City, W, 5-1, Scorers Bowyer, Wallace, Davenport (2), Wash, AT 15,323, Van Breukelen, Anderson, Gunn, Fairclough, Hart, Bowyer, Wigley, Wallace, Davenport, Thijssen, Walsh. SUB Mills.

April 25th, UEFA, A, v Anderlecht, L, 0-3, AT 38,000, Van Breukelen, Anderson, Swain, Fairclough, Hart, Bowyer, Wigley, Mills, Davenport, Hodge, Walsh. SUB Birtles.

April 28th, H, v Stoke City, D, 0-0, AT 13,625, Van Breukelen, Anderson, Swain, Fairclough, Hart, Bowyer, Wigley, Mills, Davenport, Hodge, Walsh. SUB Birtles.

May 5th, A, v Leicester City, L, 1-2, Scorer Davenport, AT 16,600, Van Breukelen, Anderson, Swain, Fairclough, Hart, Bowyer, Wigley, Davenport, Birtles, Hodge, Mills.

May 7th, H, v Watford, W, 5-1, Scorers Bowyer, Davenport (2), Hodge, (OG), AT 13,732, Van Breukelen, Anderson, Swain, Fairclough, Hart, Bowyer, Wigley, Davenport, Birtles, Hodge, Walsh. SUB Mills.

May 16th, H, v Manchester United, W, 2-1, Scorers Anderson, Birtles, AT 23,651, Van Breukelen, Anderson, Swain, Fairclough, Gunn, Bowyer, Wigley, Wallace, Birtles, Davenport, Walsh. SUB Mills.

May 18th, CC, H, v Mansfield Town, W, 3-0, Scorers Wallace (P), Davenport (2), AT 3,169, Sutton, Anderson, Swain, Fairclough, Gunn, Bowyer, Wigley, Wallace, Birtles, Davenport, Mills. SUB Walker

Camera call for the Junior Reds football squad.

Back Row (left to right) : Barry Tewson (manager), Dave Lindley, David Torrington, Derek Monks, Martin Bellamy, Martin Herd, David Spilbeck, Geoff Hart (trainer).

Front : Matthew Hutchins, Anthony Binch, Daren Morley, Stephan Ball, Anthony Limb, Paul Grainger, Roy Standage.

Mick Fallon, and son Steve, a new member of the Junior Reds.

WHERE! WHEN!

SEASON 1984-85

Back row L to R: Gary Megson, Gary Mills, Mark Smalley, Chris Fairclough, Kenny Swain, Franz Carr, Steve Murray
Middle row L to R: Ron Fenton (Asst. Manager), Trevor Christie, Johnny Metgod, Darren Hayes, Steve Sutton, Ronnie Sinclair, Paul Hart, Brian Clough (Manager)
Front row L to R: Peter Davenport, Jim McInally, Steve Hodge, Ian Bowyer, Steve Wigley, Bryn Gunn, Colin Walsh

The end of season trip to Australia had been a great success. Games were played in Perth, Adelaide, Melbourne, Brisbane and Sidney. Van Breukelen and Anderson who were both to leave the club, were among the travelling party. Venues varied, from a velodrome in Perth with 25 metres of banked concrete between the pitch and spectators, to the Melbourne cricket ground and a prestige friendly against Manchester United, where 20,000 fans looked lost in the enormous arena. Old acquaintances were renewed, Joe Watson,who had been an apprentice at the City Ground in the 1970's before emigrating to Australia and becoming the national team captain and also Torvill and Dean who were appearing in Brisbane at the same time.

Having come to terms with losing Hans van Breukelen to PSV Eindhoven, Brian Clough was dealt a further blow, when Viv Anderson contacted him after they had returned to England, to say he was turning down the offer of a new contract and would like to move on. Viv had clearly learned from the badly handled departure by John Robertson the previous season and he made sure that he would leave on the best possible terms.

After his move to Arsenal for £250,000 was completed, Clough wrote an article praising the full backs magnificent ten years service to the club, and understood why he needed a new challenge at this stage of his career.

Perhaps Clough had an inkling about Anderson, because they had already brought in a replacement, Jim McInally from Celtic, for a cut price £30,000, but the keeper's position might be more difficult to fill. McInally had been noted when Forest had played Dundee United, the player had been on loan at Tannadice.

Steve Sutton had come through the ranks and certainly looked a competent keeper, but would he be given the responsibility of being the number one choice this time. There was also the added pressure of replacing a terrace legend. After a difficult start, van Breukelen had settled into English football and become a firm fan's favourite.

The player had been overwhelmed by the final day scenes, when he was carried around the City Ground pitch after his final appearance. Like many ex Foresters, he was to be a regular returner to Nottingham, the family nature of the club and the city had that effect on players.

Van Breukelen did recommend that the club should look at the young PSV keeper that he was replacing, Hans Segers, and he duly turned up for a trial and loan spell.

With the money received from the transfers of van Breukelen and Anderson, plus the money accrued from a successful season, the manager felt confident enough to go on a mini spending spree. First in was Johnny Metgod, a Dutchman, playing for Real Madrid. Forest had initially tried to sign the player from AZ Alkmaar in 1982, but the player, not surprisingly, had opted for Spain. Keeping tabs on Metgod, Forest moved quickly when they heard he might be available. Metgod and his family moved to England and settled well to the area, though his acclimatisation to the English game, took a little longer.

Clough once said to the player: "You tackle like a butterfly, but you pass the ball like a dream." The player in common with many Dutch footballers, often had a lot to say for himself. On one occasion he had given the referee too much backchat, a trait that the manager detested, and got himself booked. By the time he had got back to the dressing room, there was a club envelope waiting for him, with a letter explaining that he had been fined half a week's wages.

He was joined by Trevor Christie, a forward who had scored plenty of goals for relegated Notts County and could be relied on for maximum effort. On joining the Reds he commented: "When

Gary Megson and Franz Carr.

Johnny Metgod signs on the dotted line.

I was at Notts, I would watch enviously as it always seemed as if Forest were jetting off somewhere. Since joining, I've already been to six countries and I've told the missus she might see me at Christmas." Trevor was soon followed by Gary Megson, who joined for a substantial fee from Sheffield Wednesday. Gary was seen as a replacement for IanBowyer, a player who could 'put his foot in', but also play as well.

Gary's stay at the City Ground was so short, that he doesn't even make the 'Who's Who' of players who played for the club, because he failed to play one competitive game. Clough had realised very quickly that he had made a mistake.

Kenny Swain recalls an idiosyncrasy of the player: "We were sitting in the dressing room before a pre-season game, when all we could hear was Gary in the toilet being violently sick. Apparently he did this before every game. Clough let out a sigh and said. 'Blow me, what have I signed here, I can't put up with this'.

Steve Hodge who had been sitting on the bench next to the manager at another pre-season game recalls a conversation between the manager and Ron Fenton: "Who is that red haired player in my midfield?" asked Clough. "Gary Megson," came the reply. "That's not the player I saw last season."- "It is boss, it's the player you signed from Sheffield Wednesday." "No Ron, you signed him, not me and I suggest you get rid of him."

A signing that went under the radar, was the capture of seventeen year old Franz Carr from Blackburn Rovers. Alan Hill had spotted him and had invited him down to the club two years previously. But because of the players age and the fact that he had already signed forms for Blackburn, they had to send him back, but Alan reassured the player that they would keep tabs on him. So when the opportunity arose, they paid £100,000 to Rovers for his signature. Franz Carr was fast and Clough liked pace, he knew that you could turn defence into attack in a blink, with pace.

In a conversation with John Barnwell that was to take place years later, Barnwell, who didn't rate Carr, asked the Forest boss what he saw in the player: "That little bugger could pick the ball up outside my penalty area and get it up to their penalty area, quicker than any player I know," was the reply.

Ian Wallace was now considered surplus to requirements and sent to France where he joined Stade Brestois. He was the last of the club's million pound players to move on, a sign of the changing financial fortunes at the club. This was despite further concerns about the state of Garry Birtles back that was only slowly responding to treatment. Young keeper Kevin Hitchcock was allowed to join Mansfield permanently after his loan spell there. However there was good news, when it was announced that Peter Davenport had signed a new long term contract and intended to buy a house in the area that would cut down on the time he spent travelling back to the North West.

Pre-season was a slog, on the back of already visiting Australia in June, they then played ten games across Europe, including hard fought encounters with Celtic and Derby, before concluding preparations in Greece, with a game against Panathinaikos. The team only arriving back in Nottingham, the Friday before the season kicked off against newly promoted Sheffield Wednesday. Hardly ideal preparation once more.

The opening game at Sheffield Wednesday was more highly charged than usual due to events happening off the pitch. The miners strike had split communities across the north of England and led to many violent clashes away from colliery sites. The conflict in it's crudest form could be reduced to striking Yorkshire against working Nottinghamshire. The police were already restricting the movement of people over the county lines and there was genuinely the threat of industrial violence on top of the normal trouble associated with football.

'Scabs,scabs, scabs', chanted the Wednesday fans at their Forest counterparts, who responded with the 'Sign on' song.

Sheffield Wednesday under manager Howard Wilkinson, were just another version of Watford. Two big forwards, get the ball forward early and get stuck in, just the sort of side that Forest struggled against. So the 3-1 defeat was not altogether a surprise. Steve Hodge turned to Metgod as they left the pitch: "How did you like that?" he asked. "I have got a stiff neck, from watching the ball sail over my head," he replied.

Things were much more to Forest's liking four days later when Arsenal, with Woodcock and Anderson in their line up visited

MY CLUB

CONTINUED FROM PAGE 22

Paul Hart (centre) clears for Forest against Sheffield Wednesday.

MEET MY TEAM

SAYS IAN BOWYER

It's time to meet the players who are spearheading Nottingham Forest's drive for the First Division Championship.

Ian Bowyer, one of the most experienced captains in the country, takes you inside the dressing room at the City Ground for a player-by-player run-down on his team-mates . . .

STEVE SUTTON: He's come out of the shadows of Peter Shilton and Hans van Breukelen to get the number one goalkeeper spot on merit. Steve's got a lot of nicknames with the lads most of which are unprintable so he is known as "Sutty" most of the time.

KENNY SWAIN: Along with Paul Hart and myself he's the elder statesman in the side — actually we all reckon we've lost our birth certificates, the former Chelsea and Aston Villa star has started well this season.

BRYN GUNN: Although he is just 26, Bryn is one of our longest serving players. With Viv Anderson going to Arsenal he has now got the chance to become first choice right-back. The boss christened him "Bucket" because he likes a drink but he is also known as "Frank Spencer" because every job he tackles at home goes wrong.

CHRIS FAIRCLOUGH: "Mamba" could emerge as one of the country's outstanding defenders and with a reasonable amount of progress he looks certain to play for England.

PAUL HART: 'Harty' reckons he used to stand on the terraces as a schoolboy and watch me play but I think it was the other way round! Since he joined us from Leeds over a year ago he just seems to get better with age.

STEVE WIGLEY: He's my room-mate and if he ever learns how to make a decent cup of tea he could go a long way in the game! His 80 yard runs give us a welcome breather, on occasions.

JOHNNY METGOD: He got the nickname "Egghead" when he joined us before the start of the season because his arrival took the pressure off any of us who've had receding hairlines and once he adjusts to life in the First Division will be a revelation.

TREVOR CHRISTIE: It's not always easy joining a club from another in the same city but Trevor has settled down extremely well since coming from Notts County. He's a player's player who will run and graft all day for you and produce his share of goals. We're working on a nickname for him.

'Egghead' in action against Arsenal this season.

PETER DAVENPORT: He was christened "Birkenhead" because for reasons best known to himself he loves the place. Football-wise, he's got off to a flier this season. He looks so sharp and he's such a natural goalscorer.

STEVE HODGE: He's now been appointed chairman of the players committee at Forest so he has got a lot of responsibility off the field as well as on it. Steve got the name "Harry" after the television character "Harry the Rat" because he is always scurrying around the field.

COLIN WALSH: He had the unenviable task of stepping into John Robertson's shoes at Forest but he is a different type of player who deserves his own identity. "Walshy" joined the married set during the summer, settled into a new house and signed a new contract.

GARY MILLS: Now happily recovered from the broken leg he received over a year ago playing in America. He was a revelation when he made his debut as a 16-year-old, played in the European Cup before he was 17 and in the Final itself a year later. He's got the nickname "Chips" because he eats so many we swear he has them for breakfast.

GARRY BIRTLES: Recovering from a back operation during the close season, and although our strikers are scoring consistently, it would be nice to have "Gaz" back again. We also miss his "play school" tricks so the sooner he gets out of the kindergarten and back to work the better.

Focus on

Full name: Peter Davenport.
Birthplace and date: I was born in Birkenhead, Merseyside, on March 24, 1961.
Height and weight: 6 feet. 11st. 5lbs.
Married: No.
Home: I still live with my parents in their Birkenhead home, although during the week I stay in a club house in Nottingham.
Car: Ford Escort XR3i.
Nickname: Dav is the most common one, although they sometimes call me Birkenhead because that's where I'm always dashing off to!

Peter Davenport

Nottingham Forest

Previous clubs: I was an amateur with Wrexham and Everton, but was playing for Cammell Laird when Forest spotted me a couple of years ago.
Team you supported as a boy: Manchester United.
Football hero of childhood: Bobby Charlton and George Best were my United idols during the late 60's, and I also liked Liverpool striker Roger Hunt (below).
Job or trade before turning pro: I was a civil servant with the Land Registry Department.
Favourite current player: Liverpool's Kenny Dalglish for his ability to create something out of nothing.
Most memorable match: The second-leg of our UEFA Cup clash with Celtic last season. They held us to a goalless draw at the City Ground, but we beat them 2-1 at Parkhead.
Biggest disappointment: Being beaten by Anderlecht in last season's UEFA Cup Semi-Final.
Superstitions: I don't have any.
International honours: None.
Club honours: None.
Favourite other sports: Golf, tennis and cricket.

Favourite other sports person: Golfer Jack Nicklaus (above). He has a tremendous will to win and has won everything in the game but remained so modest.
Hobbies: Messing about with my home computer and playing any sport.
Favourite actor/actress: Henry Fonda and Jane Seymour.
Favourite TV shows: A Question Of Sport, Hill Street Blues, Porridge.
Favourite musicians: Paul McCartney, Lionel Ritchie, Stevie Wonder.
Biggest influence on career: All my family, particularly my father, for all their support and encouragement.
Ambitions for 1984-85: To win something with Forest.
Long-term ambitions: Just to be a successful footballer.

Shoot!

Trevor Christie.

Heartache at The City Ground AS THE REDS FALL AT THE FIRST HURDLE.....

Nottingham. Forest ran out 2-0 victors, with the first home goal of the season coming from the left boot of Metgod, usually only reserved for standing on, according to the player.

This was followed by two hat tricks in the next couple of games, as first, Davenport bagged all three in the victory over Sunderland, followed by his strike partner Trevor Christie in a 5-0 win at Aston Villa, a result that took Forest to the top of an admittedly early table. After the game, Villa manager Graham Turner came into the Forest dressing to congratulate the team and offered to give Clough £100,000 for Wigley and Bowyer, quick as a flash Bomber came back with: "Wigley's got to be worth more than £5,000!"

Forest once again decided to experiment with a Sunday fixture, on paper not an overly attractive one against Luton But once again the Nottingham public showed their support for the idea, an above average 18,605 turned up to witness a 3-1 win that again took them back to the top and two points clear.

Nigel Clough, the manager's son had been turning out for Heanor Town in the Midland League. He had been showing promise, and a couple of other clubs including Derby had been sniffing around. Alan Hill told the manager that fans would never forgive him if Forest missed out. So Nigel was given the chance to train at the club and turn out for the reserves. The manager left the details of this to Ron Fenton, for obvious reasons.

The UEFA Cup pitted Forest against Belgian opposition once more, this time Bruges and another opportunity for thousands of Reds' fans to make the trip. However there was to be no extended run in the competition this year and they went out in the first round. For a free scoring side, they barely created a chance over both games, failing to score in either tie. But Bruges were little better, managing only one goal themselves in the second leg in Belgium, and that was in the last minute, but it proved to be enough. They were on the end of another poor refereeing decision, when Davenport had a goal disallowed at the other end, robbing them of progressing on away goals.

Steve Wigley.

Ian Bowyer.

Already out of one cup competition, Forest looked to make progress in the Milk Cup against Second Division Portsmouth again over two legs. Despite losing the first game 1-0 at Fratton Park, they had little difficulty turning the tie around, winning the return 3-0. Portsmouth had an energetic player called Neil Webb who caught the eye.

After a bright start to the season, things just didn't seem to be clicking, injuries of course played their part but the new faces were not making the expected impact. When Liverpool rolled up for the club's first home live TV game they were slipping, but that was nothing compared to the poor form their opponents were in. Liverpool were down at the bottom, in sixteenth place with only two wins in eleven games. An injury to Paul Hart, meant that Metgod was pushed back to partner Fairclough in defence, whilst Hodge returned to his preferred position in the middle. Hodge had been pushed wide left to accommodate Metgod and Bowyer, and didn't like it. Although he was to still score twelve goals, he wanted to play down the middle where he could constantly be part of the action, rather than waiting for someone to feed him the ball. Liverpool of course, chose this game to re-discover their

THE REDS GO ON THE RAMPAGE

Davenport nets against Sunderland.

Then celebrates.

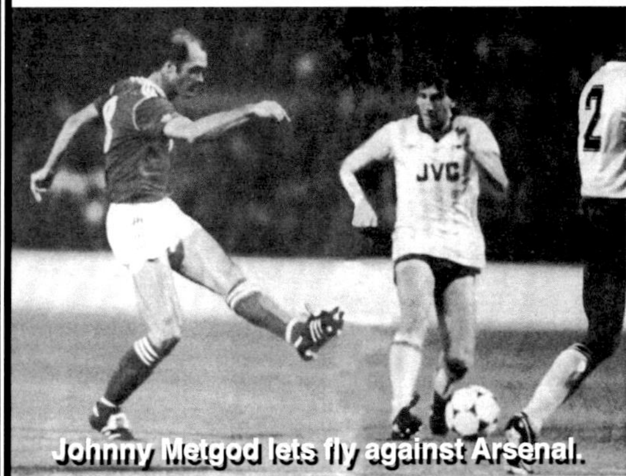

Johnny Metgod lets fly against Arsenal.

Steve Hodge scores against Norwich.

All eyes on the ball against Arsenal.

Trevor Christie takes the crowds' acclaim.

1. Davenport rounds the Luton keeper.

2. Then cooly slides the ball home.

3. Then turns to celebrate.

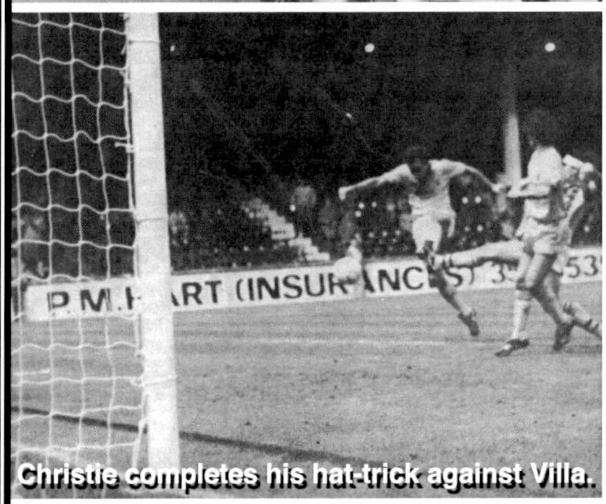
Christie completes his hat-trick against Villa.

More action from the Norwich game.

Hodge beats the diving Luton keeper.

Focus on CHRIS FAIRCLOUGH

Nottingham Forest

Full name: Chris Fairclough (there is more but I'm not letting on).
Birthplace and date: Nottingham, April 12, 1964.
Height and weight: 5ft 11ins. 12 stone 4lbs.
Married: No.
Home: I'm living with my parents in Nottingham.
Car: Ford Orion.
Nicknames: Mamba and Chief.

Peter Davenport

Team you supported as a boy: No one particularly.
Football hero of childhood: Kenny Burns.
Favourite current player: Peter Davenport... apart from when he goes past me in training.
Most memorable match: Beating Celtic in last season's UEFA Cup at Parkhead.
Biggest disappointment: Losing to Anderlecht in last season's UEFA Cup Semi-Final and losing to Wimbledon in this season's F.A. Cup.
International honours: Two England Under-21 caps, in Turkey and Israel.
Club honours: None as yet.
Superstitions: I do have a few but I don't want to talk about them.
Favourite other sports: I like all sports but particularly tennis. I'm after Ian Bowyer's crown because he's reckoned to be the best player in the club.
Favourite other sports person: John McEnroe... he's got tremendous talent.
Hobbies: I enjoy driving.
Favourite actors: John Hurt and Rod Steiger.
Favourite musicians: Alison Moyet and Sade.
Favourite TV shows: Auf Wiedersehen, Pet.

Biggest influence on career: Obviously Brian Clough but in my school days I got a lot of help from Brian Bates, Trevor Paterson, Alex King, Graham Cordell and Graham Sulley.
Ambitions for 1985: After the disappointments we've had in the Cups, we want to finish high enough in the League to qualify for Europe.
Long term ambitions: Hopefully to break through on the full international scene and help put a trophy back in the cabinet at Forest.

John McEnroe

Shoot!

Clemence acrobatically keeps out this effort.

Davenport has the last laugh, as he lobs the Spurs' keeper.

Steve Hodge with the first against Pompey.

Davenport scores against Leicester.

Davenport sends the Leicester keeper the wrong way.

Ian Bowyer in action.

It's the 89th minute as Johnny Metgod steps up to take this free kick at Manchester United.

A split second later and it's in the top corner of the net...GOAL!

METGOD'S MAGIC MOMENT

Steve Hodge beats the United keeper Gary Bailey.

Gary Mills completes the fight back with the equaliser.

It's Clough Mark II as young Nigel makes his debut...

Aussie, Alan Davidson gets his first sight of snow!!

form and strolled to a 2-0 win.

Forest's interest in the Milk Cup disappeared after the next round, a 1-1 home draw with Sunderland, led to them being eliminated after a replay 1-0 at Roker Park. There were talking points from both games, in the first Bryn Gunn was substituted after only twenty one minutes, when he played a reckless pass that led to Sunderland's goal, whilst Paul Raynor, making only his second appearance, was sent off in the North East.

The manager had stuck by Steve Sutton, despite reservations in some quarters, but after the keeper was blamed for a 2-1 home defeat, he took him out of the firing line. Davenport who had already scored, escaped blame although he missed two far easier chances.

Hans Segers came in for the following game, a 3-1 win at Coventry and retained his place for the rest of the season. At this time, there was little to choose between the pair. Segers was small for a keeper and didn't particularly stand out, and it would be difficult to remember a performance where you could say that he single-handedly won the points. The manager was really at fault for not going out and bringing in a top class keeper. After all, the club's success over the previous eight years had been built from having a commanding goalkeeper.

Forest once more pushed a fixture back to a Sunday, this time local rivals Leicester were the visitors. Davenport scoring both goals in a 2-1 victory. In a sign of the times, there was fighting in the upper tier of the East Stand, as some supporters migrated to seating areas of the ground. This match also saw the thawing of relations between the manager and John Robertson, who along with his wife, sat in the directors box as guests of the club.

Alan Davidson an Aussie, became the sixth debutant of the season when he made his bow against Watford. He replaced Kenny Swain and formed a new full back partnership with Jim McInally. Davidson was considered to be the best Australian player of his generation, but he didn't last long. He always seemed to be ill or injured, with a temperament or body that didn't seem suited to the harsh world of professional English football. A stress fracture of the back, sustained during a friendly in Iraq, was to put him out for the season.

The 3-2 win over Manchester United, treated fans to their first sight of a Metgod free kick special. Forest were trailing 2-0 to a couple of first half goals from Gordon Strachan. The unlikely fight back began when Hodge chased a through ball to fire home off a post on the hour mark. Gary Mills brought the scores level after a smart turn and shot from a Davenport pull back, before Johnny brought the house down with a last minute winner, wheeling away with what was to become his trademark celebration.

On the face of it, losing 5-0 at Everton in the next game looks disastrous, but the scoreline doesn't tell the whole story. Everton would go on to win the title this season, but they also had an edge that often strayed over the boundaries of acceptable. Gary Mills had suffered a couple of really bad injuries during his short career, and he had only just returned from a broken leg. So when he was the recipient of a crude challenge by Graeme Sharp that once more broke his leg, his fellow players were outraged. Sharp was not sent off, but Chris Fairclough was, for exacting some sort of revenge for his mate. Down to ten men, they stood little chance.

There was an amusing incident to relate from the night before this game. The squad were staying overnight and Kenny

Cloughie

SPEAKING HIS MIND

My son's got it!

I honestly could not understand what all the fuss was about when my younger son Nigel got into our first team at Forest.

I think I must have taken a few people by surprise when I named him for his debut against Ipswich ... and there were more surprises when I left him out for the following game against Aston Villa.

There were so many photographers at our ground for the Villa match, I thought Fleet Street had moved up to Nottingham.

But I did my job by leaving him out because I thought he hadn't really had a kick against Ipswich.

He's a better chauffeur than he is a striker at the moment because he gets the job of ferrying me around.

But he's only 18 — he can trap a ball, pass well and get the occasional goal. He's also got a big heart and it might help him make it.

Nigel didn't really get a kick against Ipswich.

THE TITLE -or else!

THERE'S one thing that might just persuade me to carry on in football when my contract with Nottingham Forest expires next year.

I have not really looked beyond 1986 but I might be tempted to carry on if I can see the development of a side capable of putting a few trophies in the showcase again.

We've been without a piece of silverware for four years at Forest ... and that's too long. But if in the course of the next 18 months we can put together a side capable of winning the League, then I might leave the pension alone for a bit longer.

Seeing the emergence of young players into household names has always been a cause for immense satisfaction for me and we've got a few players at Forest who fit into that category.

Chris Fairclough is one, Peter Davenport is another and beneath the surface of the first team, there are one or two youngsters who have the talent to follow them.

I dropped a bit of a clanger when I said that Fairclough would be the first coloured centre-half to play for England because at his age he could have done without me putting unfair pressure on him.

But although it knocked his form back slightly thinking about what I had said, he's now showing the maturity that you don't associate with someone of his age.

Peter Davenport has made great strides over the last 12 months and I was not kidding when I told manager Bobby Robson that he is good enough to go into an England squad straight away.

I'm not in the habit of recommending players for the sake of it but I know what I am doing in Davenport's case.

He's the sort of striker who excites a manager and if we can get him to sign a new contract, find a few more like him and Fairclough, then we might be in with a bigger shout of winning the title again.

And, as I say, that might just get me to hang around a bit longer — if they'll still have me by then.

Clark can take my job

I was thrilled to bits for Frank Clark when he got a brief moment in the spotlight by tasting F.A. Cup glory with Third Division Orient.

It wasn't for that reason that I put his name forward as a contender to take over from me when I'm ready to step down — or am kicked out — as manager of Nottingham Forest.

Frank, like my first team coach at the City Ground Ron Fenton, is the type of person I would not hesitate in recommending for the job.

They're both men of integrity, know what is required of the position and they've both served a fair old apprenticeship.

I've no doubt Frank has found it tough with little Orient but he's managed to put a smile on their football and their bit of joy in the Cup is well deserved.

If he turns out to be half as good a manager as he was a player he can't fail.

Newcastle thought he was finished when he joined me at Forest but I doubt whether I've made many better signings in my time.

Frank (light strip) was one of my best signings for Forest.

THE HODGE AND DAVENPORT SHOW

Forest new signing Jim McNally in action.

You can tell Steve Hodge has just scored.

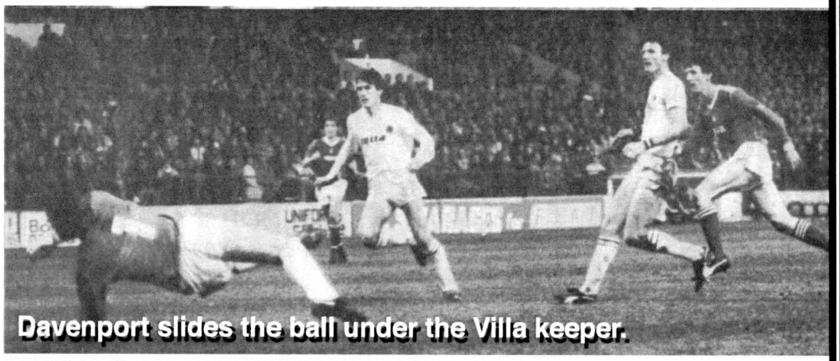

Davenport slides the ball under the Villa keeper.

Hodge beats Peter Shilton from close range.

Action from the Ipswich game.

Steve Hodge with the first goal against QPR.

Peter Davenport beats the diving Villa keeper Nigel Spink.

Swain who was from Liverpool, decided to visit an old friend, and the manager and players tagged along. Being Christmas they decided to sing a carol outside the door, the expression on Duncan McKenzie's face was priceless, this was life under Brian Clough.

December the 26th 1984, would be one of the proudest days in the life of the manager. This was the day that he saw Nigel Clough make his first team debut at home to Ipswich Town wearing the number nine shirt. It might not have been the greatest game, nor the highest crowd, but it was certainly an important staging post in the club's history. Fenton and O'Kane had thought he was ready for weeks, but the manager was wary about throwing him in too soon. The Clough name would have as many negatives as positives. Nigel showed a couple of nice touches, but he was to have to wait until much later in the season for a run of matches.

Forest had another Christmas home game three days later against Aston Villa and it turned out be virtually a re-run of the Manchester United game. Two goals down, a stirring fight back, a Johnny Metgod free kick and a late winner, it was just a pity that there were only 17,000 there to witness it.

Snow was to cause big disruptions to fixture lists in January. Forest would play four consecutive FA Cup games, as league games fell foul of the weather. The first, a home draw with Newcastle must have given some satisfaction to Gary Megson, who scored the visitors' goal, but Ian Bowyer equalised with a smart header.

The replay went to extra time at St James' Park, before another goal from Bowyer and Trevor Christie gave the Reds a 3-1 victory. The manager said that he was so sick and tired of the team making such a slow start to matches, he was thinking of giving his half time team talk before the game instead.

If there was one team that they wanted to avoid, it would be Wimbledon, but that is who they drew in the fourth round. A goalless draw in Nottingham, but you would have needed an abacus to count of the number of chances that Forest missed. It was pretty much the same story at Plough Lane, but the Wombles only needed one chance to clinch the tie 1-0, the Cup dreams over for yet another year. At least Garry Birtles could look forward to the new year with optimism, as it looked like that he could put his back problems behind him and challenge for a first team spot once more.

Steve Hodge was becoming more than a little disenchanted with life at the club. Always a team player, he didn't like being forced to play wide to accommodate Johnny Metgod. He knew his strengths were in getting into the box to support the attack and by playing wide he felt he was missing out. Colin Walsh was struggling with confidence, so Steve was charged with replacing him. There were rumours of interest from other clubs, Manchester United was mentioned, but he was particularly concerned that this change of position could harm his international prospects.

The snow returned with a vengeance in February. It was all hands to the pumps as even the office staff were expected to help clear the pitch so that the home game against Queens Park Rangers could go ahead. Clough also invited a number of striking miners down and they were rewarded with free tickets, soup and hamburgers. The pitch turned out to be almost perfect under the snow and a good performance coupled with a 2-0 win was a good result all round.

Almost immediately the squad set off for a couple of games in Iraq. Brian Clough decided to miss out on the opportunity of meeting Saddam Hussein and went to Spain instead, leaving Ron

Norwich City.

Steve Hodge and Johnny Metgod battle for the ball against Norwich City.

West Ham United.

Paul Hart in an aerial challenge against West Ham as Forest press for an equaliser.

Southampton.

Steve Sutton watches intently as Forest clear their lines against Southampton.

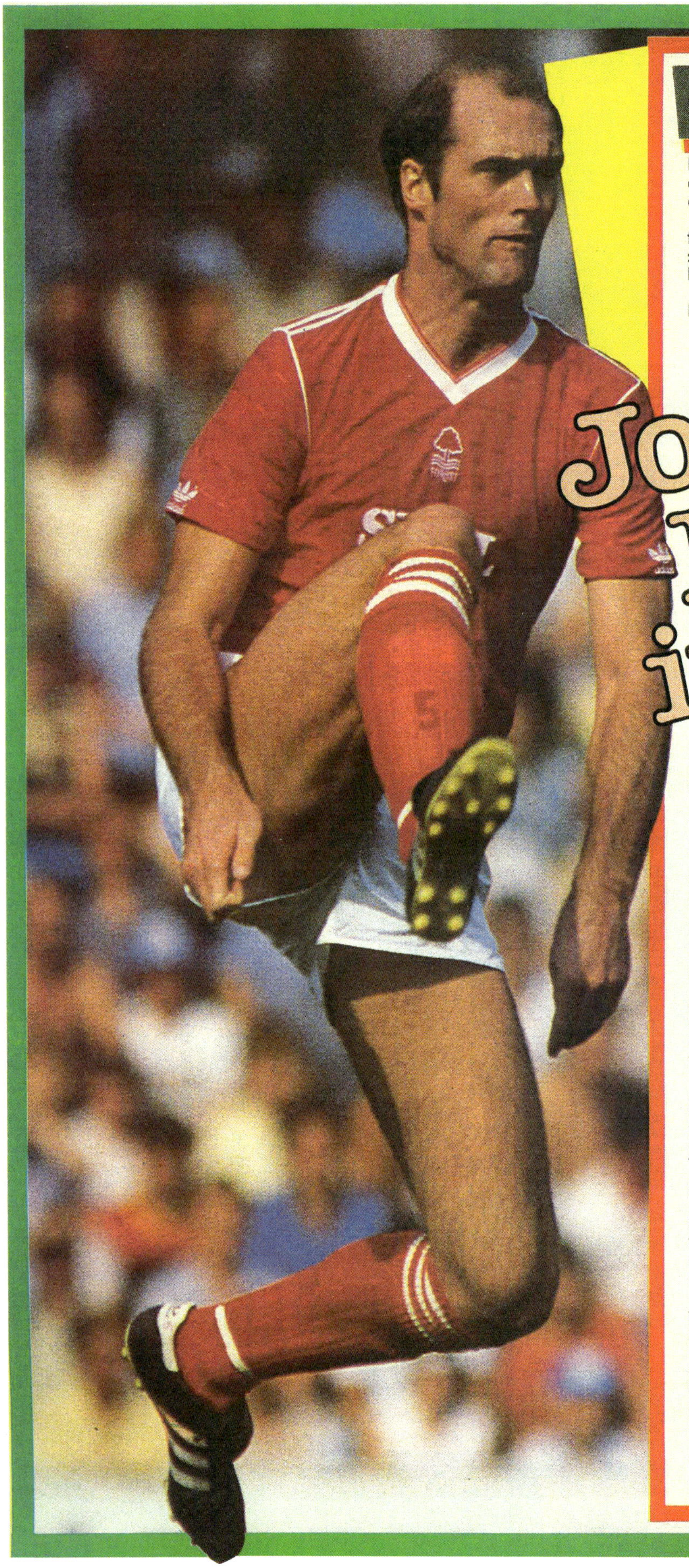

Johnny likes it hot!

WHEN Johnny Metgod goes on a lap of honour it takes his Nottingham Forest team-mates some time to catch him! The Dutch international, currently top of the pops with the City Ground fans, has been striding out, arms aloft, with a consistency that's beginning to alarm opponents.

The 26-year-old midfield player joined Forest from Real Madrid during the summer, and the £225,000 Brian Clough paid out is beginning to look like peanuts.

Metgod took a little while to settle into the Football League, but it's no coincidence that Forest's surge back into the title zone goes hand in glove with the Dutchman's return to form.

Hard in the tackle and capable of delivering the short and long pass with tremendous accuracy, he has given Forest a new dimension. Then, of course, there are those famous free-kicks bent "Platini" style over walls and away from clawing fingers.

He sank Manchester United and gutted Aston Villa with identical free-kicks before haring away to celebrate, his colleagues in vain pursuit.

"I feel a tremendous sense of release since coming to Forest," he says. "I spent so much of my two years with Real playing as sweeper and although I gave everything I had to make things work out, they didn't.

"I did not enjoy the football in Spain and my own role was too negative. If the manager at Forest wanted me to play at the back I would have no worries. But I believe I am doing a good job in midfield at the moment."

Metgod has no problems dealing with the physical side of the English game.

"Football in Holland can be hard and in Spain it is simply too rough and uncontrolled. Here, the game is hard but it is fair. Referees are good and the whole standard of football is competitive and enjoyable."

Metgod's international aspirations have burst to life again after a spell on the outside looking in.

"I have played for Holland against England and I have been proud of my international opportunities. Now I want to earn a place in the side again and if I do well with Forest that can happen."

The Forest lads are getting used to those long exhausting runs that follow a Metgod 'special' . . . in fact they don't mind one bit!

Nigel Clough heads home the first senior goal of his career against Watford.

Hodge the Wednesday keeper falls on the ball.

This effort just goes past the post.

A goalmouth scramble against Sheffield Wednesday.

Riley blasts over the West Ham bar.

YET ANOTHER SEASON COMES TO A CLOSE

Ogrizivic foils Steve Hodge.

Chris Fairclough goes close with this header against West Ham.

Riley tries to round keeper Hodge.

David Campbell.

Steve Hodge with a right foot effort against Everton.

Birtles header enters the Chelsea net.

Steve Hodge and Peter Davenport.

Garry Birtles and Kevin Ratcliffe of Everton.

Nigel Clough.

Metgod lets fly.

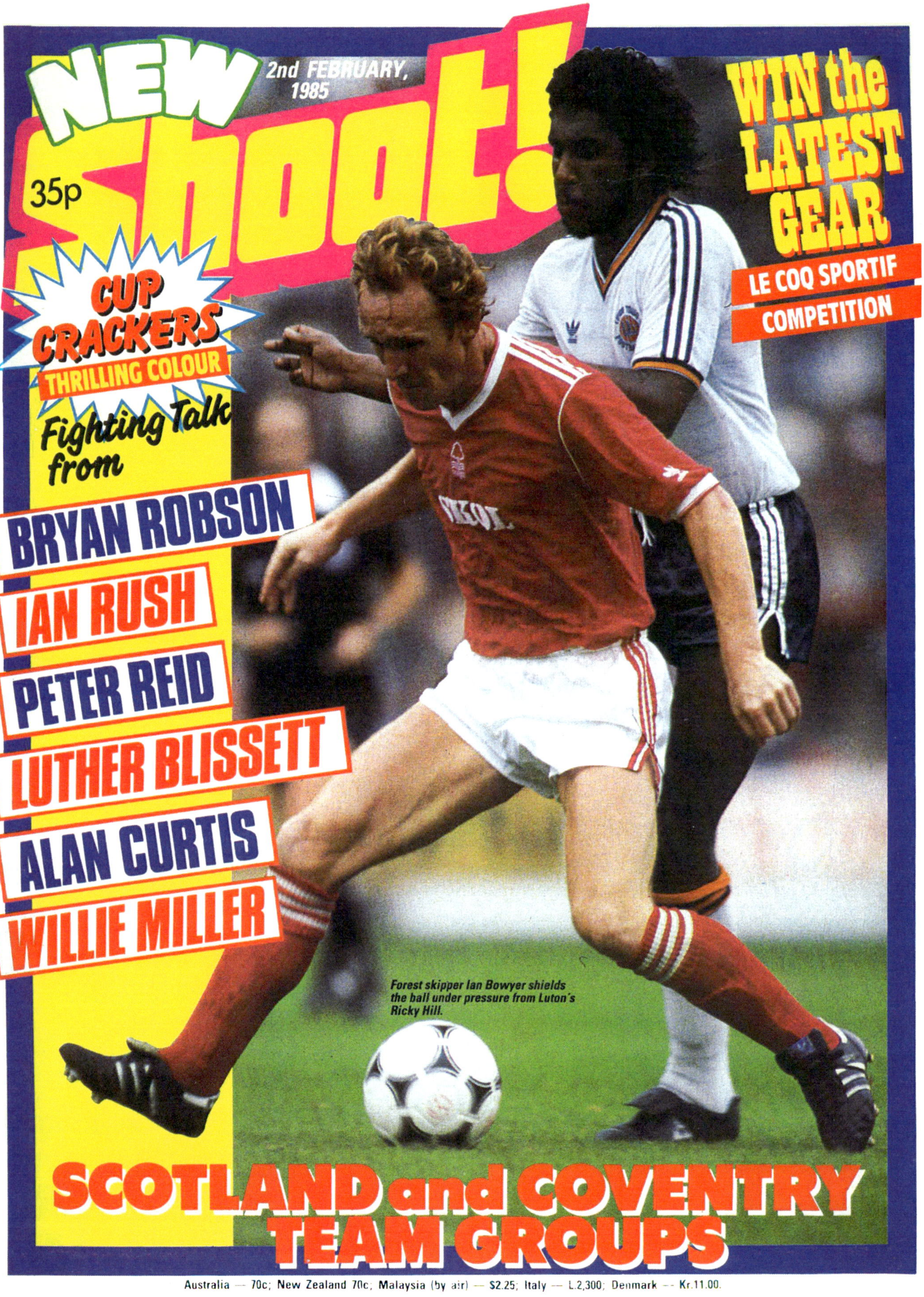
NEW
Shoot!
2nd FEBRUARY, 1985
35p
WIN the LATEST GEAR
LE COQ SPORTIF COMPETITION
CUP CRACKERS
THRILLING COLOUR
Fighting Talk from
BRYAN ROBSON
IAN RUSH
PETER REID
LUTHER BLISSETT
ALAN CURTIS
WILLIE MILLER
Forest skipper Ian Bowyer shields the ball under pressure from Luton's Ricky Hill.
SCOTLAND and COVENTRY TEAM GROUPS
Australia — 70c; New Zealand 70c; Malaysia (by air) — $2.25; Italy — L.2,300; Denmark — Kr.11.00.

**Jim McInally
Player of the Year.**

Fenton to do the honours. Ken Swain remembers meeting the dictator, but has always wondered whether it really was him, as it was rumoured that fearful of assassination, he often used 'body doubles' to stand in for him.

Trevor Christie had scored a few goals for the club. He definitely had a good attitude, but he really wasn't a Forest type of player. His ball control didn't compare with Birtles and Davenport, in truth he just fell a little short of the standard needed. But it was still a surprise that he was sold to Derby for £100,000, another loss of money on a transfer. This meant that of the three major summer signings, only Metgod remained and even he wasn't an unqualified success at the present moment.

He showed touches of class, especially from dead ball situations, but he was still taking his time to adjust to the special needs of the English game. This meant that Ian Bowyer was having to shoulder more than his fair share of responsibility and sometimes the midfield was being overrun.

At the same time that Christie was sold to Derby, Steve Sutton was making the same journey, albeit on loan. Forest had just completed the permanent signing of Hans Segers, so it wasn't looking likely that Sutton was going to regain his place, so he figured that the chance to put himself in the shop window was his best option.

Because of a fixture backlog, there were still fifteen matches to play and forty five points to play for. A top four finish and European qualification wasn't out of the question, but the team needed to find some consistency. A loss at home to West Brom was followed by a 4-1 victory at Stoke in front of the division's lowest attendance of the season, 7,000, before West Ham scored their first goal in eleven visits to the City Ground and left with a 2-1 win.

After months of speculation about his future, it was announced that Brian Clough had signed a new long term contract. The main motivation he said when explaining his decision was that he wanted to be around when this group of players won something. Working with these young players had enthused him about the game once more. As if to prove this point, there were another two more debutants, two young Irish lads. First to make his bow was forward David Campbell and he was quickly followed by fullback Gary Fleming, there seemed to be an almost inexhaustible supply of talent coming through.

There was delight for Garry Birtles when he scored his first goal for almost a year against Chelsea, a fine looping header. Could he now put eighteen months of injury worry behind him? But the team couldn't find any consistency and remained stubbornly just outside a group of teams challenging at the top.

Nigel Clough was given the chance to claim the number nine shirt beginning with a game at Kenilworth Road against Luton. This time he looked far more assured. He scored the first of his 131 goals a week later against Watford, a brave diving far post header, captured for posterity by a local photographer.

The final home game against Everton, (already crowned champions), at least provided Forest the chance of revenge after the events at Goodison Park earlier in the season. Everton, unbeaten in twenty eight games, lost to a Garry Birtles tenth minute goal.

Forest finished the season in ninth place, a massive twenty six points behind the champions. There were green shoots as always, the number of young players progressing through to the first team, and in all there were nine debutants, not including Gary Megson who never played a competitive first team game. Jim McInally, another of the club's bargains, had taken his time to tie down the right back position, but when he had, his form was so good that he was awarded the fans' Player of the Year trophy, picking up 51% of the votes.

Most worryingly however, there seemed to be no end to the slide in attendances, as the season's average of 17,071 was the lowest since the dark days of Division Two in the 1974 - 75 season.

Even with the club severely hampered by a lack of money, could Brian Clough persuade the board to somehow find the cash, and back him in the transfer market?

FOREST

APPEARANCES TEAM LINE-UPS

Aug 25th, A, v Sheffield Wednesday, L, 3-1, Scorer Davenport, AT 31,925, Sutton, Swain, Bowyer Fairclough, Hart, Metgod, Wigley, Hodge, Christie, Davenport, Walsh. SUB Mills.

Aug 29th, H, v Arsenal, W, 2-0, Scorers Metgod, Davenport, AT 18,215, Sutton, Gunn, Swain, Fairclough, Hart, Bowyer, Wigley, Metgod, Christie, Davenport, Hodge.

Sept 1st, H, v Sunderland, W, 3-1, Scorers Davenport (3), AT 15,760, Sutton, Gunn, Swain, Fairclough, Hart, Bowyer, Wigley, Metgod, Christie, Davenport, Hodge.

Sept 5th, A, v Aston Villa, W, 5-0, Scorers Bowyer, Christie (3), Hodge, AT 17,730, Sutton, Gunn, Swain, Fairclough, Hart, Bowyer, Wigley, Metgod, Christie, Davenport, Hodge. SUB Mills.

Sept 8th, A, v Queens Park Rangers, L, 0-3, AT 13,507, Sutton, Gunn, Swain, Fairclough, Hart, Bowyer, Wigley, Metgod, Christie, Davenport, Hodge.

Sept 16th, H, v Luton Town, W, 3-1, Scorers Davenport, Hodge (2), AT 18,605, Sutton, Gunn, Swain, Fairclough, Hart, Bowyer, Wigley, Metgod, Christie, Davenport, Hodge.

Sept 19th, H, UEFA, v Bruges, D, 0-0, AT 18,307, Sutton, Gunn, Swain, Fairclough, Smalley, Bowyer, Wigley, Metgod, Christie, Davenport, Walsh.

Sept 22nd, A, v West Ham, D, 0-0, AT 17,434, Sutton, Gunn, Swain, Fairclough, Smalley, Bowyer, Wigley, Metgod, Hodge, Davenport, Walsh.

Sept 25th, LC, A, v Portsmouth, L, 0-1, AT 20,409, Sutton, Gunn, Swain, Fairclough, Smalley, Bowyer, Wigley, Metgod, Hodge, Davenport, Walsh. SUB Mill.

Sept 29th, H, v Norwich City, W, 3-1, Scorers Christie, Hodge, (OG), AT 15,166, Sutton, McInally, Swain, Gunn, Fairclough, Bowyer, Wigley, Metgod, Christie, Davenport, Hodge. SUB Mills.

Oct 3rd, UEFA, A, v Bruges, L, 0-1, AT 2,983, Sutton, Gunn, Swain, Fairclough, Hart, Bowyer, Mills, Metgod, Christie, Davenport, Hodge.

Oct 6th, H, v Stoke city, D, 1-1, Scorer Davenport (P), AT 14,129, Sutton, Gunn, Swain, Fairclough, Hart, Bowyer, Wigley, Metgod, Christie, Davenport, Hodge. SUB Walsh.

Oct 10th, LC, H, v Portsmouth, W, 3-0, Scorers Gunn, Wigley, Hodge, AT 18,182, Sutton, Gunn, Swain, Fairclough, Hart, Bowyer, Wigley, Metgod, Christie, Davenport, Hodge. SUB Mills.

Oct 13th, A, v West Bromwich Albion, L, 1-4, Scorer Bowyer, AT 13,056, Sutton, Gunn, Swain, Fairclough, Hart, Bowyer, Wigley, Metgod, Christie, Davenport, Hodge. SUB Mills.

Oct 20th, A, v Newcastle United, D, 1-1, Scorer Hodge, AT 28,252, Sutton, Gunn, Swain, Fairclough, Hart, Bowyer, Wigley, Metgod, Christie, Davenport, Hodge. SUB Mills.

Oct 28th, H, v Liverpool, L, 0-2, AT 19,838, Sutton, Gunn, Swain, Metgod, Fairclough, Bowyer, Mills, Hodge, Christie, Davenport, Walsh.

Oct 31st, LC, H, v Sunderland, D, 1-1, Scorer Christie, AT 14,291, Sutton, Gunn, Swain, Metgod, Fairclough, Bowyer, Mills, Hodge, Christie, Davenport, Walsh. SUB Wigley.

Nov 3rd, A, v Southampton, L, 0-1, AT 17,818, Sutton, Mills, Swain, Metgod, Fairclough, Bowyer, Wigley, Hodge, Raynor, Riley, Walsh.

Nov 6th, LC, A, v Sunderland, L, 0-1, AT 23,184, Sutton, Mills, Swain, Metgod, Fairclough, Bowyer, Wigley, Hodge, Raynor, Riley, Walsh.

Nov 10th, H, v Tottenham Hotspur, L, 1-2, Scorer Davenport, AT 21,306, Sutton, Mills, Swain, Metgod, Fairclough, Bowyer, Wigley, Hodge, Raynor, Davenport, Walsh.

Nov 17th, A, v Coventry City, W, 3-1, Scorers Walsh, Riley, (OG), AT 9,895, Segers, Mills, Swain, Metgod, Fairclough, Bowyer, Wigley, Hodge, Raynor, Davenport, Walsh. SUB Riley.

Nov 15th, H, v Leicester City, W, 2-1, Scorers Davenport (2) (1P), AT 21,463, Segers, Mills, Swain, Metgod, Fairclough, Bowyer, Wigley, Hodge, Riley, Davenport, Walsh.

Dec 1st, A, v Watford, L, 0-2, AT 17,758, Segers, Davidson, Swain, Fairclough, Hart, Gunn, Mills, Metgod, Davenport, Bowyer, Hodge.

Dec 8th, H, v Manchester United, W, 3-2, Scorers Mills, Metgod, Hodge, AT 25,902, Segers, Davidson, Swain, Fairclough, Hart, Bowyer, Mills, Metgod, Riley, Davenport, Hodge.

Dec 15th, A, v Everton, L, 0-5, AT 22,487, Segers, Mills, Swain, Fairclough, Hart, Bowyer, Wigley, Metgod, Riley, Davenport, Hodge. SUB Walsh.

Dec 22nd, A, v Sunderland, W, 2-0, Scorers Wigley, Christie, AT 21,235, Segers, McInally, Swain, Fairclough, Hart, Bowyer, Wigley, Metgod, Christie, Davenport, Hodge.

Dec 26th, H, v Ipswich Town, W, 2-0, Scorers Metgod, Hodge, AT 17,123, Segers, McInally, Swain, Fairclough, Hart, Bowyer, Wigley, Metgod, Clough, Davenport, Hodge.

Dec 29th, H, v Aston Villa, W, 3-2, Metgod, Davenpor (2), AT 17,676, Segers, McInally, Swain, Gunn, Hart, Bowyer, Wigley, Metgod, Christie, Davenport, Hodge.

Jan 1st, A, v Chelsea, L, 0-1, AT 21,552, Segers, McInally, Davidson, Gunn, Fairclough, Walsh, Wigley, Metgod, Christie, Davenport, Hodge.

Jan 6th, FAC, H, v Newcastle United, D, 1-1, Scorer Bowyer, AT 23,582, Segers, McInally, Davidson, Gunn, Fairclough, Bowyer, Wigley, Metgod, Christie, Davenport, Hodge.

Jan 9th, FAC, A, v Newcastle United, W, 3-1, Scorers Bowyer, Christie, Davenport (3), AT 25,166, Segers, McInally, Davidson, Gunn, Fairclough, Bowyer, Wigley, Metgod, Christie, Davenport, Hodge.

Jan 26th, FAC, H, v Wimbledon, D, 0-0, AT 17,184, Segers, McInally, Swain, Fairclough, Hart, Bowyer, Wigley, Metgod, Birtles, Davenport, Hodge.

1984 - 1985 DIVISION 1 TABLE

TEAMS	P	W	D	L	F	A	W	D	L	F	A	PTS
1 Everton	42	16	3	2	58	17	12	3	6	30	26	90
2 Liverpool FC	42	12	4	5	36	19	10	7	4	32	16	77
3 Tottenham H	42	11	3	7	46	31	12	5	4	32	20	77
4 Manchester U	42	13	6	2	47	13	9	4	8	30	34	76
5 Southampton	42	13	4	4	29	18	6	7	8	27	29	68
6 Chelsea	42	13	3	5	38	20	5	9	7	25	28	66
7 Arsenal	42	14	5	2	37	14	5	4	12	24	35	66
8 Sheffiled W	42	12	7	2	39	21	5	7	9	19	24	65
9 Nottingham F	42	13	4	4	35	18	6	3	12	21	30	64
10 Aston Villa	42	10	7	4	34	20	5	4	12	26	40	56
11 Watford	42	10	5	6	48	30	4	8	9	33	41	55
12 W.B.A	42	11	4	6	36	23	5	3	13	22	39	55
13 Luton T	42	12	5	4	40	22	3	4	14	17	39	54
14 Newcastle U	42	11	4	6	33	26	2	9	10	22	44	52
15 Leicester C	42	10	4	7	39	25	5	2	14	26	48	51
16 West Ham U	42	7	8	6	27	23	6	4	11	24	45	51
17 Ipswich T	42	8	7	6	27	20	5	4	12	19	37	50
18 Coventry C	42	11	3	7	29	22	4	2	15	18	42	50
19 Q.P.R	42	11	6	4	41	30	2	5	14	12	42	50
20 Norwich C	42	9	6	6	28	24	4	4	13	18	40	49
21 Sunderland	42	7	6	8	20	26	3	4	14	20	36	40
22 Stoke C	42	3	3	15	18	41	0	5	16	6	50	17

WHO? WHAT!

FACTFILE

RESULTS LEAGUE TABLE

Jan 30th, FAC, A, v Wimbledon, L, 0-1, AT 10,348, Segers, McInally, Swain, Fairclough, Hart, Bowyer, Wigley, Metgod, Birtles, Davenport, Hodge. SUB Walsh.

Feb 2nd, A, v Norwich City, W, 1-0, Scorer Davenport, AT 14,669, Segers, McInally, Swain, Fairclough, Hart, Walsh, Wigley, Metgod, Clough, Davenport, Hodge.

Feb 9th, H, v Queens Park Rangers, W, 2-0, Scorers Metgod, Hodge, AT 11,991, Segers, McInally, Swain, Fairclough, Hart, Walsh, Wigley, Metgod, Birtles, Davenport, Hodge.

Feb 23rd, H, v Southampton, W, 2-0, Scorers Davenport (P), Hodge, AT 14,752, Segers, McInally, Swain, Fairclough, Hart, Bowyer, Wigley, Metgod, Birtles, Davenport, Hodge.

March 2nd, A v Liverpool, L, 0-1, AT 35,696, Segers, McInally, Swain, Fairclough, Hart, Bowyer, Wigley, Metgod, Birtles, Davenport, Hodge. SUB Riley.

March 9th, H, v Newcastle United, D, 0-0, AT 17,425, Segers, McInally, Swain, Fairclough, Hart, Bowyer, Wigley, Metgod, Birtles, Davenport, Hodge.

March 16th, H, v West Bromwich Albion, L, 1-2, Scorer Davenport, AT 12,663, Segers, McInally, Swain, Gunn, Hart, Bowyer, Wigley, Metgod, Birtles, Davenport, Hodge. SUB Riley.

March 20th, H, v Sheffield Wednesday, D, 0-0, AT 17,648, Segers, McInally, Swain, Fairclough, Hart, Bowyer, Wigley, Hodge, Riley, Davenport, Mills.

March 23rd, A v Stoke City, W, 4-1, Scorers Hart, Hodge, Riley, Davenport (P), AT 7,453, Segers, McInally, Swain, Fairclough, Hart, Bowyer, Wigley, Hodge, Riley, Davenport, Metgod. SUB Mills.

March 30th, H, v West Ham, L, 1-2, Scorer Hodge, AT 13,560, Segers, McInally, Swain, Fairclough, Hart, Bowyer, Wigley, Hodge, Riley, Davenport, Metgod. SUB Campbell.

April 6th, A, v Ipswich Town, L, 0-1, AT 16,296, Segers, McInally, Swain, Fairclough, Hart, Bowyer, Wigley, Metgod, Birtles, Davenport, Hodge. SUB Mills.

April 10th, H, v Chelsea, W, 2-0, Scorers Metgod, Birtles, AT 14,666, Segers, McInally, Swain, Fairclough, Hart, Bowyer, Wigley, Metgod, Birtles, Hodge, Mills.

April 13th, A v Arsenal, D, 1-1, Scorer Mills, AT 24,152, Segers, Fleming, McInally, Fairclough, Hart, Bowyer, Wigley, Metgod, Clough, Hodge, Mills.

April 20th, H, v Coventry City, W, 2-0, Scorers Mills, (OG), AT 12,990, Segers, Fleming, McInally, Fairclough, Hart, Bowyer, Wigley, Metgod, Davenport, Hodge, Mills. SUB Clough.

April 24th, A, v Luton Town, W, 2-1, Scorers Mills, Hodge, AT 10,156, Segers, McInally, Swain, Fairclough, Hart, Bowyer, Mills, Metgod, Clough, Davenport, Hodge. SUB Birtles.

April 27th, A, v Leicester City, L, 0-1, AT 13,886, Segers, McInally, Swain, Gunn, Hart, Bowyer, Mills, Metgod, Clough, Birtles, Hodge. SUB Walsh.

May 4th, H, v Watford, D, 1-1, Scorer Clough, AT 12,649, Segers, McInally, Swain, Gunn, Hart, Bowyer, Mills, Metgod, Clough ,Birtles, Hodge. SUB Wigley.

May 6th, A, v Manchester United, L, 0-2, AT 43,334, Segers, McInally, Swain, Walker, Hart, Bowyer, Wigley, Mills, Clough , Birtles, Hodge.

May 11th, H, v Everton, W, 1-0, Scorer Birtles, AT 18,784, Segers, McInally, Swain, Walker, Hart, Bowyer, Mills, Metgod, Clough , Birtles, Hodge.

May 17th, A, v Tottenham Hotspur, L, 0-1, AT 20,075, Segers, McInally, Swain, Walker, Hart, Bowyer, Mills, Metgod, Birtles, Davenport, Hodge.

Brian Clough presents Peter Davenport with the manager's Player of the Season award.

WHERE! WHEN!

SEASON 1985-86

Back row L to R: Nigel Clough, Colin Walsh, Brian Rice, Ian Butterworth, Des Walker, Neil Webb, Gary Mills.
Middle row L to R: Ron Fenton (Asst. Manager), Bryn Gunn, Steve Sutton, Johnny Metgod, Hans Segers, Alan Davidson, Chris Fairclough, Brian Clough (Manager).
Front row L to R: Garry Birtles, John Robertson, Ian Bowyer, Steve Hodge, Peter Davenport, Jim McInally, Steve Wigley, Stuart Pearce.

If you had thought that football couldn't get much lower, then you were in for a shock. Just eighteen days after the disastrous fire at Bradford, the Heysel Stadium in Brussels, was the venue for the European Cup final between Juventus and Liverpool, and millions of people saw the sickening scenes played out live in their front rooms, as television beamed the images to a world wide audience.

Put aside the fact that the stadium was not fit for purpose, the events that took place that night were a disgrace, as Liverpool fans caused multiple deaths amongst fans who happened to be standing in the next section, by charging indiscriminately into them. Anyone who travelled to football matches during this era, knew that the media image of the cheery Scouser was a load of rubbish, as a significant minority of their followers robbed and fought their way across, not only this country, but Europe as well. The criminal enquiry found Liverpool fans solely to blame and twenty four people were charged with manslaughter and extradited to stand trial.

The upshot of this, was that all English teams were to be banned, not only from taking part in European competition, but they were not even allowed to play friendly matches on the continent. There was no timescale on this banning order, it would only be rescinded when the authorities were satisfied that there was unlikely to be a repeat. The immediate effect on Forest was that they had to cancel all of their pre-season plans and arrange fixtures in England. That is why the names of Bournemouth, Weymouth, Portsmouth and Brighton, replaced Bilbao, Munich and Lisbon.

This season on the face of it was to be a middling nothing sort of campaign. It is only when looking back to review the events, that you can clearly see the progress and the building blocks being put in place, that were to culminate in the second period of success that Brian Clough was to have at the club.

There were a couple of outgoings to report. Paul Raynor joined Huddersfield, whilst Kenny Swain left to captain Portsmouth. Kenny had absolutely embraced his time with the club and especially the manager. Every player would have their disagreements with the boss at some time, but to Kenny, he felt that it was an absolute privilege to work with him. The fun times far out weighing anything else. As the player says: "There might have been some that doubted his motives, but all I ever saw, was a genuine, honest and generous person." The player recalls one of their final times together, when he and his wife Lily were invited to the Clough household just before he left. "It was obviously an emotional time for me and I am not ashamed to admit that when Lily and I left Brian's house that day, we were in tears. Anyway, he said, 'must dash, because I've got to go and sign your replacement'. Who? I asked, 'young lad at Coventry, Stuart Pearce'. He replied."

With the progress that had been made by Chris Fairclough and Des Walker, it was also felt that they could allow Paul Hart to move on, he joined Sheffield Wednesday. Paul is another who really enjoyed his time at the club. Despite often being the subject of the manager's criticism, he took it on board and I think it is fair to say that the football philosophy that he took into his coaching career, was nurtured at the City Ground.

There is a common misconception that Stuart Pearce was the makeweight in the joint deal that also took Ian Butterworth from Coventry to Nottingham. Not so, Alan Hill who was heavily involved in the signing explains the background: "We had seen the player and taken a liking to him, and although he wasn't a youngster, that didn't bother us. We had bought several players who had also missed the boat and been late

Stuart Pearce **Brian Rice** **Ian Butterworth** **Neil Webb** **John Robertson**

starters. I travelled to Coventry on a match day, and caught up with the player as he was parking his car. I explained who I was and would he be interested in joining us. He gave me his number and I said we would be in touch. That evening we phoned him and I put the gaffer on. 'Do you want to play for me son? 'Yes, good', and that was it."

Stuart Pearce and Ian Butterworth weren't the only signings to be made. Alan Hill again provides a fascinating insight in to the way football works: "We wanted to sign Neil Webb, but we also knew that he had other options, with Aston Villa being desperate to sign the player. We had already tapped him up months before, but we wanted him to meet the gaffer, so when we played Tottenham in London for the final game of the season, we invited the player and his wife to join us for a meal the night before and he worked his usual charm. I remember bumping in to Alan Ball the Portsmouth manager at the game the next day, hoping he hadn't got word about what had happened."

Brian Rice from Hibernian was another signing that cost money. He had been spotted by Liam O'Kane whilst playing for Hibs in a pre-season game. The two clubs couldn't agree a fee, so it went to a tribunal where Forest got stitched up. The fee was higher than the figure they were originally looking for, but after producing 'evidence' from another Scottish club about how much they would have paid, the tribunal settled on £175,000.

John Blackley, the Hibernian manager said: "I hope this sends a message out to other English clubs that they can't come up here and take our talent on the cheap." Clough was really angry, he had been assured that the fee would be much lower, and probably wouldn't have gone through with the deal for an untried youngster if he had known what the outcome would be.

The final signing needed no introduction. After two years away, John Robertson returned to the place he should never have left. He had been released on a free transfer by Derby, and Clough was quick to pick him up. Whether sentiment played a role in the manager bringing him home, he wouldn't admit it, merely stating that he had brought him to show the others how to play.

Robertson though had no doubts, either about returning or the amount of involvement he was likely to get with the first team: "I have always been a little insecure, and I knew that by returning to the City Ground I would have to prove myself all over again, I wouldn't walk back into the team. My game had declined at Derby and I wasn't getting any younger, but it was the right thing to do."

The squad for the upcoming season not only looked stronger, but also was greater in numbers. With the investment made, the manager and the committee would be looking for an improvement on last year.

With the signing of Neil Webb, Steve Hodge had expected to move on, so it was a surprise to him that when the season started, not only was he still in Nottingham, but in the side playing in his favoured central position. The team began with a useful draw on the artificial pitch at Luton, then followed this up with a home defeat to Sheffield Wednesday, 1-0 and a clean sheet for Paul Hart on his return. Brian Clough couldn't abide the way Howard Wilkinson, the Wednesday manager sent his team out to play. After the game he shouted to the Owls' boss: "Howard, you'll get the game done away with, playing football like that!"

However on the Friday, as Steve was preparing to get changed for training, the manager caught him and said that Graham Turner, The Aston Villa manager, was in his office waiting to speak to him. Clough said: "I think you should go, make yourself a few bob". With that, the player's seven years at the club he supported, were over, but he couldn't help recalling what the manager had said to him when he had handed in a written transfer request: "Now remember young man, that anything that happens to you now, is because of that letter."

Ian Butterworth and Des Walker began the season as the central defensive partnership. Chris Fairclough had picked up an injury during pre-season and would miss the whole of the campaign, as the medical team just couldn't put their finger on the real problem. Butterworth was not really a Clough type of centre half. He really liked the head it and kick it types, in truth a bit of a bastard. Hadn't he once said to Dave Needham, that if he was looking for someone to go out for a drink with, he would choose him, but for football it would be Larry Lloyd.

With so many new faces, it was not a surprise that the team struggled to gel. They did get their first win of the season at home to Southampton, courtesy of another Metgod free kick, but their second successive away game on an artificial pitch at Queens Park Rangers resulted in another loss.

Garry Birtles couldn't care if he never plays another game at centre-forward in his life. Nottingham Forest's newly converted centre-half insists: "I'm happy to stay in defence for the rest of my career."

After nearly ten years of leading the attack for Forest and Manchester United, Birtles was surprisingly switched to defence for the Milk Cup tie at Bolton in October.

And the 29-year-old reckons the change of role has given him a new lease of life.

Explains Garry: "I don't miss the glory of scoring goals in the least. So long as the side is winning and I'm playing well enough to be included, I'm perfectly happy.

"I reckon I only had a couple more years in me as a striker. Playing with your back to goal and taking all those knocks and kicks eventually begins to take its toll.

"Now I'm seeing things the other way round. But of course I don't foul forwards like other defenders!"

But Garry admits he is still terrified at the prospect of making a tackle in the penalty-area.

"The thought of giving away a penalty frightens me more than anything. Commit a foul in your opponents' box and it doesn't really matter. But upend someone in your own area and you're in big trouble."

One tackle which particularly pleased the former £1million striker came in the final minute of Forest's 2-1 win against West Bromwich Albion last month.

"Garth Crooks had worked his way into the area and was going for goal," Birtles recalls. "It was absolutely essential I got my timing right. I held off for as long as possible because I didn't want to dive in and give them a last minute penalty. But in the end I had to commit myself and thankfully I won the ball cleanly."

Birtles FRIGHTENED and loving it

Birtles was the star of the show during Forest's 2-1 win against WBA.

That match-winning tackle clinched Birtles' tag as Man of the Match — during which he also contributed to Neil Webb's opening goal with a neat header.

"I'm only doing my old job the other way round," he insists. "Look how Kenny Burns made his point: he slammed in goals for Birmingham as a centre-forward and was outstanding as a centre-half for Scotland at the same time.

"David Cross asked me what the hell I was doing at the back when we played at Bolton," recalls Birtles with chuckle. "And my old Forest partner Tony Woodcock pulled my leg in much the same way during our Arsenal game."

But does Garry prefer to face a striker who is quick and darting like Crooks and Woodcock, or a direct powerhouse finisher like Andy Gray, another famous name shut out by the Birtles skill?

"I never think in those terms. That's the fast lane to being half defeated before you start. I just take them as they come."

WIN, LOSE & DRAW

Steve Hodge's last game against Sheff Weds.

Davenport with Reds' only goal against Man Utd.

Johnny Metgod is a picture of concentration as he takes this free kick against Southampton.

Clough and Davenport.

Des Walker at Anfield.

Birtles flicks on at Leicester.

A goal line scramble against the Owls.

Neil Webb bravely scores away at Leicester.

Davenport's fine left foot effort, finds the net at Filbert Street.

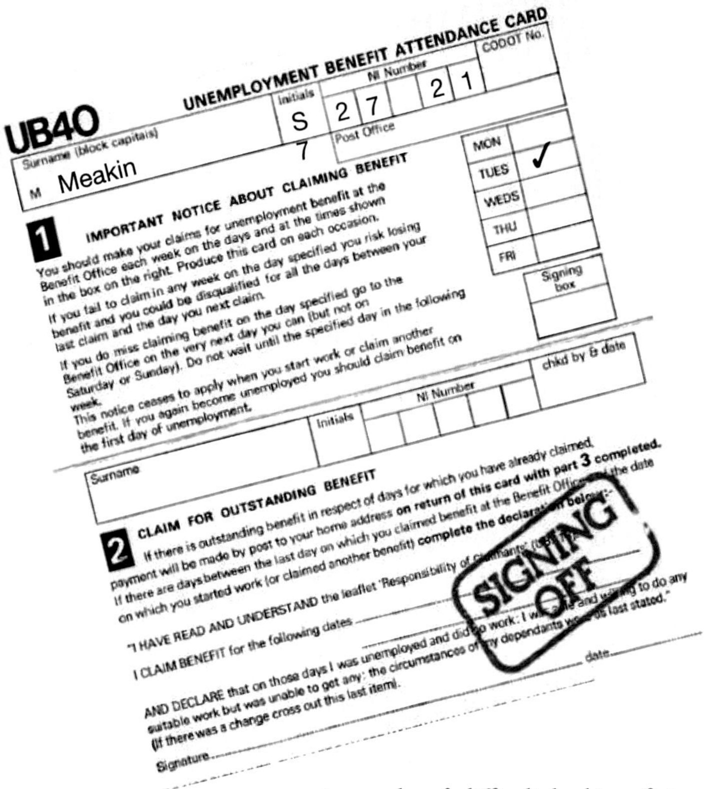

UB40 UNEMPLOYMENT BENEFIT ATTENDANCE CARD

Surname (block capitals) M Meakin | Initials S 7 | NI Number 2 7 2 1 | CODOT No. | Post Office

MON | TUES ✓ | WEDS | THU | FRI | Signing box

1 IMPORTANT NOTICE ABOUT CLAIMING BENEFIT

You should make your claims for unemployment benefit at the Benefit Office each week on the days and at the times shown in the box on the right. Produce this card on each occasion.

If you fail to claim in any week on the day specified you risk losing benefit and you could be disqualified for all the days between your last claim and the day you next claim.

If you do miss claiming benefit on the day specified go to the Benefit Office on the very next day you can (but not on Saturday or Sunday). Do not wait until the specified day in the following week.

This notice ceases to apply when you start work or claim another benefit. If you again become unemployed you should claim benefit on the first day of unemployment.

Surname | Initials | NI Number | chkd by & date

2 CLAIM FOR OUTSTANDING BENEFIT

If there is outstanding benefit in respect of days for which you have already claimed, payment will be made by post to your home address **on return of this card with part 3 completed.** If there are days between the last day on which you claimed benefit at the Benefit Office and the date on which you started work (or claimed another benefit) **complete the declaration below:-**

"I HAVE READ AND UNDERSTAND the leaflet 'Responsibility of Claimants'

I CLAIM BENEFIT for the following dates

AND DECLARE that on those days I was unemployed and did no work: I was able and willing to do any suitable work but was unable to get any; the circumstances of my dependants were as last stated."

(If there was a change cross out this last item).

Signature date

SIGNING OFF

A couple of difficult looking fixtures against Manchester United and Liverpool returned no points, making this, officially the worst start to a campaign since Brian Clough had joined the club. Only four points from a possible eighteen, down in twentieth spot. The attendance at Anfield was only 27,135, it wasn't only Forest fans who were turning their backs on football. The manager had tried to integrate Robbo back into the side, but it just wasn't working. Then Brian Rice was given the number eleven jersey, making his debut against Liverpool, before the position began alternating between him and Colin Walsh, though Robbo was to sporadically appear in the line up.

A 3-0 win at Leicester stopped the rot, Webb, Davenport and a first goal for Rice gave the impression it was easy, but Forest were again grateful for another penalty save from Hans Segers.

Forest were concerned about falling attendances and introduced a novel scheme, beginning with the next home game against Tottenham, to help the unemployed attend. When you were out of work and signing on, you were given a card called a UB40 (that is what the group were named after) to present at the dole office. Forest decided to offer reduced admission to supporters on presentation of their card at a turnstile at the Bridgford End, and instead of paying £2.50, you would only pay £1.50. The club hoped that this wouldn't be abused, but it was a common sight for cards to be passed through the railings for multiple people to use, it lasted a couple months before it was stopped.

The home defeat to Tottenham, to yet another late goal from Chris Hughton, led to the manager making a rare public apology to the chairman Maurice Roworth about the team's poor start, but even then, there was barbed criticism of others: "I wonder how many of his nine fellow directors can look him straight in the eye and say they are giving him their undivided loyalty?"

Throughout his whole tenure at the club, it was always felt that many committee members, wouldn't mind seeing Forest fail, if it meant that the manager was brought down a peg or two. Clough would take great satisfaction whenever these 'small men' were forced out. The manager and Derek Pavis were often at loggerheads and it wouldn't be long before the manager had the ammunition he needed to have him removed.

The manager liked to have a settled side, but at that time, he couldn't decide on his best eleven. McInally who had been a great success the previous season, wasn't playing well and lost his place to Des Walker, who was moved from the centre, whilst Metgod dropped back to take on the sort of 'sweeper' role. Nigel Clough had been given the centre forward position, alongside Peter Davenport, meaning that Birtles wasn't in the team.

Results slowly began to pick up, as they surely were bound to, with such a strong team. The average age of 22 years and 188 days for the team selected to play Watford, was the youngest ever in the club's history, and even this would be lowered twice more later in the season. Eighteen year old Franz Carr was to make his debut three days later in a 4-0 win over Bolton in the Milk Cup, (they were to progress 7-0 on aggregate).

Hans Segers' run as first choice keeper was about to come to an end. He was injured after thirteen minutes of the game at West Ham, by which time Forest were already two goals down. Neil Webb took the gloves and his first action was to pick the ball out of the net, as the Hammers scored again. It looked as if they were to be on the wrong end of a thrashing, four down before the hour mark, but with a spirited fight back, (two goals from Clough and Metgod), a 4-2 defeat ended up being considered a positive.

Seven successive victories followed, although two of these were in the Milk Cup. First up was a 3-1 win against Ipswich and a first goal for Stuart Pearce. Pearce was already a fans' favourite, prepared to fling himself into any challenge. The manager had words of advice for the player, telling him to stay on his feet more when making a tackle.

Villa Park at this time was proving to be a lucky ground for the Reds, and they achieved a 2-0 win there, but it was a chastening day for Steve Hodge, as he unsurprisingly received lots of abuse from Forest fans who taunted him throughout. Franz Carr made his first league start and made an instant favourable impression. So much so, that Forest sold Steve Wigley to Sheffield United the following week.

After beating Bolton in the Milk Cup, Forest were drawn away to play Derby in the next round. Because of previous crowd trouble, the police initially refused to cover the game, unless it was made an afternoon kick off, but after negotiations, they agreed they would attend. Before this game, the good form continued with a couple more outstanding wins. Steve Sutton who had patiently bided his time was superb at Newcastle, saving a Peter Beardsley penalty in a 3-0 win. City Ground spectators were then treated to their first glimpse of Franz Carr in a 3-2 victory over Arsenal. He made an immediate impression. It might be a cliché, but his pace was electrifying and the Gunners just couldn't handle him. The two goals that Arsenal scored, were in the final minute, and couldn't hide the fact that they had been second best for the entire game.

Garry Birtles had now got himself back in the team, not at centre forward, but at centre half, as the manager thought that they were missing Metgod in midfield. So fans were treated to the experience of Birtles marking his old striking partner, Tony Woodcock, out of the game.

Derby County away, their 'Cup Final.' Lower league opposition and a potential banana skin was handled with aplomb. Despite going 1-0 down, they showed their class and two goals

Brian Rice evades this challenge from Roberts of Spurs.

Campbell pokes in against Watford.

Another Davenport Goal!

The unusual sight of Neil Webb in the goalkeeper's Jersey against West Ham, after Hans Segers went off injured.

Pearce has scored against Ipswich.

Nigel Clough gives the Watford keeper no chance.

Nigel Clough is foiled by the Tottenham keeper.

A typical Ian Bowyer goal against Ipswich.

AUTUMN ACTION!

1. Neil Webb flings himself forward.

2. watching as his header flies past the Albion keeper.

Davenport curls this effort in to the Arsenal net.

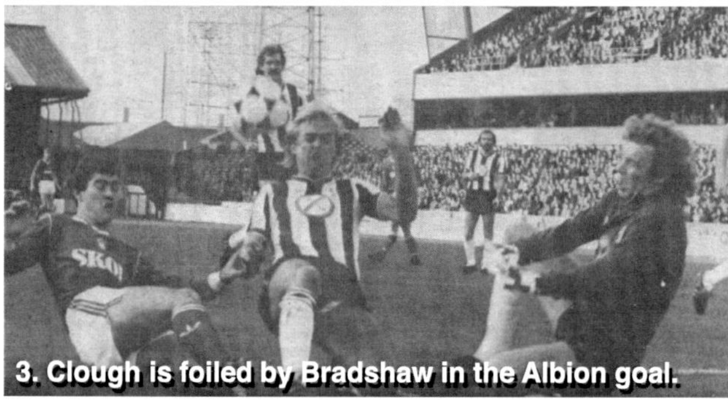

3. Clough is foiled by Bradshaw in the Albion goal.

Neil Webb goes sprawling in the Albion box.

Davenport completes his hat-trick against Arsenal.

Nigel Clough takes a leaf out of the Metgod free kick manual and curls this effort past the Luton defence, and in to the net.

Ronnie Fenton and Brian Clough.

KOP THAT!

1. Grobbelaar is beaten by Neil Webb.

2. The Forest player takes the applause.

Nigel Clough.

BRIAN RICE

JOHN ROBERTSON

HANS SEGERS

DES WALKER

BRETT WILLIAMS

STEVE WIGLEY

FRANZ CARR

NIGEL CLOUGH

GARY FLEMING

Franz Carr coolly puts the Reds ahead at the Baseball Ground.

CARR RIDE to VICTORY at DERBY

The rare sight of a Metgod header, clinching the tie for Nottingham Forest.

Focus on NEIL WEBB
FOREST

Full name: Neil John Webb.
Birthplace and date: Reading on 30th July, 1963.
Height and weight: 6ft.; 12st. 12lb.
Married: Yes, to Shelley. We married during the summer.
Home: We are moving in November into a four-bedroom detached house.
Car: Alfa Romeo.
Nickname: Webby, for obvious reasons.
Previous clubs: Reading and Portsmouth.
Team you supported as a boy: Tottenham.

Pele, Webb's childhood hero.

The former Portsmouth star scores his first goal in Division One.

Football hero of childhood: Pele, I still watch films of him, and Dutchman Johan Cruyff.
Favourite current player: Glenn Hoddle. He has tremendous skill and passing ability.
Most memorable match: Scoring on my League debut for Forest in the opening game of the season against Luton.
Biggest disappointment: Injuring an ankle when I was 17 — I thought it was the end of the world.
Superstitions: None.

International honours: Ten England youth caps and one Under-21 cap.
Club honours: Third Division Championship medal with Portsmouth in 1982-83.
Favourite other sports: Athletics and snooker.
Favourite other sports star: Seb Coe, a superb athlete.
Hobbies: Listening to music.
Favourite actor and actress: David Jason and Felicity Kendall.
Favourite TV shows: Bill Cosby and Cheers — they both make me laugh.
Favourite musicians: I like soul and jazz.
Biggest influence on career: My father and the rest of my family who have always offered their support.
Ambitions for 1985-86: To establish myself with Forest.
Long-term ambitions: To be successful with Forest and hopefully to do well enough to get into the England side.

Shoot!

from Metgod, a header from a Carr cross, then Carr himself slotting home the winner to earn instant cult status, putting the Rams firmly in their place. Ian Bowyer had been granted a testimonial year for his ten years service, despite the break at Sunderland, and his organising committee were arranging a series of events to celebrate this. The first was a fans' special at the supporters club, where Stuart Pearce revealed his skills as a bingo caller and John Robertson unveiled his comedy routine. John thought that he was so funny, that they had trouble getting the microphone off him.

The win over West Brom, 2-1, was the seventh in a row, and was instrumental in Brian Clough receiving his first manager of the month award for four years, his sixteenth in total, but as always seems to happen to the recipient, they lost the next game 4-2 at Stamford Bridge. Ken Smales was given the rare privilege of sitting on the bench after he had not been allocated a seat in the stand after a mix up.

The reward for beating Derby was an awkward looking trip to London to face QPR in the Milk Cup. The first game unusually was abandoned after floodlight failure, but the lights really went out on the Reds' cup aspirations the following week, after a 3-1 loss. Most of the action was condensed into the last three minutes, two goals for Rangers and a sending off for Davenport. Although Rangers' first goal, a penalty, was given after an offence that clearly took place outside the box. The skid mark was visible to everyone but the referee.

Results continued to be inconsistent and the team hovered around mid-table as a result. The last six matches of the year produced two wins, two draws and two defeats. An injury to Pearce meant that Birtles even had to play left back on one occasion, but Brett Williams, another seventeen year old was called on to fill in until Stuart's return. With Gary Fleming at right back, they became the youngest full back pairing in the club's history.

The stand out game during this period was against champions elect Liverpool. It may have finished 1-1, but the Reds were only denied a win after an acrobatic penalty save by Bruce Grobelaar, in front of a healthy Christmas crowd in excess of 27,000.

As the club entered the New Year, there were further optimistic signs, a 5-2 win over Coventry City, after being two goals down and then a well deserved 3-0 victory at White Hart Lane over Tottenham, courtesy of a couple of Davenport goals. But elimination in the Third Round of the FA Cup to Division Two Blackburn Rovers, brought a premature end to the season. The first game against Rovers at the City Ground, a 1-1 draw, had been played out against the backdrop of a snowstorm, the replay was even more disappointing, a deserved 3-2 loss.

Brian Clough enjoyed a love hate relationship with some committee members. There were those he disliked because he thought they were 'amateurs', and involved for the wrong reasons, but there were also those who thought that he wielded too much power and should be more respectful to those who employed him. One such committee man was Derek Pavis, a successful self made business man, who was a strong character in his own right. Derek had been associated with the club for over twenty years, but there was a skeleton in his closet. Back in the 1960's, he had been accused of, and found guilty of offering a bribe to the Nottingham Forest wing half, Jeff Whitefoot to lose a game. He had somehow managed to overcome this and remained with the club, but the manager was always on the look out for an excuse to force him out.

The opportunity came after the manager heard about an event that occurred on the directors' coach to an away fixture at Old Trafford. Forest were considered the underdogs for this fixture, so in what they perhaps considered fun, Frank Allcock and Derek Pavis were offering odds of 7-1 against a Reds' victory. Fellow directors Fred Reacher and Pete Atkins took them up on this offer. But after Forest gained a magnificent come from behind win, Clough heard about the incident, and then exploded at what he perceived as a lack of support. As a result, Pavis was forced out and in an action that was seen by many as a way to get back at Clough, he set up camp over the river and bought Notts County.

Whether the incident on the bus was a harmless bit of fun and blown out of all proportion, you can never be 100% sure, but one thing was for certain, Derek Pavis was an astute business man and when Forest entered another period of economic uncertainty in the early nineties, his acumen and money would have been useful, after all, many committee members were loath to even consider putting their own money in to help the club, whereas Pavis showed at County, he had the money and was prepared to put his money where his mouth was.

When Queens Park Rangers were humbled 4-0 the following week, suddenly the team were up to sixth place, but immediately two defeats and a draw dropped them back to tenth, although they were not helped by a return of the icy weather, that meant they went without a fixture for almost four weeks from February to March.

There was plenty of news off the pitch. Firstly Jim McInally who had shown so much promise, was transferred to Coventry, although he only managed one game at Highfield Road, before returning to Scotland. But the really big news came when the

WINTER WARMERS

A Christmas Cracker for Webb against Coventry City.

Did you see that?

Colin Walsh can't miss against QPR.

Webb beats Barron in the Rangers' goal.

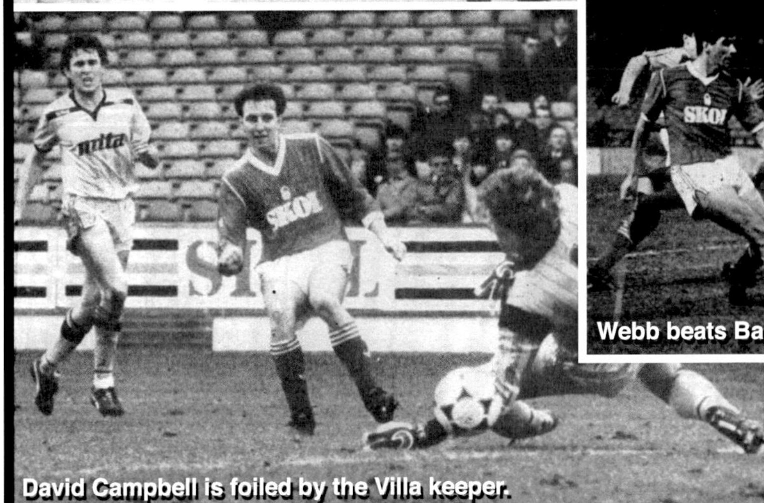

David Campbell is foiled by the Villa keeper.

Franz Carr from close range against QPR

Action from the Aston Villa game.

An ice bound City Ground for the visit of Newcastle.

Johnny Metgod tussles with the Queens Park Rangers defence

club were forced to accept a bid from Manchester United for Peter Davenport. The club needed money, there had been no progress in either cup competition, whilst crowds were down in the low 10,000's. The manager made his displeasure known about the sale, but deep down he knew the financial reality and didn't kick up too much fuss. Commenting on the situation he said: "I don't know how long we can go on finding players, selling them and trying to build a successful side. Potential England strikers don't grow on trees, although some people at this club might think otherwise, but maybe one day, they will realise this is not the case." The fee was perhaps a little low at £575,000, but Forest were desperate, and with the player again expressing his desire to move back to the North West, Forest were unable to generate a bidding war on the player.

Specialists thought that they had finally got to the root of Chris Fairclough's injury problems, although this would mean another operation and writing off the whole season, but at least the player's career didn't look in jeopardy now. Alan Davidson, the Australian had never settled and was released to return home and prepare for the World Cup.

The team line-up was continually rotated, although the signs of partnerships within the team were growing, injuries permitting. Walker and Metgod in central defence, Pearce and Fleming at full back and Clough and Birtles upfront. Bowyer usually played, but several players such as Brian Rice and Colin Walsh, never seemed to do quite enough to become regulars.

Back on the pitch, a least there was a good game to report on. A 4-3 victory over Leicester City, a match in which there was never more than one goal between the two sides, but an attendance of only 14,844 served to emphasise the financial realities facing the club. At least the team were in no danger of relegation, the situation in the West Midlands was far worse. The relegation positions were filled by Albion, Birmingham City and Aston Villa.

April the 2nd, and a re-arranged game against West Ham United, who surprisingly had found the consistency to challenge for the title. A larger than average attendance, plus a wider audience courtesy of a visit from the BBC television cameras, were to witness one of the free kicks of the decade. Five minutes before half time, Forest were awarded a foul, about thirty yards out from the Bridgford End goal. Five in the defensive wall, including a couple of Reds players, but the Hammers weren't concerned , they had giant keeper Phil Parkes in goal. Johnny Metgod, who already had several fine free kick goals to his name was the only candidate. He carefully retreated perhaps ten paces before beginning his run up. The player himself said that he had never struck a ball sweeter. It may have looked as if it passed just over the head of Parkes, but he never even saw it. Some free kicks use finesse, this particular one used brute force. Every Forest fan of a certain age, can surely remember the Metgod celebration afterwards. The 2-1 defeat for West Ham halted their momentum and probably cost them the title that year.

Incredibly, despite losing Davenport to Manchester United, Forest remained unbeaten for the rest of the campaign, a run of twelve matches. This might have included seven drawn games, but a more settled side gave real hope for the future. In a further indication of declining attendances, the 1-1 draw at Highbury against Arsenal was watched by only 15,098 spectators.

Forest were to finish the season in a comfortable eighth place, twenty points adrift of Liverpool who regained their title. Nigel Clough was top scorer with fifteen goals and also the recipient of the Player of the Year award. The average attendance had fallen to only 16,497, but this was far from being the worst in the league.

If the club could keep hold of it's best young talent, good times, in the form of trophies might not be too far away.

Johnny Metgod receives the County Cup trophy.

1. Carr advances on the Leicester goal.

2. Knocks it past the keeper.

3. Then turns away after scoring.

Webb fires home against Birmingham.

Another Metgod headed goal against Birmingham.

Nigel Clough back on penalty taking duties, sends the Birmingham keeper the wrong way,

Ghostbuster

Brian Rice gives the Reds all the points against West Ham.

Blockbuster

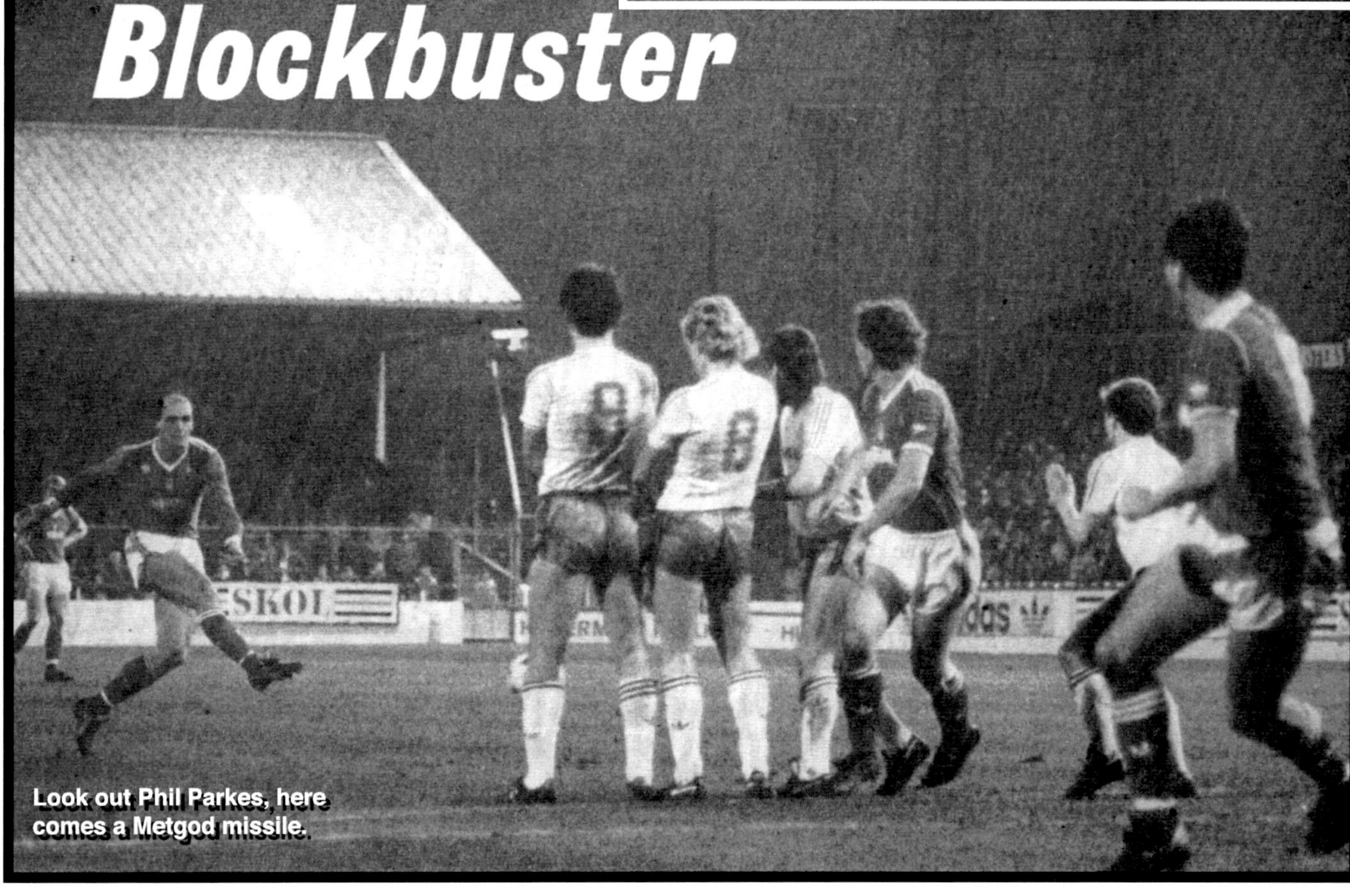

Look out Phil Parkes, here comes a Metgod missile.

★★★ FOREST

APPEARANCES   TEAM LINE-UPS

Aug 17th, A, v Luton Town, D, 1-1, Scorer Webb, AT 11,318, Segers, McInally, Pearce, Butterworth, Walker, Hodge, Mills, Webb, Birtles, Davenport, Robertson.

Aug 21st, H, v Sheffield Wednesday, L, 0-1, AT 18,367, Segers, McInally, Pearce, Butterworth, Walker, Hodge, Wigley, Webb, Birtles, Davenport, Robertson.

Aug 24th, H, v Southampton, W, 2-1, Scorers Metgod, (OG), AT 12, 643, Segers, McInally, Pearce, Butterworth, Walker, Webb, Wigley, Metgod, Birtles, Davenport, Robertson.

Aug 27th, A, v Queens Park Rangers, L, 1-2, Scorer Webb, AT 10,748, Segers, McInally, Pearce, Butterworth, Walker, Webb, Wigley, Metgod, Clough, Birtles, Robertson. SUB Mills.

Aug 31st, H, v Manchester United, L, 1-3, Scorer Davenport, AT 26,274, Segers, McInally, Pearce, Butterworth, Walker, Webb, Wigley, Metgod, Clough, Birtles, Davenport. SUB Bowyer.

Sept 3rd, A, v Liverpool, L, 0-2, AT 27,135, Segers, Butterworth, Pearce, Walker, Metgod, Bowyer, Wigley, Webb, Birtles, Davenport, Rice. SUB Clough.

Sept 8th, A, v Leicester City, W, 3-0, Scorers Webb, Davenport, Rice, AT 14,247, Segers, Butterworth, Pearce, Walker, Metgod, Bowyer, Wigley, Webb, Birtles, Davenport, Rice. SUB Clough.

Sept 11th, CC, H, v Notts County, L, 1-2, Scorer Carr, AT 2,207, Segers, Butterworth, Pearce, Walker, Metgod, Bowyer, Wigley, Webb, Clough, Davenport, Carr. SUBS Campbell, Fleming.

Sept 14th, H, v Tottenham Hotspur, L, 0-1, AT 17,554, Segers, Butterworth, Pearce, Walker, Metgod, Bowyer, Wigley, Webb, Clough, Davenport, Rice.

Sept 21st, H, v Watford, W, 3-2, Scorers Clough, Davenport, Campbell, AT 12,921, Segers, Butterworth, Pearce, Walker, Metgod, Bowyer, Wigley, Webb, Clough, Davenport, Rice. SUB Campbell.

Sept 25th, LC, H, v Bolton Wanderers, W, 4-0, Scorers Campbell (2), Clough, Rice, AT 10,530, Segers, Butterworth, Pearce, Walker, Metgod, Campbell, Wigley, Webb, Clough, Davenport, Rice. SUB Carr.

Sept 28th, A, v West Ham, L, 2-4, Scorers Metgod, Clough, AT 14,540, Segers, Butterworth, Pearce, Walker, Metgod, Bowyer, Mills, Campbell, Clough, Davenport, Webb. SUB Walsh.

Oct 5th, H, v Ipswich Town, W, 3-1, Scorers Pearce, Bowyer (2), AT 12,200, Sutton, McInally, Pearce, Butterworth, Walker, Bowyer, Metgod, Campbell, Clough, Davenport, Robertson. SUB Birtles.

Oct 8th, LC, A, v Bolton Wanderers, W, 3-0, Scorers Clough, Davenport, Rice, AT 4,010, Sutton, Mills, Pearce, Butterworth, Birtles, Webb, Wigley, Metgod, Clough, Davenport, Rice. SUB Walsh.

Oct 12th, A, v Aston Villa, W, 2-0, Scorers Clough, (OG), AT 15,315, Sutton, Mills, Pearce, Butterworth, Birtles, Webb, Carr, Metgod, Clough, Davenport, Rice.

Oct 19th, A, v Newcastle United, W, 3-0, Scorers Davenport (2), Rice, AT 23,151, Sutton, Mills, Pearce, Butterworth, Birtles, Webb, Carr, Metgod, Clough, Davenport, Rice.

Oct 26th, H, v Arsenal, W, 3-2, Scorer Davenport (3), AT 17,756, Sutton, Mills, Pearce, Butterworth, Birtles, Webb, Carr, Metgod, Clough, Davenport, Rice. SUB Walker.

Oct 30th, LC, A, v Derby County, W, 2-1, Scorers Carr, Metgod, AT 22,226, Sutton, Mills, Pearce, Butterworth, Birtles, Webb, Carr, Metgod, Clough, Davenport, Rice. SUB Walker.

Nov 3rd, H, West Bromwich Albion, W, 2-1, Scorers Webb, Davenport, (P), At, 19,610, Sutton, Mills, Pearce, Butterworth, Birtles, Webb, Carr, Metgod, Clough, Davenport, Rice.

Nov 9th, A, v Chelsea, L, 2-4, Scorers Clough (2), AT 17,743, Sutton, Mills, Pearce, Butterworth, Birtles, Webb, Carr, Metgod, Clough, Davenport, Rice. SUB Walker.

Nov 16th, H, v Manchester City, L, 0-2, AT 15,140, Sutton, Mills, Pearce, Butterworth, Birtles, Webb, Carr, Metgod, Clough, Davenport, Rice. SUB Walker.

Nov 23rd, A, v Everton, D, 1-1, Scorer Clough, AT 27,860, Sutton, McInally, Pearce, Walker, Butterworth, Webb, Mills, Metgod, Clough, Davenport, Walsh.

Nov 25th, LC, A, v Queens Park Rangers, L, 1-3, Scorer Clough, AT 13,052, Sutton, McInally, Pearce, Walker, Birtles, Webb, Mills, Metgod, Clough, Davenport, Walsh.

Dec 1st, H, v Oxford United, D, 1-1, Scorer Davenport (P), AT 15,317, Sutton, McInally, Pearce, Walker, Birtles, Webb, Mills, Metgod, Clough, Davenport, Walsh.

Dec 7th, A, v Sheffield Wednesday, L, 1-2, Scorer Webb, AT 22,496, Sutton, McInally, Pearce, Walker, Birtles, Bowyer, Carr, Webb, Clough, Davenport, Walsh.

Dec 14th, H, v Luton Town, W, 2-0, Scorers Clough, Webb, AT 12,078, Sutton, McInally, Pearce, Walker, Butterworth, Bowyer, Carr, Metgod, Clough, Webb, Robertson. SUB Walsh.

Dec 20th, A, v Southampton, L, 1-3, Scorer Carr, AT 12,500, Sutton, McInally, Birtles, Walker, Butterworth, Bowyer, Carr, Webb, Clough, Walsh, Robertson. SUB Metgod.

Dec 26th, A, v Birmingham City, W, 1-0, Scorer Webb, AT 10,378, Sutton, McInally, Williams, Walker, Birtles, Bowyer, Metgod, Webb, Clough, Davenport, Robertson. SUB Walsh.

Dec 28th, H, v Liverpool, D, 1-1, Scorer Webb, AT 27,141, Sutton, Mills, Williams, Walker, Birtles, Bowyer, Metgod, Webb, Clough, Davenport, Robertson. SUB Walsh.

Jan 1st, H, v Coventry City, W, 5-2, Scorers Metgod, Webb (3), Davenport, AT 13,860, Sutton, Mills, Williams, Walker, Birtles, Bowyer, Metgod, Webb, Clough, Davenport, Robertson. SUB Walsh.

Jan 4th, FAC, H, v Blackburn Rovers, D, 1-1, Scorer Birtles, AT 15,772, Sutton, Mills, Williams, Walker, Birtles, Bowyer, Metgod,

1985 - 1986 DIVISION 1 TABLE

TEAMS	P	W	D	L	F	A	W	D	L	F	A	PTS
1 Liverpool FC	42	16	4	1	58	14	10	6	5	31	23	88
2 Everton	42	16	3	2	54	18	10	5	6	33	23	86
3 West Ham U	42	17	2	2	48	16	9	4	8	26	24	84
4 Manchester U	42	12	5	4	35	12	10	5	6	35	24	76
5 Sheffield W	42	13	6	2	36	23	8	4	9	27	31	73
6 Chelsea	42	12	4	5	32	27	8	7	6	25	29	71
7 Arsenal	42	13	5	3	29	15	7	4	10	20	32	69
8 Nottingham F	42	11	5	5	38	25	8	6	7	31	28	68
9 Luton T	42	12	6	3	37	15	6	6	9	24	29	66
10 Tottenham H	42	12	2	7	47	25	7	6	8	27	27	65
11 Newcastle U	42	12	5	4	46	15	5	7	9	21	41	63
12 Watford	42	11	6	4	40	25	5	5	11	29	40	59
13 Q.P.R	42	12	3	6	33	31	3	4	14	20	44	52
14 Southampton	42	10	6	5	32	22	2	4	15	19	44	46
15 Manchester C	42	7	7	7	25	20	4	5	12	18	31	45
16 Aston Villa	42	7	6	8	27	18	3	8	10	24	39	44
17 Coventry C	42	6	5	10	31	26	5	5	11	17	36	43
18 Oxford U	42	7	7	7	34	28	3	5	13	28	53	42
19 Leicester C	42	7	8	6	35	35	3	4	14	19	41	42
20 Ipswich T	42	8	5	8	20	24	3	3	15	12	31	41
21 Birmingham C	42	5	2	14	13	25	3	3	15	17	48	29
22 W.B.A	42	3	8	10	21	36	1	4	16	14	53	24

★★★★ WHO? WHAT!

FACTFILE

RESULTS LEAGUE TABLE

Webb, Clough, Davenport, Robertson. SUB Walsh.

Jan 11th, A, v Tottenham Hotspur, W, 3-1, Scorers Davenport (2), Walsh, AT 19,043, Sutton, Butterworth, Williams, Walker, Birtles, Bowyer, Metgod, Webb, Clough, Davenport, Walsh. SUB Robertson.

Jan 13th, FAC, A, v Blackburn Rovers, L, 2-3, Scorers Birtles, Walsh, AT 11,710, Sutton, Butterworth, Williams, Walker, Birtles, Bowyer, Metgod, Webb, Clough, Davenport, Walsh.

Jan 18th, A, v Manchester United, W, 3-2, Scorers Clough, Walsh (2), AT 46,717, Sutton, Fleming, Williams, Walker, Metgod, Bowyer, Carr, Webb, Clough, Davenport, Walsh.

Feb 1st, H, v Queens Park Rangers, W, 4-0, Scorers Carr, Webb, Walsh (2), AT 11,538, Sutton, Fleming, Williams, Walker, Metgod, Bowyer, Carr, Webb, Clough, Davenport, Walsh.

Feb 8th, H, v Newcastle United, L, 1-2, Scorer Walsh, AT 15,388, Sutton, Fleming, Williams, Walker, Metgod, Bowyer, Carr, Webb, Clough, Davenport, Walsh. SUB Campbell.

March 8th, A, v Ipswich Town, L, 0-1, AT 12, 658, Sutton, Fleming, Williams, Walker, Metgod, Bowyer, Carr, Webb, Clough, Davenport, Rice. SUB Campbell.

March 15th, H, v Aston Villa, D, 1-1, Scorer Clough (P), AT 12,993, Segers, Fleming, Williams, Walker, Birtles, Bowyer, Mills, Campbell, Clough, Webb, Walsh. SUB Metgod.

March 22nd, H, v Leicester City, W, 4-3, Scorers Bowyer, Carr, Clough (2), AT 14,484, Sutton, Fleming, Williams, Walker, Metgod, Bowyer, Carr, Campbell, Clough, Birtles, Rice.

March 29th, A, v Coventry City, D, 0-0, AT 9,500, Sutton, Fleming, Williams, Walker, Metgod, Bowyer, Carr, Campbell, Clough, Birtles, Rice.

March 31st, H, v Birmingham City, W, 3-0, Scorers Metgod, Webb, Clough (P), AT 12,134, Sutton, Fleming, Pearce, Walker, Metgod, Bowyer, Campbell, Webb, Clough, Birtles, Rice. SUB Walsh.

April 2nd, H, v West Ham, W, 2-1, Scorers Metgod, Rice, AT 17,498, Sutton, Fleming, Pearce, Walker, Metgod, Bowyer, Carr, Webb, Clough, Campbell, Rice.

April 5th, A, v West Bromwich Albion, D, 1-1, Scorer Metgod, AT 7,901, Sutton, Fleming, Pearce, Walker, Butterworth, Walsh, Carr, Campbell, Clough, Metgod, Rice.

April 8th, A, v Arsenal, D, 1-1, Scorer Campbell, AT 15,098, Sutton, Fleming, Pearce, Walker, Metgod, Bowyer, Carr, Campbell, Clough, Webb, Walsh.

April 12th, H, v Chelsea, D, 0-0, AT 18,055, Sutton, Fleming, Pearce, Walker, Metgod, Bowyer, Carr, Webb, Clough, Campbell, Walsh.

April 19th, A, v Manchester City, W, 2-1, Scorers Webb, Campbell, AT 19,715, Sutton, Fleming, Pearce, Walker, Metgod, Bowyer, Carr, Webb, Clough, Campbell, Walsh. SUB Butterworth.

April 21st, A, v Watford, D, 1-1, Scorer Clough, AT 11,510, Sutton, Fleming, Pearce, Walker, Metgod, Rice, Carr, Webb, Clough, Campbell, Walsh.

April 26th, H, v Everton, D, 0-0, AT 30,171, Sutton, Fleming, Pearce, Walker, Metgod, Walsh, Carr, Webb, Clough, Campbell, Rice.

May 3rd, A, v Oxford United, W, 2-1, Scorer Clough (2), AT 11,845, Sutton, Fleming, Pearce, Walker, Metgod, Walsh, Carr, Webb, Clough, Campbell, Rice.

May 7th, CC, A, v Mansfield Town, W, 1-0, Scorer Birtles, AT 3,165, Sutton, Butterworth, Pearce, Walker, Metgod, Clough, Carr, Webb, Birtles, Mills, Rice.

May 8th, CC, H, v Notts County, W, 2-0, Scorers Carr, Rice, AT 1,752, Sutton, Butterworth, Pearce, Walker, Metgod, Clough, Carr, Webb, Birtles, Mills, Rice. SUBS Wiliams, Murray

Franz Carr is foiled during the last game of the season against Everton.

WHERE! WHEN!

SEASON 1986-87

Back row L to R: Colin Walsh, Garry Birtles, Steve Sutton, Ian Butterworth, Hans Segers, Brian Rice, Ian Bowyer.
Middle row L to R: Ron Fenton (Asst. Manager), David Campbell, Stuart Pearce, Gary Mills, Johnny Metgod, Neil Webb, Mark Smalley, Liam O'Kane (Trainer).
Front row L to R: Des Walker, Nigel Clough, Gary Fleming, Franz Carr, Brett Williams.

The most significant aspect of pre-season came when the club's accounts were published for the period 1985-86, and they showed a profit of £473,000, compared to a loss of £627,000 the previous tax year. The manager had splashed out on an early spending spree the previous summer, but had then managed to balance the books by selling six players, whilst bringing in only one further player. The sheer number of youngsters coming through had greatly contributed to this. If the club had had to go and buy talent such as Des Walker and Nigel Clough on the open market, they wouldn't have been able to afford it. Other clubs in a similar position, such as West Brom and Ipswich had tried to replace their stars with cheaper journeyman signings and been relegated as a result.

Over the years, there had been many calls for a restructuring of the divisions, particularly at the top of the game, where it was considered that players were being forced to play too many games. And on the financial side, many First Division chairman thought that the top clubs deserved a greater 'slice of the pie'. So it wasn't altogether surprising when it leaked out that talks were taking place about a new Super League containing the countries best teams, with a new television deal and perhaps no promotion and relegation.

These discussions were at a very low level initially, but the Football League had reacted to these talks with their own innovations. As we have seen, the top clubs were worried about the number of games that they were playing, so it was decided that the First Division would be reduced from twenty two teams to twenty over a period of two years. This would be achieved by relegating three teams and only promoting two. As Ken Smales pointed out, those teams that had also been moaning about falling incomes, would have to replace the money lost from two home games a season.

But the most startling change was to be the introduction of 'Play Offs', for the final promotion spot in each division.

Unlike the system used in the present day, the first two years of the play offs included the third bottom team in the First Division, along with the second, third and fourth placed teams in Division Two, thus giving the third worst team the chance to retain their higher status. Both the semi finals and finals were played on a two legged home and away basis, with away goals counting double in the circumstances of an aggregate draw.

Two substitutes would now be allowed in all cup matches, therefore a back up keeper could be included if clubs wished.

Kennilworth Road, the home of Luton Town, had seen the worst football related riots in years the previous season, when followers of their FA Cup visitors Millwall, had reacted to being eliminated from the competition, by smashing the ground up and fighting with Police. In response to this, Luton, who were under the chairmanship of David Evans, the local Conservative MP, decided to ban away supporters completely and introduced a home members scheme to make it work.

Although many could see the logic in the argument, this meant that not only would Luton enjoy the advantage of an artificial pitch but also the total crowd support for home games. The matter came to a head when they drew Cardiff at home in the Littlewoods Cup (renamed after the new sponsors) and were threatened with expulsion if they did not allow Cardiff fans to attend. Luton decided to withdraw from the competition instead.

Although the balance was looking better, there would

be no new signings this pre-season, although there was the welcome sight of Chris Fairclough continuing his return to fitness. Ian Bowyer had been awarded another years contract, but it was goodbye to the City Ground for perennial stand in Bryn Gunn, who left to join Peterborough United. Over eleven years stalwart service, he had accumulated 159 appearances and was the proud possessor of a European Cup winners medal.

There was also to be a different kit supplier for the new season. Umbro, who were beginning a big marketing push, replaced Adidas and the result was a smart v-neck shirt, with black and white neck detail and Home Ales in white across the chest, as the main sponsor.

The ban on clubs playing and preparing for the new season on the continent had been lifted and Forest returned to their regular routine of visiting Scandinavia and Holland. They were joined by an old face, Archie Gemmill, who had been promoted to first team coaching duties.

Fifteen games were played in total, the quality of the opposition varied greatly from lower league Danish sides such as Bromoella to Utrecht of the Netherlands. This mini tour culminated in a City Ground clash with Moscow Torpedo three days before opening day, the club's first encounter with Russian opposition.

Unlike the previous season when their routine had been curtailed, this time there was no chance that they would be 'under cooked,' and would begin the season on fire, although you wouldn't have predicted this after an opening day 2-0 reverse at Everton. But even this doesn't tell the whole story, as they hit the woodwork twice before falling behind, earning plaudits from the Merseyside crowd for an adventurous approach.

Brian Clough was able to name a virtually unchanged team for the first twelve fixtures and after a comprehensive 4-0 home defeat of newcomers Charlton Athletic, (who had won promotion despite being exiled to Selhurst Park), they were less convincing in a 1-1 draw with Watford.

But after fine away wins at Southampton and West Ham, they then absolutely smashed Aston Villa 6-0, with a couple of goals each for Webb and Birtles, a win that put them on top of the table. When they followed this up with their second six goal haul in London the following week, beating Chelsea 6-2, the sports writers were all over the 'second coming' of Brian Clough. This appeared to be a different type of Clough team, far less experience, more youthful and attack minded. There were hat tricks for both Garry Birtles and Neil Webb, Neil had now scored eight times already. It was also the first time that two players had scored hat tricks in the same First Division game for the Reds since Leicester Fosse had been beaten 12-0 in 1909.

Neil Webb admits that he had a lot to learn when he joined the club. Used as a forward or wide player by Portsmouth, he was now being used as a box to box type midfielder. The manager regularly criticised his tackling ability, but as a young player prepared to learn, he was now developing into a future England international.

A couple of enticing fixtures against Arsenal and Manchester United, proved that the Nottingham public would still come out to support a successful team. Over 25,000 saw the 1-0 win over Arsenal, Nigel Clough with the only goal, but the manager showed his displeasure at Forest fans cheering the sight of Arsenal's Charlie Nicholas being stretchered off. Stuart Pearce who had taken over penalty taking duties from Clough, missed from the spot. When Man Utd rolled into town, there was a magnificent 35,000 in attendance, but Forest were deprived of a deserved win after a late Bryan Robson goal, although they retained top spot.

After progressing serenely through to the second round of the Littlewoods cup after a 3-0 aggregate win over Brighton, they encountered their first setback of the season, losing 3-1 to a poor Leicester side, but once again there were extenuating circumstances. Ian Bowyer had to go in goal after an injury to Sutton and Des Walker made a couple of howlers to gift the Foxes the points. The injury to the unfortunate Sutton again opened the way for Hans Segers to reclaim his spot. Steve was so unlucky with injuries, they often occurred just when he was showing his best form.

Stuart Pearce was late to professional football. He had been playing part-time for Wealdstone before joining Coventry. Even after joining Forest, he still wasn't totally confident that he would enjoy a long career, so he decided to keep his hand in by continuing with his trade as an electrician on the side. If you open the Forest programme against Brighton, you will find an advert for S. Pearce Electrician. Stuart says he was a good one, but an ex teammate at Coventry, Kirk Stephens will tell you of the time when he narrowly avoided injury when a chandelier fixed above his bed crashed down.

Colin Walsh had been playing on a week to week contract after turning down an initial offer. When the two parties couldn't agree, he decided that his future would be away from the City Ground and he joined Charlton for a fee of £125,000. At the same time, Ian Butterworth was also considered surplus to requirements and allowed to join Norwich, initially on loan. With Chris Fairclough back on the scene, he was down the pecking order.

Notts County after two successive relegations had the begging bowls out again. Forest agreed to play them in a benefit game to raise funds. Once more there were more Forest Fans than Notts even for their own charity game in a crowd of only 3,229.

Forest travelled to South London in what was to be the first of three cup meetings with Crystal Palace, they were to meet later in the season in the FA Cup as well. On the first occasion, they fought out a hard earned 2-2 draw, before completing the job 1-0 in the replay. Clough the scorer.

Forest were beginning to show a soft underbelly, they had lost at Leicester, then Oxford and then Coventry, and for an attacking side they were not converting their chances on the road. Luckily they were still picking up points in Nottingham, two successive 3-2 victories over Sheffield Wednesday and Wimbledon, both bogey teams kept them in second place, but an uncharacteristic 4-2 defeat at Luton, three goals conceded in the opening seventeen minutes, continued the poor run of away league form.

No such problem in the Littlewoods Cup though, a resounding 5-0 win at Bradford City, played at the Odsall Stadium, the home of the Bradford Bulls, City's temporary home after the fire at Valley Parade. There was yet another debutant in Lee Glover, aged only sixteen. Lee was a centre forward very much in the mould of John O'Hare, brave and with a good touch, it often seemed as if he was a manager's favourite, keeping his place in later years seemingly at the expense of better players.

Nottingham Forest continued their policy of playing friendlies and testimonials, the players much preferred to play rather than train, except when there was a lot of travelling

Brian Rice
Gary Mills

Metgod's volley at the Goldstone Ground, Brighton.

Webb hooks home against Charlton.

Webb on target again.

Birtles scores against Charlton.

Neil Webb has just scored against Charlton.

Bowyer with his first of the Season against Watford.

Birtles evades this challenge to score against Villa.

Nigel Clough in action against Aston Villa.

Webb scores against Villa.

Birtles and Webb.

Fleming shakes Clough

Nigel Clough and transfer-listed Franz Carr have grabbed the headlines as Nottingham Forest's young pretenders have gone on the rampage this season.

But the youngster who has probably impressed manager Brian Clough more than any other is Northern Ireland full-back Gary Fleming.

He's just celebrated his 20th birthday but is showing the kind of maturity that has had Clough heaping praise on his young shoulders.

Says Clough: "I've been delighted with the way the young man has set his stall out to make a career for himself in the game.

"He's breaking his neck to stay in our side and there's no doubt he got into the team – and is staying there – on merit.

"Last season I was expecting to have to give him a rest, as you do with most youngsters. But he proved to be the exception to the rule.

"He kept battling away, stuck at his job and ended up by almost getting on the Northern Ireland plane to Mexico."

Fleming's international entry was not delayed long, however. He was called up for his debut in the European Championship qualifier with England at Wembley in October.

Now he's hoping to add to that Irish experience but insists his priority is still to hold down a place in Clough's side.

'Chance'

He admits: "I don't know what it's like at other clubs but you can never be sure of your place at Forest.

"The boss has shown in the past that he's always willing to give anyone a chance no matter what age they are and there are plenty more good youngsters coming through at the club.

"All you can do is try to produce your best every week and I've been delighted to play the number of games that I have done over the last 12 months.

"I suppose it meant something to me that the boss was willing to let Jim McInally and Ian Butterworth leave the club because they were players who were capable of holding down the right-back position.

"I know I've still got a lot to learn but it's great to be able to do that in the First Division. Once you get a taste of first team football you don't want to let it go.

"The run I've had in the side has certainly given me a lot more confidence.

"My natural game has always been to get forward and while I was more concerned with doing the defensive job when I first got into the team, I like to think that I am now making a greater contribution in the opposition's half.

"The biggest problem I've got is going on the overlap and trying to keep up with Franz Carr!"

Stuart Pearce Des Walker Chris Fairclough Franz Carr Nigel Clough Neil Webb

The club's England internationals, pose in their caps for the camera.

involved. So the embarrassment Brian Clough felt when his team lost 6-1 at Plymouth was acute on more than one level, as he said: "I will never forget this result because the chairman took the bother to travel ten hours on the bus with us, and because a lovely man, and a great friend of mine, an ex manager of Sunderland called Allan Brown was my guest. Conceding five goals in the first thirty minutes is beyond my comprehension."

So in football's usual way, how can you explain that they went straight to White Hart Lane and beat Spurs 3-2, coming from behind to do so. Tottenham had also been boosted by a half-time show from Chas 'n' Dave, who got the fans going.

More player movement at the City Ground, Brian Rice who had been unable to force his way into the team on a regular basis, joined Grimsby Town on loan. Brian was obviously a skilful player, he possessed a sweet left foot, but there was no getting away from the fact that he didn't seem to relish the physical side of the game. Brian Clough had been prepared to accept this trait in a player, after all he had got the best out of an ex Forest winger called Alan Hinton at Derby, who had been nicknamed Gladys by supporters, but he demanded moral courage, that is taking responsibility within the game.

Ian Butterworth also headed out of the door, back to Norwich City, this time on a permanent deal bringing in another £150,000.

Einar Aas had kept in touch with the club, and it was on his recommendation that they gave a trial and subsequently offered a deal to Kjetil Osvold a Norwegian international who was a free agent. Because Norway were outside of the EU, once more the club encountered difficulties in obtaining a work permit, so much so that the deal was almost scuppered.

As the pitches got heavier around Christmas time, Forest were about to begin their worst spell of the season at the most inopportune time. League points were dropped to Southampton, even after Saints' keeper had been inconvenienced by breaking his nose in a collision with Garry Birtles, and worse still at Norwich, where they were one nil up and absolutely cruising, before a deflected goal and a mistake from Fairclough turned the game on it's head.

Injuries in the forward line meant another youngster got his chance against Liverpool in the first game of the New Year. Local lad Phil Starbuck made a scoring start to his career, although it was not a winning one as Ian Rush ruined his day with an 88th minute equaliser. Forest could still be described as title challengers, despite having slipped slightly, they were still in touching distance in fourth place.

The next two fixtures were both cup encounters and ultimately disappointing. First up was a return to Selhurst Park to meet Crystal Palace in the FA Cup. It was a freezing day no doubt, but Forest fans were surprised to see several players in black tights and gloves, particularly so when one of them was Nigel Clough. Forest were undone by an up and coming Palace player called Ian Wright who in tandem with Mark Bright, caused the Reds' defence no end of problems.

Ten days later they were out of the Littlewoods Cup as well, this time at the hands of Arsenal. Forest were hit by a second minute Charlie Nicholas goal, before a further effort from Martin Hayes just before half time sealed their fate. Although having plenty of the ball, Forest weren't really able to fashion any clear opportunities and exited the competition in rather tame fashion.

Forest did bounce back however, after seven games without a win. They defeated Everton at home in the live Sunday game, Webb with the only goal, before returning for the third time in the season to Selhurst Park, this time to face Charlton and return with a clinical 1-0 win.

Harold Allcock, Al to his friends, who had served the club for fifty years in many capacities, including chairman, passed away at the age of eighty four. Considered an anachronism by the manager, his death still represented a further break with the club's past. He had seen his first game in 1910, it just seemed as if the club's original values were being continually eroded by the increasing financial pressures on the game.

Hans Segers after losing his place to Steve Sutton, was sent out on loan to Stoke City. With his departure the club was five players down from the start of the season. Osvold had still not received his clearance to play, so re-enforcements were needed. Clough again showed that he was not afraid to trawl the lower leagues for additions. Colin Foster, a 6'4" centre half joined on a trial basis, with Mark Smalley travelling in the opposite direction.

If Forest were doing well, there would never be any criticism of himself or the players for taking a few days re-charging batteries in the sunshine. But if results are poor, everybody had an opinion. Forest returned from Tenerife to face Chelsea, admittedly they played poorly and lost 2-1, but the manager had to remind everyone that only three of the starting line up had actually been away. Rumours began to circulate that several Forest players weren't happy. Franz Carr, whose father had a rather fractious relationship with Clough was one of them, but this was put to bed when the player

Carr's first goal against Brighton.

Clough with the only goal against Rangers.

SUNSHINE AND ACTION

Joy for Birtles, as he gives Forest the lead against Manchester United.

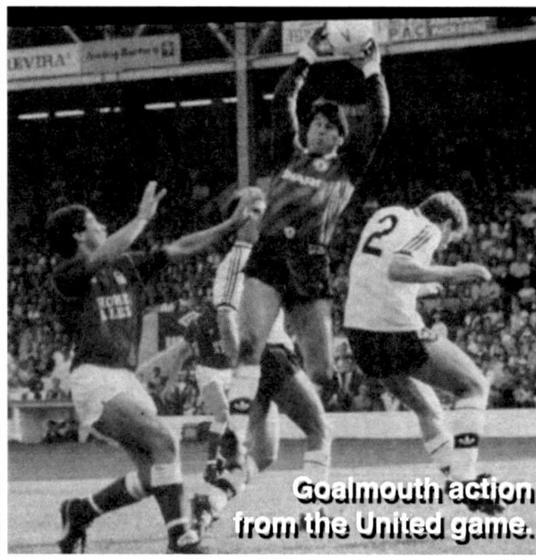

Goalmouth action from the United game.

Birtles with a late equaliser against Crystal Palace.

Clough again scores the only goal against Arsenal.

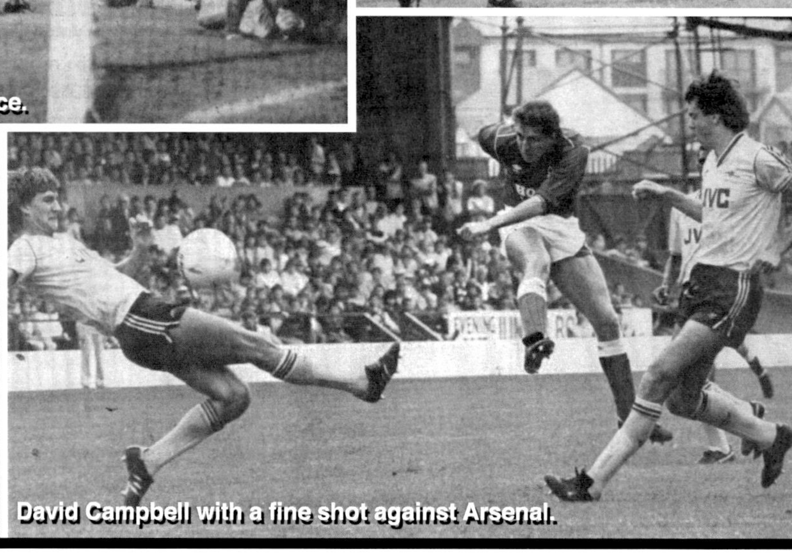

David Campbell with a fine shot against Arsenal.

Focus on DES WALKER

Nottingham Forest

Full name: Desmond Walker.
Birthplace and date: Hackney, East London on November 26, 1965.
Height and weight: 5ft 11ins. 11st 5lbs.
Married: No.
Home: Three bedroom semi-detached just outside Nottingham.
Car: None at the moment.
Nickname and reason for it: 'Dessy' and 'Pappa' because the lads once heard me call out to my father.

Previous clubs: None.
Team you supported as a boy: Tottenham.
Football hero of childhood: Glenn Hoddle (I bet that makes him feel old).
Favourite current player: Manchester United's Paul McGrath — he's the best defender I've seen around.
Most memorable match: My Forest debut against Everton in March, 1984. We won 1-0.
Biggest disappointment: Being out through injury for almost the entire 1984-85 season.

Superstitions: I'm not really superstitious but I never go onto the field last.
International honours: Two England Under-21 caps.

Club honours: None yet — but hopefully that will change at the end of the season.
Favourite other sports: Tennis and snooker.

Favourite other sports person and why: Daley Thompson — a superb athlete and a winner.
Hobbies: Playing snooker and listening to music.
Favourite actor/actress: Clint Eastwood and Faye Dunaway.
Favourite TV shows: The Cosby Show and switching off EastEnders.
Favourite musicians: I'm a soul fan — 'Five Star' and 'Change' are my favourites.
Biggest influence on career and why: All the Forest coaching staff and former Forest coach John Sheridan, who had faith in me in my early days.
Ambitions for 1986-87: To win something with Forest.
Long-term ambitions: To be happy, successful and play football as long as I can.

Neil Webb bravely scores against Sheffield Wednesday.

Birtles with the winner against the Owls.

Another Metgod free kick special, this time against Wimbledon.

Birtles narrowly misses against Spurs.

Birtles scores from a corner kick.

A METGOD SPECIAL!!

Birtles denied by his old mate Shilton.

Gary Mills still can't get the ball past Saints' keeper Peter Shilton.

Forest's *fast* Learner

It takes more than just a hatful of goals to satisfy Brian Clough.

Even a strike rate better than any other midfield man in the country has not been enough to keep Neil Webb in the Forest boss' good books.

"We know he will always score goals, but there are other aspects of his trade which Webb still has to learn," says Clough.

And the former Reading and Portsmouth star agrees.

"I'm the kind of player who needs a rocket from time to time, and you can be certain that the boss obliges me on that score," laughs Webb.

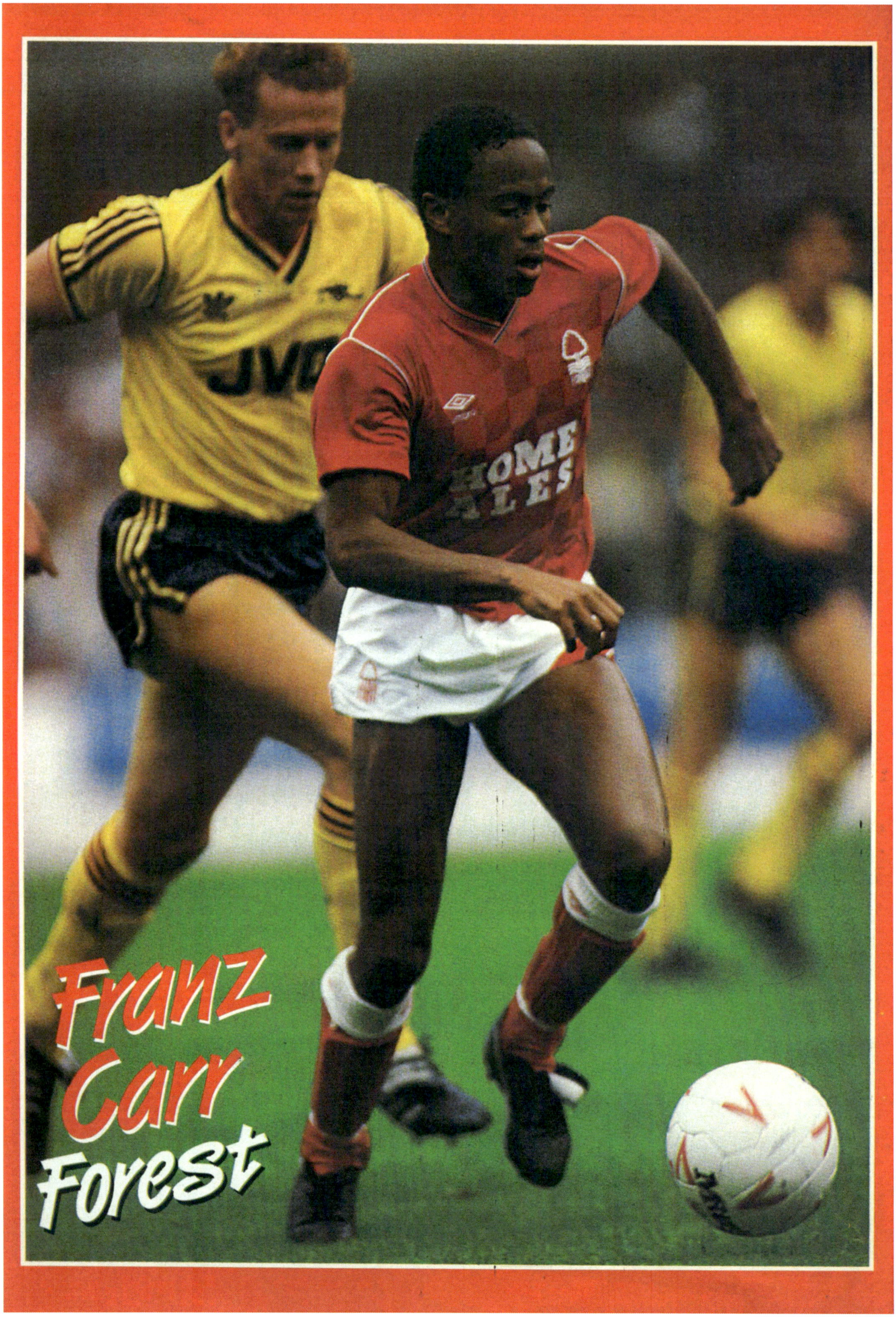
Franz
Carr
Forest

NON STOP ACTION

An unusual view of this free kick against Chelsea.

The Chelsea defence stands firm.

Webb with the only goal against Everton.

Birtles makes no mistake.

Everton take desperate measures to stop Clough.

Clough fires in to the Luton net.

Bowyer rescues a point against Luton.

A debut goal for Phil Starbuck against Liverpool.

Nigel Clough challenges Pat Terry of Watford.

signed a new contract. Franz Carr's father did say though: "I don't mind how he speaks to my son, but if he talks to me like that, I will sort him out." The other players were said to be Chris Fairclough, Johnny Metgod and Neil Webb, although the situation with Webb was different, as he was supposed to have been unsettled by other players when attending England get togethers.

Ken Smales then announced that he was stepping down from his role as club secretary after twenty five years. Ken had seen it all at Forest, initially joining the club in the late 1950's as assistant secretary to Noel Watson, after he had decided that life as a professional cricketer was a little too precarious. Ken spanned the period from Billy Walker to Brian Clough, both of whom had run the club in their own authoritarian way, both being successful. Ken originally had misgivings about the appointment of Brian Clough, because they had had several run ins over the years, not least the fiasco over the on off transfer of Ian Moore to Derby, but he was the first to admit that he had been wrong, perhaps basing all that he knew about the man, from the media.

They grew to have an exceptional working relationship. Both from Yorkshire, as long as you did your job properly, everything was fine and dandy. Once more the club appointed from within, assistant secretary Paul White, once a Forest apprentice was given the job, in a popular move.

Brian Clough liked what he saw with Colin Foster and completed the transfer for a cut price £50,000, (because the player was out of contract at the end of the season), but then he also splashed out a further £275,000 on Paul Wilkinson from Everton. Paul was similar to Garry Birtles, tall and rangey, an all round centre forward, not prolific in front of goal, but more than capable. One of the first things he did was to give the rest of the players a humorous story at his expense.

After losing 2-0 at Old Trafford where he made his debut, the players set off immediately for Gatwick for a flight to take them to Majorca. By the time they were ready to board the plane, there was no sign of the new boy, who had said that he was going to get some food. He eventually turned up at Reading hospital after the police had taken him there with suspected concussion.

David Campbell who had enjoyed a bright start to the season, had fallen out of favour and gone to Notts County on loan in an attempt to rekindle his career, but Brian Rice returned from Grimsby and found himself back in the team for the goalless draw with Coventry, before losing his place once more to Kjetil Osvold who was now cleared to play. The writing looked on the wall for Garry Birtles though, as it seemed as if Wilkinson had been signed to replace him, and with his contract expiring in the summer could this be the end of the road? Ian Bowyer too had found himself on the sidelines, but he did have an offer of a new deal if he wished, although the manager had told him that he was unlikely to start many games. Ian, like many of his ex colleagues fancied a shot at management, and was hoping that something might come up.

Following a fine win 2-0 win over Tottenham, Forest travelled to Manchester City on the Easter Monday. City were desperate for points in an attempt to stave off relegation. The game was played out to a chorus of protest at what was seen as gross mismanagement of their club. These protests continued after the game outside the main entrance, and as police struggled to maintain control, the Forest players were taken out of a side entrance to avoid the situation.

The season was to end on a sour note after a pitch invasion by Forest fans, led to trouble with followers of Newcastle United. Memories of the injustice of 1974 still ran deep.

Because the season had begun so brightly, there was obviously an air of anti-climax about how things had turned out. But unlike many other clubs of a similar stature such as Leeds United and Manchester City who were in crisis, there seemed an order in place at the club. Supporters might get annoyed when another player was allowed to leave, but at the moment, there always seemed to be a better one ready to step in.

Average crowds had increased by 2,000, bucking the national trend, and the Junior Reds section continued to go from strength to strength, ending the season with over 2,500 members. Des Walker was voted player of the year, whilst Nigel Clough not only played the most games, but was also top scorer once more with sixteen goals.

All that was left of the season was to say goodbye to Reds' legend Ian Bowyer, who bowed out after his testimonial game against Derby County and also Garry Birtles who was also leaving after not being offered a new contract.

CLOUGH ON TARGET

Clough turns away after Metgod scores against Spurs.

Clough heads home against Oxford.

Nigel Clough's second against Oxford United.

No joy for Johnny Metgod against Coventry City.

Birtles goes close against City.

Neil Webb has just scored against Tottenham.

FOREST

APPEARANCES TEAM LINE-UPS

Aug 23rd, A, v Everton, L, 0-2, AT 35,198, Sutton, Fleming, Pearce, Walker, Metgod, Bowyer, Carr, Webb, Clough, Birtles, Campbell.

Aug 27th, H, v Charlton Athletic, W, 4-0, Scorers, Webb (2), Clough, Birtles, AT 12,970, Sutton, Fleming, Pearce, Walker, Metgod, Bowyer, Carr, Webb, Clough, Birtles, Campbell. SUB Mills.

Aug 30th, H, v Watford, D, 1-1, Scorer Bowyer, AT 14,709, Sutton, Fleming, Pearce, Walker, Metgod, Bowyer, Carr, Webb, Clough, Birtles, Campbell.

Sept 2nd, A, v West Ham, W, 2-1, Scorers Webb, Clough, AT 21,305, Sutton, Fleming, Pearce, Walker, Metgod, Bowyer, Carr, Webb, Clough, Birtles, Campbell.

Sept 6th, A, v Southampton, W, 3-1, Scorers Webb (2), Birtles, AT 14,604, Sutton, Fleming, Pearce, Walker, Metgod, Bowyer, Carr, Webb, Clough, Birtles, Campbell.

Sept 13th, H, v Aston Villa, W, 6-0, Scorers Carr, Webb (2), Clough, Birtles (2), AT 17,045, Sutton, Fleming, Pearce, Walker, Metgod, Bowyer, Carr, Webb, Clough, Birtles, Campbell. SUB Mills.

Sept 20th, A, v Chelsea, W, 6-2, Scorers Webb (3), Birtles (3), AT 20,171, Sutton, Fleming, Pearce, Walker, Metgod, Bowyer, Carr, Webb, Clough, Birtles, Campbell. SUB Mills.

Sept 24th, LC, A, v Brighton, D, 0-0, AT 13,266, Sutton, Fleming, Pearce, Walker, Metgod, Bowyer, Carr, Webb, Clough, Birtles, Campbell. SUB Mills.

Sept 27th, H, v Arsenal, W, 1-0, Scorer Clough, AT 25,371, Sutton, Fleming, Pearce, Fairclough, Metgod, Bowyer, Carr, Webb, Clough, Birtles, Campbell. SUB Mills.

Oct 4th, H, v Manchester United, D, 1-1, Scorer Birtles, AT 35,828, Sutton, Fleming, Pearce, Walker, Metgod, Bowyer, Carr, Webb, Clough, Birtles, Campbell.

Oct 8th, LC, H, v Brighton, W, 3-0, Scorers Pearce (P), Carr (2), AT 16,036, Sutton, Fleming, Pearce, Walker, Metgod, Mills, Carr, Webb, Clough, Birtles, Campbell. SUBS Rice, Andrews.

Oct 11th, A, v Leicester City, L, 1-3, Scorer Birtles, AT 18,402, Sutton, Fleming, Pearce, Walker, Metgod, Bowyer, Carr, Webb, Clough, Birtles, Campbell. SUB Mills.

Oct 18th, H, v Queens Park Rangers, W, 1-0, Scorer Clough, AT 17,199, Segers, Fleming, Pearce, Walker, Metgod, Bowyer, Carr, Campbell, Clough, Birtles, Mills.

Oct 25th, A v Oxford United, 1-2, Scorer Pearce (P), AT 10,219, Segers, Fleming, Pearce, Walker, Metgod, Bowyer, Carr, Webb, Clough, Birtles, Campbell. SUB Fairclough.

Oct 29th, LC, A, v Crystal Palace, D, 2-2, Scorers Pearce (P), Birtles, AT 12,020, Segers, Butterworth, Pearce, Walker, Fairclough, Bowyer, Carr, Webb, Clough, Birtles, Metgod. SUB Mills.

Nov 1st, H, v Sheffield Wednesday, W, 3-2, Scorers Pearce (P), Webb, Birtles, AT 23,303, Segers, Butterworth, Pearce, Walker, Metgod, Bowyer, Carr, Webb, Clough, Birtles, Mills.

Nov 5th, LC, H, v Crystal Palace, W, 1-0, Scorer Clough, AT 13,029, Segers, Butterworth, Pearce, Walker, Metgod, Campbell, Carr, Webb, Clough, Birtles, Mills.

Nov 8th, A, v Coventry City, L, 0-1, AT 16,089, Segers, Butterworth, Pearce, Walker, Metgod, Bowyer, Carr, Webb, Clough, Birtles, Mills.

Nov 15th, A, v Luton Town, L, 2-4, Scorers Bowyer, Birtles, AT 11,097, Segers, Butterworth, Pearce, Walker, Metgod, Bowyer, Carr, Webb, Clough, Birtles, Mills.

Nov 19th, LC, A, v Bradford City, W, 5-0, Scorers Metgod, Carr, Clough, Mills, Fairclough, AT 16,009, Segers, Butterworth, Williams, Walker, Metgod, Bowyer, Carr, Webb, Clough, Birtles, Mills. SUBS Fairclough, Glover.

Nov 22nd, H, v Wimbledon, W, 3-2, Scorers Clough (P), Metgod, (OG), AT 15,575, Segers, Butterworth, Williams, Walker, Metgod, Bowyer, Carr, Webb, Clough, Birtles, Mills.

Nov 29th, A, v Tottenham Hotspur, W, 3-2, Scorers Pearce (P), Fairclough, Webb, AT 30,042, Segers, Fleming, Pearce, Walker, Fairclough, Metgod, Carr, Webb, Clough, Birtles, Mills.

Dec 6th, H, v Manchester City, W, 2-0, Scorers Carr, Birtles, AT 19,129, Segers, Fleming, Pearce, Walker, Fairclough, Metgod, Carr, Webb, Clough, Birtles, Mills.

Dec 13th, A, v Newcastle United, L, 2-3, Scorers Carr, Starbuck, AT 26,191, Segers, Fleming, Pearce, Walker, Fairclough, Bowyer, Carr, Metgod, Clough, Starbuck, Webb.

Dec 20th, H, v Southampton, D, 0-0, AT 15,394, Segers, Fleming, Pearce, Walker, Fairclough, Webb, Carr, Metgod, Clough, Birtles, Mills.

Dec 26th, A, v Norwich City, L, 1-2, Scorer Pearce, AT 22,131, Segers, Fleming, Pearce, Walker, Fairclough, Bowyer, Carr, Metgod, Clough, Campbell, Webb.

Dec 28th, H, v Luton Town, D, 2-2, Scorers Bowyer, Clough, AT 20,273, Segers, Fleming, Pearce, Walker, Fairclough, Bowyer, Carr, Webb, Clough, Campbell, Mills.

Jan 1st, H, v Liverpool, D, 1-1, Scorer Starbuck, AT 32,854, Segers, Fleming, Pearce, Walker, Fairclough, Bowyer, Carr, Webb, Clough, Starbuck, Mills.

Jan 3rd, A, v Aston Villa, D, 0-0, AT 19,159, Sutton, Fleming, Pearce, Walker, Fairclough, Bowyer, Carr, Webb, Clough, Starbuck, Mills.

Jan 11th, FAC, A, v Crystal Palace, L, 0-1, AT 11, 618, Segers, Fleming, Williams, Walker, Fairclough, Bowyer, Metgod, Webb, Clough, Starbuck, Mills. SUB Campbell.

Jan 21st, LC, A, v Arsenal, L, 0-2, AT 38,617, Sutton, Fleming, Pearce, Walker, Fairclough, Bowyer, Carr, Webb, Clough, Metgod, Mills.

Jan 25th, H, v Everton, W, 1-0, Scorer Webb, AT 17,009, Sutton, Fleming, Pearce, Walker, Fairclough, Bowyer, Carr, Webb, Clough, Metgod, Mills.

Jan 31st, A, v Charlton Athletic, W, 1-0, Scorer

1986 - 1987 DIVISION 1 TABLE

TEAMS	P	W	D	L	F	A	W	D	L	F	A	PTS
1 Everton	42	16	4	1	49	11	10	4	7	27	20	86
2 Liverpool FC	42	15	3	3	43	16	8	5	8	29	26	71
3 Tottenham H	42	14	3	4	40	14	7	5	9	28	29	71
4 Arsenal	42	12	5	4	31	12	8	5	8	27	23	70
5 Norwich C	42	9	10	2	27	20	8	7	6	26	31	68
6 Wimbledon	42	11	5	5	32	22	8	4	9	25	28	66
7 Luton T	42	14	5	2	29	13	4	7	10	18	32	66
8 Nottingham F	42	12	8	1	36	14	6	3	12	28	37	65
9 Watford	42	12	5	4	38	20	6	4	11	29	34	63
10 Coventry C	42	14	4	3	35	17	3	8	10	15	28	63
11 Manchester U	42	13	3	5	38	18	1	11	9	14	27	56
12 Southampton	42	11	5	5	44	24	3	5	13	25	44	52
13 Sheffield W	42	9	7	5	39	24	4	6	11	19	35	52
14 Chelsea	42	8	6	7	30	30	5	7	9	23	34	52
15 West Ham U	42	10	4	7	33	28	4	6	11	19	39	52
16 Q.P.R	42	9	7	5	31	27	4	4	13	17	37	50
17 Newcastle U	42	10	4	7	33	29	2	7	12	14	36	47
18 Oxford U	42	8	8	5	30	25	3	5	13	14	44	46
19 Charlton A	42	7	7	7	26	22	4	4	13	19	33	44
20 Leicester C	42	9	7	5	39	24	2	2	17	15	52	42
21 Manchester C	42	8	6	7	28	24	0	9	12	8	33	39
22 Aston Villa	42	7	7	7	25	25	1	5	15	20	54	36

WHO? WHAT!

Clough, AT 5,050, Sutton, Fleming, Pearce, Walker, Fairclough, Bowyer, Carr, Webb, Clough, Metgod, Mills.

Feb 7th, A, v Watford, D, 1-1, Scorer Birtles, AT 15,173, Sutton, Fleming, Pearce, Walker, Fairclough, Bowyer, Carr, Webb, Clough, Birtles, Mills.

Feb 14th, H, v West Ham, D, 1-1, Scorer Birtles (P), AT 19,373, Sutton, Fleming, Williams, Walker, Fairclough, Bowyer, Carr, Webb, Clough, Birtles, Mills.

Feb 28th, H, v Chelsea, L, 0-1, AT 18,317, Sutton, Fleming, Williams, Walker, Fairclough, Bowyer, Carr, Metgod, Clough, Birtles, Mills.

March 7th, H, v Oxford United, W, 2-0, Scorer Clough (2), AT 12,298, Sutton, Fleming, Pearce, Walker, Fairclough, Bowyer, Carr, Webb, Clough, Birtles, Mills. SUB Metgod.

March 14th, A, v Queens Park Rangers, L, 1-3, Scorer Metgod, AT 11,896, Sutton, Fleming, Pearce, Walker, Fairclough, Bowyer, Carr, Metgod, Clough, Birtles, Mills. SUB Starbuck.

March 17th, A, v Arsenal, D, 0-0, AT 18,353, Sutton, Walker, Pearce, Metgod, Fairclough, Bowyer, Carr, Webb, Clough, Birtles, Mills. SUB Foster.

March 22nd, H, v Leiceter City, W, 2-1, Scorers Carr, Clough, AT 18,679, Sutton, Fleming, Pearce, Walker, Fairclough, Bowyer, Carr, Metgod, Clough, Birtles, Mills.

March 28th, A, v Manchester United, L, 0-2, AT 39,182, Sutton, Fleming, Pearce, Walker, Fairclough, Bowyer, Wilkinson, Metgod, Clough, Birtles, Mills. SUB Foster.

April 4th, H, v Coventry city, D, 0-0, AT 13,507, Sutton, Fleming, Pearce, Walker, Fairclough, Bowyer, Mills, Metgod, Clough, Birtles, Rice.

April 14th, A, v Sheffield Wednesday, W, 3-2, Scorers Clough (2), Rice, AT 18,597, Sutton, Fleming, Pearce, Walker, Foster, Bowyer, Carr, Metgod, Clough, Wilkinson, Rice.

April 18th, A, v Liverpool, L, 0-3, AT 37,359, Sutton, Fleming, Pearce, Walker, Foster, Bowyer, Carr, Metgod, Clough, Wilkinson, Rice. SUB Mills.

April 20th, H, v Norwich City, D, 1-1, Scorer Clough, AT 14,446, Sutton, Fleming, Pearce, Walker, Foster, Bowyer, Carr, Metgod, Clough, Wilkinson, Mills. SUB Fairclough.

April 25th, A, v Wimbledon, L, 1-2, Scorer Pearce (P), AT 5,012, Sutton, Fleming, Pearce, Walker, Foster, Fairclough, Mills, Metgod, Clough, Wilkinson, Osvold. SUB Starbuck.

May 2nd, H, v Tottenham Hotspur, W, 2-0, Scorers Metgod, Webb, AT 19,837, Sutton, Walker, Pearce, Foster, Fairclough, Metgod, Mills, Webb, Clough, Wilkinson, Osvold.

May 4th, A, v Manchester City, L 0-1, At 21,405, Sutton, Walker, Pearce, Foster, Fairclough, Metgod, Mills, Webb, Clough, Wilkinson, Osvold. SUB Riley.

May 9th, H, v Newcastle United, W, 2-1, Scorers Pearce (P), Foster, AT 17,788, Sutton, Walker, Pearce, Foster, Fairclough, Metgod, Mills, Webb, Clough, Wilkinson, Osvold.

Cherished rewards of modest man

Ian Bowyer

SEASON 1987-88

Back row L to R: Phil Starbuck, Terry Wilson, Steve Chettle, Neil Webb, Brian Rice, Lee Glover.
Middle row L to R: Liam O'Kane (Trainer), Paul Wilkinson, Colin Foster, Steve Sutton, Hans Segers, Billy Stubbs, David Campbell, Ron Fenton (Asst. Manager)
Front row L to R: Nigel Clough, Kjetil Osvold, Des Walker, Brian Clough (Manager), Stuart Pearce, Franz Carr, Gary Fleming.

Could this finally be the season when Brian Clough returned to the winners' table? With the departure of Messr's Smales, Bowyer and Birtles, the only remaining links with the successful European Cup winning side was the manager himself and Archie Gemmill, one of his coaches. Brian Clough knew that he needed a trophy to finally put an end to the accusation that he wasn't the same manager without Peter Taylor by his side.

Six players left the City Ground during this pre-season. Ian Bowyer got the offer that he was hoping for, a player coaches role at Hereford United, whilst Garry Birtles and Gary Mills teamed up with ex Forest favourite John Barnwell, who was managing over the Trent at Notts County, where Derek Pavis was now the club owner.

The two major player losses were Chris Fairclough and Johnny Metgod, who both moved on to Tottenham Hotspur. Losing Fairclough was unfortunate, and in the player's eyes totally avoidable. Chris had been grateful for the support that the club had given him over the period that he was out injured, but he said, that despite many requests, the club just would not open contract talks, let alone offer him a new one. The manager had been slow in the past at tying down contracts, often using this type of situation to test out a player's loyalty. John Robertson reported that he too had been feeling vulnerable with no offer on the table, when Peter Taylor had approached him about joining Derby. There was also the usual story of home grown players often being less financially rewarded than newcomers. So by the time that the manager got around to dealing with the situation, it was too late and Fairclough had agreed to join Spurs.

The case of Johnny Metgod was subtly different. The player had once played for Real Madrid, and Tottenham were seen as a bigger club than the Reds, so although the player and his family were settled in Nottingham the lure of London proved to be too great.

Clough knew that Metgod could play, but he wasn't the most consistent of performers. In midfield he didn't dominate games to such an extent that he was undroppable, he had often been moved back in to defence, and when he played in defence it was exactly the same, he had good games, but physically he often wasn't up for the battle. If you were looking for the best sweeper in the club, it would always be Des Walker. So the manager was left with a player who wasn't irreplaceable and when Spurs came in with an offer of £250,00, he didn't stand in the player's way, although in an ideal world he would have kept him.

To fans, it is always a matter of black and white, they weren't really bothered about 'balancing the books'. The sale of players was made worse by the promotion and apparent resurgence of Derby County. Under the 'moneyed' new ownership of Robert Maxwell, they had embarked on a buying spree, including big names such as Mark Wright and ex Forest star Peter Shilton, so Forest supporters began to feel that the club's position as the top team in the East Midlands might be under threat.

Shipstones were unveiled as the team's new shirt sponsor and Liam O'Kane was rewarded for his work with the reserves by being promoted to first team coach. Archie Gemmill meanwhile, was now given sole control of the reserves and Stuart Pearce was to take the captains armband.

Because of all the negativity surrounding the game, the

Neil Webb and Des Walker pictured with the first team shirts, now featuring the club's new sponsor Shipstones.

Conservative government was looking at ways they might legislate to make the game more appealing to stay away fans. Violence and bad behaviour was considered to be the main reason that spectators weren't attending matches. Despite protests from the football authorities that they could administer the game, the Government pressed ahead with plans to introduce members only areas that would restrict the possibility of away fans infiltrating and causing trouble, after all, Luton had gone the whole way, their whole ground was members only, with away fans banned. It was decided initially that clubs had to create members areas totalling 15% of capacity, so Forest set aside the Lower Executive Stand seating area and the Pavilion Road side of the Bridgford End as the club's member only areas. The main concern in football was that this scheme would deter people who just decided on a whim to take in a game.

As preferred by the manager, a pre-season training camp was set up in Denmark, followed by a series of very low key games to build up fitness. There was a school of thought that the training could have been a little tougher, it often took Forest a few games to find their feet, but Clough himself was of the opinion that it was a long season and the players would play themselves into fitness. There was a chance to meet up with old adversaries Malmo in the final warm up game, but the Swedes ran out 2-0 winners on this occasion.

The manager again seemed unsure about who his number one keeper would be, Segers and Sutton were alternating throughout pre-season, until Sutton got the nod when the league campaign began. David Campbell was given another opportunity in midfield, whilst Walker and Foster were the preferred centre back partnership. Clough and Wilkinson up front looked nailed on to be in the starting line-up

Charlton Athletic, the Reds' first opponents of the season, had been forced away from their true home ground at the Valley for several years, whilst arguments raged with the local council about how they could be accommodated. The Valley was positioned slap bang in the middle of a residential area and there did not seem to be any rush by the authorities to help. They were based at Selhurst Park, the home of Crystal Palace and many fans were boycotting games, partly due to the difficulties in getting to one of the most awkward London grounds to visit.

In the circumstances they had done wonders to reach the top flight, but how long they would be able to sustain it on the meagre gates they were able to attract was unclear. Even for an opening day fixture, they could only manage 6,000 and they only reached that figure because Forest took over 2,000 to back them. Forest might have conceded an early penalty but they were by far the better team, and two second half goals, (the equaliser a 60th minute diving header from Lee Glover), was followed seven minutes later by a thirty yard curler from Nigel Clough that clinched the points.

Lee Glover was a manager's favourite, Stuart Pearce was not alone in being surprised when he was picked ahead of more in form players, but also that the manager sometimes seemed loathed to criticise him. The manager did like a brave player though, who was prepared to play with his back to a defender.

Despite often being slow starters, on this occasion, Forest were to make a fine start to the season, with only one defeat in the opening fourteen games. Watford were beaten 1-0, a Pearce penalty was enough, then Everton came and left with a 0-0 draw. Goal chances were few, but despite losing Fairclough, the defence was looking firm and organised,

English football was becoming less parochial every season, Forest had their Dutch and Scandinavian imports, but Newcastle went one better when they paraded their new Brazilian signing Mirandinha before the St James' Park encounter with the Reds. Nigel Clough was unimpressed and it was his first half goal that gave Forest the points.

Hans Segers had once more replaced Steve Sutton in goal, but that was only because the unfortunate Sutton had picked up another minor injury in training, but two poor games were to signal the end of the Dutch keeper's career at the City Ground. The first a 3-3 draw with Southampton after Forest had led 3-1 and the second a 4-3 defeat at Stamford Bridge, again after Forest threw away a two goal lead. Segers didn't look confident and his lack of height was causing him problems with crosses and unsettling the defenders in front of him.

More significantly, two more young players forced their way into the team. Steve Chettle, although primarily thought of as a centre half came into the team at right back to challenge Gary Fleming whose form had dipped and Terry Wilson came from virtually nowhere to take Campbell's place in midfield. Scottish born Wilson was an assured ball player, skilful but not afraid to put his foot in. He immediately looked the 'real deal'. Yet again the manager's bravery in fast tracking players into the first team should not be underestimated. Terry scored

A FINE START TO THE SEASON

The opening goal of the season from Lee Glover.

A goal fit to win any football match, as Nigel Clough (out of picture), curls this effort past Charlton keeper Bolder.

A penalty from Pearce gives Forest a victory over Watford.

Terry Wilson with a fine long range goal against Coventry City.

Stuart Pearce the new free kick specialist against the Saints.

Clough misses out against the Gunners.

Webb volleys home against Southampton.

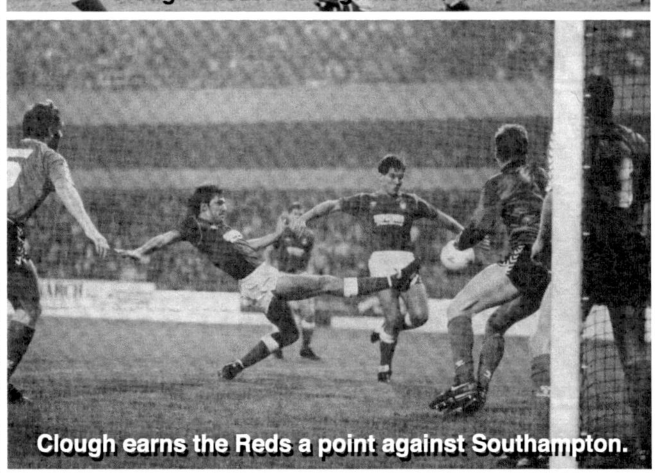
Clough earns the Reds a point against Southampton.

I've let down Forest

says Nigel Clough

Nigel Clough has been Nottingham Forest's leading scorer for two successive seasons ... but he's far from satisfied.

The 21-year-old striker is hungry for more of the kind of action that made his father one of the most prolific goalscorers in the history of the game.

By modern day standards, his track record is reasonably impressive. He scored 18 goals in his first full season and followed up with another 16 last year.

Now he's set his sights higher, and in his first ever interview he argues: "If you are earning your living in the game as a First Division striker I think your target for a season should be 20.

"If you reach that figure I think you can comfortably say you are doing your job. It's tough but it's realistic.

"Hopefully I can do it this season if I keep clear of injuries but it's difficult to set targets or make promises in this game. At the end of the day, scoring is not the be all and end all for me.

"I would happily settle for scoring less goals if it meant the team was successful. I get almost as much pleasure from creating goals as scoring them.

'Consistency'

"The thing I look for more than goals is consistency of performance. If you can maintain a certain standard over the course of a season then goals will come."

A regular in the England Under-21 team, Clough's class and composure will surely lead him one day into Bobby Robson's senior squad.

For the time being he's happy playing a significant part in Forest's bid to end their seven-year search for honours.

Adds Nigel: "A lot of people were ready to have a go at us during the summer when we lost a few players, but we might surprise those critics sooner rather than later.

"Forest might not be the most experienced side in the First Division but most of the players who got us to the top of the table this time last year are still with us and have learned from that experience.

"We ran out of steam a little bit but hopefully we can get into the same kind of rhythm again and keep it going longer."

33

his first goal on his full debut at Coventry, an expertly driven shot from the edge of the area that helped the team to a 3-0 victory. Brian Rice was also restored to the team in place of Lee Glover and such was his form, he was to keep his place for the rest of the season.

There was a palpable buzz around the City Ground now, the lessons of last season had been absorbed and there was a real feeling that finally they were able to compete for honours. Neil Webb, who had been given a new nickname by Pearce of 'chunky', was now playing a slightly different role, in that he was restricting his forward runs to make sure that he was not forgetting his defensive duties. He may not be getting his name on the score sheet as often, but his value to the team had increased.

Eight games were played across September and October with only two goals conceded. Progress was made in the Littlewoods Cup at the expense of Hereford United, by an aggregate score of 6-1. The tie had meant an early return to the City Ground for Ian Bowyer, as he captained the visitors and by the time the two sides met in the second leg, he had been appointed manager after Hereford had sacked John Newman.

The Hereford game was sandwiched by another couple of impressive away wins. The first came at Carrow Road, where Norwich were despatched 2-0 courtesy of a couple of Neil Webb goals, but it was two weeks later at the Baseball Ground that Forest put Derby firmly in their place. The score might have only been 1-0 in the first East Midlands league clash for eight years, but it was a game the Reds never looked like losing.

After the Derby game, many of the Forest players disappeared off on international duty, both for the senior sides and under 21's. The manager was on tenterhooks the whole time, the season could be de-railed by a couple of injuries. In the meantime he added to the Forest squad with yet another swoop on the lower leagues. He had taken a fancy to a twenty four year old Irish striker playing for Doncaster Rovers called Tommy Gaynor. Tommy had only been in the country for twelve months after joining Rovers from Limerick City and he wasn't even starting every game in the Fourth Division side, but yet again Brian Clough pulled off a master stroke and Forest picked up the player for only £25,000. When Tommy joined, it was the end of David Campbell's Forest career, he left to join up with Colin Walsh at Charlton.

Brian Clough need not have been concerned about how the players would react to the international break, they returned with two consecutive 3-0 home victories. First up were Sheffield Wednesday, Clough, Carr and Wilkinson were the scorers, whilst Owls centre forward Lee Chapman was sent off for use of an elbow.

The next game must have given the manager a great deal of satisfaction for several reasons. Chris Fairclough and Johnny Metgod had left to further their careers at Tottenham, but it looked like they had made a bad decision after goals from Carr, Webb and Clough had given Forest an easy victory. Only Fairclough actually played in this game, Metgod had already lost his place several weeks earlier.

Clough had been upset that his friend David Pleat had been forced to resign by the Tottenham directors, after a Sunday newspaper had published a lurid story about the Spurs' manager and his liking for visiting red light districts. Always loyal to those who were loyal to him, Clough let it be known that he felt that they should have stuck by him.

After the start that they had made to the season, it came as a jolt when Forest made a tame exit from the Littlewoods Cup at the hands of Second Division Manchester City, in a very disappointing and out of character 3-0 scoreline. City fans had not been optimistic about their own team's chances, only 15,000 bothered to turn up, but a team that were having such a poor time of it in the League, raised their game against a full strength Reds line up.

Forest returned to Manchester just four days later to take on United and this time they were far more convincing, earning a 2-2 draw. The second goal, a firmly struck free kick from Stuart Pearce had extra significance in that it was the club's 5,000 league goal.

City Ground supporters could now be fairly certain that they were in for an afternoon's entertainment whenever they attended. They were treated to another nine goals in the next two home game, Portsmouth were crushed 5-0 and Neil Webb had no qualms about celebrating a goal against his old team mates. Forest followed this up with four unanswered goals against Queens Park Rangers and a first senior hat-trick for Nigel Clough, who was now adding more goals to the all round threat he brought to the team. The other goal came from Tommy Gaynor who had been given an early first team chance after Paul Wilkinson had been ruled out for several weeks with a knee injury.

Calvin Plummer had left the City Ground several years previously when his opportunities had been limited due to the emergence first, of Steve Wigley and then Franz Carr. His career had faltered and after unsuccessful spells with Chesterfield, Derby and Barnsley, he had been plying his trade in Finland. After returning to England, he had asked Brian Clough if he could train with the club to maintain his fitness. The manager agreed and signed him on a non contract basis, that would also allow him to play for the reserves. The player's belief was re-kindled back at the club where he had begun his career and he found himself back in the manager's plans for a while. His second debut came at Plough Lane against Wimbledon, where he really should have capped his return with a goal, but he did find the net a week later in a 2-0 win over Oxford United.

Brian Clough always maintained that he would have loved a crack at managing at international level. The chances of him

Wilkinson taps in against Wednesday.

Carr hooks in the third against the Owls.

THE GOOD START CONTINUES

Clough opens the scoring.

Wilson against Portsmouth.

Wilkinson slides the ball under the Pompey keeper.

No sentiment as Webb scores against his old team.

Franz Carr from close range against Spurs.

Nigel Clough's first senior hat-trick.

Goal No.1

Goal No.2

Goal No. 3 as Nigel completes his hat-trick against QPR.

Tommy Gaynor scores against Coventry.

No way through for Brian Rice against the packed Newcastle defence.

Gaynor with his second against the Sky Blues

Lee Glover scores against Orient in the Cup.

Colin Foster dives to connect with this cross against Charlton.

Calvin Plummer on the mark against Halifax.

THE CUP RUN BEGINS!

Foster opens the scoring against Chelsea.

Brian Clough & Alan Hill

ever being offered the England job were now getting remote, but when the Football Association of Wales approached him about managing them, he was interested enough to meet up to discuss the opportunity. When they suggested that he could even do the job on a part-time basis, he appeared to be very interested. As with many incidents in the career of Brian Clough, there is a back story to this whole episode as well.

Alan Hill and the manager were not strangers to regularly falling out with each over the twenty years they worked together. Alan was never afraid to stand his corner with the boss and this period was one of the times they had fallen out.

Alan had left the club during the summer, to head up youth development at Notts County. Clough was not best pleased, firstly because Alan was good at his job and secondly because Derek Pavis was crowing about what he saw as getting 'one over', his old adversary. Cloughie was in regular contact with Alan about returning, but he always said: "I have a contract and I am going to honour it." However when Clough approached him with an offer to be assistant manager for Wales, it was a different matter.

Alan takes up the story: "We met to discuss it, and he explained that Forest had agreed that he could do both jobs, but that he wanted me to be his full time assistant for Wales, taking care of things whilst he was at Forest. He said that if I didn't agree, he would turn down the job. The deal would have been great for me, more money and a car, so after thinking about it I agreed and tendered my resignation at Notts County. They graciously accepted, knowing how much it would mean to me to take up the Wales position. Cloughie then told me that I should turn up for a press conference to be held at the City Ground in a couple of days time."

"I arrived booted and suited, ready for the media, but when I met Brian and he was dressed casually, I knew something was up. Brian said: 'The Forest board have now said that they won't allow me to do both jobs, so I am going to have to turn it down'. Where does that leave me? I asked. 'Well you can come back and work here', he replied."

Alan, even to this day thinks that Clough was never going to take the Wales job and that it was just a ruse to get him away from Pavis. Notts County appealed that they had been tricked into accepting Hill's resignation and the F.A. agreed, ruling that Forest must pay them £25,000 in compensation.

Forest seemed to be the only top flight club that saw the benefit in scouring the lower and non league arena for talent, so when Grantham manager, ex Red Martin O'Neill, recommended that they should take a look at Gary Crosby, they were open to the idea. Crosby had only been at Grantham for eight weeks, but Forest liked what they saw and snapped him up. Gary was another right winger, not super fast in the Franz Carr mould, but he had a couple of tricks including a step-over and he was more thoughtful than many wingers were, when it came to crossing the ball.

Forest reached the giddy heights of second in the table after winning 2-0 at one of their bogey grounds Highbury, when they defeated Arsenal on Boxing Day. Nigel Clough played in his 112th consecutive game as the Reds celebrated victory, after goals from Wilson and Pearce.

Not everyone was impressed though, writing in the Daily Mirror, Harry Harris reported that, 'Forest's victory was as exciting as a plate of cold fish and chips,' and the Daily Mail's Jeff Powell called Forest, 'boring and cynical'. The Reds never seemed to get any praise from the London press. Brian Clough would have been far more pleased by referee Neil Midgely's comments as he wrote in an article about the increasing bad behaviour surrounding football. 'There is definitely an upsurge in player violence, but Nottingham Forest were an exception and a pleasure to referee'.

'Boring' Nottingham Forest returned to action just two days later and thumped Coventry City 4-1, including a couple from Tommy Gaynor who looked like he had made the step up from the lower leagues with ease. Forest were rewarded with a couple of bumper crowds over Christmas. More than 31,000 watched the Coventry game, followed by 28,000 who attended against Newcastle, although the majority weren't happy with the result, going down to a Mirandinha inspired Newcastle 2-0.

Colin Foster, another of those picked up for comparative peanuts from Orient, was singled out for praise by the manager, but as was often the case, there was a caveat: "Sometimes he thinks he is Franz Beckenbauer, but he has got to learn that there is a time and place for that, sometimes you should put in to the back of the stand."

Forest began their FA Cup campaign with a visit to Yorkshire, to play Halifax Town. For fans, the dilapidated Shay Ground was an eye-opener, but it turned out to be great fun, a 4-0 victory and the sight of Paul Wilkinson being carried shoulder high off the pitch, as if he had scored the winning goal in the final itself.

Calvin Plummer was in the middle of a run of twelve consecutive appearances for the first team, by far the longest he had ever enjoyed and he was scoring as well. He followed up a

goal against Halifax with another in a 2-2 draw with Charlton. This game also saw the debut of Gary Crosby, who in the space of four months had gone from playing local football in Lancashire, to appearing in front of 20,000 spectators.

Calvin Plummer was to have one more significant impact on the team's fortunes, before he faded away once more. He was instrumental in helping turn around an FA Cup tie at Orient that the Reds looked to be losing, scoring the winner with a brave volley after Lee Glover had equalised.

The whole club looked in fine fettle, the first team returned to second place after beating Chelsea 3-2, the reserves and youth team were top of their respective leagues, whilst the youngsters had also fought their way through to the fourth round of the FA Youth Cup and yet another of their number, Darren Wassall had made his first team debut as well.

West Midlands rivals Birmingham City stood in Forest's way in the FA Cup. A massive following saw Gary Crosby score the only goal, but it took a strong rearguard action to keep out the Blues. Steve Sutton in particularly, was in fine form. Steve had just been voted the Player of the Month for the third successive month and by now was considered to be one of the best and most consistent keepers in the division. Outside of St Andrews, there were running battles between rival supporters.

If Forest thought they might be rewarded with a home tie in the next round of the F.A. Cup, they were to be doubly disappointed, not only were they drawn away again, but also faced very difficult opposition in the shape of Arsenal. Forest had already been to Highbury in the league and won, so there was no fear and they would also be backed by 10,000 fans who would be massed on the Clock End terrace.

The match is fondly remembered by players and fans alike for two wonderful goals. The first a fine right foot strike from Paul Wilkinson after a subtle turn and lay-off from Clough, and the second featured another sublime piece of skill from Nigel Clough on the half way line. Facing his own goal he turned and immediately saw Brian Rice breaking through the middle, the pass was inch perfect and the player didn't have to break stride. Rice advanced on Lukic the Arsenal keeper and waited for him to commit himself and as the keeper went down, the red haired left winger coolly chipped the ball over him and into the net. Two nil, it looked all over, but there was almost a sting in the tail. Arsenal boss George Graham threw on beanpole striker Niall Quinn and also pushed Tony Adams up front as well. The last five minutes were like the Alamo, as high ball after high ball was pumped into the Forest box. A goalmouth scramble after a corner gave Rocastle the chance to pull one back in the 89th minute and with virtually the last kick of the game, Alan Smith failed to connect from a knockdown, barely a yard from the goal line.

Forest were now through to their first FA Cup semi-final since 1967. Apart from the Reds, the other teams left in the draw were Liverpool, Wimbledon and Luton Town, so it was obvious who Forest would like to avoid, but as in the European Cup draw of 1978, Forest were paired with Liverpool in a game to be played at Hillsborough, Sheffield.

Stuart Pearce recalls his disappointment: "If we had got either of the other two, we would have fancied ourselves to go through. Although we could match Liverpool on our day, they were in truth always a couple of players too good for us."

With the club's bank balance in a very healthy state, Clough swooped on a couple of players with an eye for the future. First through the door was Nigel Jemson who joined from Preston North End for £150,000. Teenage Jemson had also been chased by Manchester United and was in fact in the middle of a trial at Old Trafford when the deal was done. Nigel said he chose Forest because of Cloughie and because he thought that his chances of first team action were better at a club that was actively encouraging younger players. The second incomer was Garry Parker, a left sided midfield player from Hull City, who set the club back £265,000. Neither player was considered likely to stake a place this season.

Perhaps emboldened by success on the pitch, Brian Clough launched in to a tirade at the press over a couple of matters. The first concerned the players, he was fed up of them denigrating team performances, and after the win at Arsenal, he was upset that his son Nigel had been picked out for special praise, when it was an all round team effort. The second gripe was a personal issue. David Moore of the Daily Mirror had used a photograph of Brian Clough's house and advertised his address to accompany an article that he had written about the manager: "How would he feel if someone had done the same to him", Clough said, "if his family were sitting there, knowing that they could be targets." Clough vowed to find out details

F.A. CUP 5TH ROUND

BIRMINGHAM CITY 0

NOTTINGHAM FOREST 1

Gary Crosby goes sprawling.

Nigel Clough hooks this effort just wide.

Stuart Pearce and Colin Foster present the defensive barricade which has carried Nottingham Forest into second place in the League. "This team are the most honest bunch of professionals I've ever worked with," says Brian Clough. "I haven't been so excited about a side of mine for years." Captain Pearce and man mountain Foster would agree.

Wilkinson's rocket at Highbury in the F.A. Cup.

Paul Wilkinson and Brian Rice celebrate the Cup victory over Arsenal.

JOY AT HIGHBURY

Brian Rice deftly lifts the ball over the advancing Lukic.

Grobbelaar foils Gary Crosby in the act of shooting.

Nigel Clough grounded, still scores against Derby.

Nigel Clough calmly slots the ball past the Tottenham keeper Bobby Mimms.

By Duncan Hamilton

AS NOTTINGHAM FOREST can now testify, the old saying really is true: There is nothing worse than losing an FA Cup semi-final.

It would not have been such a demoralising experience for them if Liverpool had initiated a slaughter. The fact Forest came so desperately close to matching the champions apparent adds to the agony.

On a subdued journey home, the defeat, not unnaturally, consumed the significant consolation prize Forest were able to take from a tie which belonged at Wembley.

What happened at Hillsborough is not the end for them, merely a beginning.

With the title all but wrapped up, it seems inconceivable that such a potent force as Liverpool will be beaten by Wimbledon.

But the impending double winners have seen enough to know that Forest are going to be waiting for them on every corner next season and there is no legitimate reason why the outcome then cannot be vastly different.

Forest...1 Liverpool...2

FOREST: Sutton, Chettle, Pearce, Walker, Foster, Wilson, Crosby, Webb, Clough, Wilkinson, Rice. Subs not used: Fleming, Glover.
LIVERPOOL: Grobbelaar, Gillespie, Ablett, Nicol, Spackman, Hansen, Beardsley, Aldridge, Houghton, Barnes, McMahon. Subs not used: Johnston, Molby.
Referee: G Courtney, Spennymoor.
Attendance: 51,627.
Goals: Liverpool — Aldridge 13, 52mins. Forest — Clough 67min.
Goal attempts on target: Forest 3, Liverpool 5.
Goal attempts off target: Forest 5, Liverpool 6.
Corners: Forest 3, Liverpool 3.
Bookings: Liverpool — Ablett, Gillespie, Aldridge.
FOREST MAN OF THE MATCH — NIGEL CLOUGH.

Clough, it should be stressed, was masterful with ... more fluent than anything Liverpool offered, except for

about the journalist and reciprocate. Several weeks later, it was reported that a poster had gone up in Clough's local Post Office doing just that.

Back to action on the pitch, there were still thirteen league games and an FA Cup semi-final to look forward to. First there was a loss to Queens Park Rangers on their plastic pitch, followed by draws at home to Manchester United and away at Tottenham, before the visit of Derby to the City Ground.
Normally this would have been the highlight of the season, but on this occasion, it was a pretty low key affair, even if it did produce a 2-1 win and a couple of goals for Nigel Clough. More worryingly was the goal drought affecting Paul Wilkinson, he had now failed to find the net in a league game since November and although he might be contributing, his lack of goals was putting extra pressure on Nigel Clough.

There was to be a dress rehearsal for the FA Cup when Liverpool visited the City Ground, just three days after the Derby game. Hopes went sky high after a 2-1 victory that was utterly emphatic and that could have been even greater but for a Clough penalty miss. Liverpool were never in it until they were gifted a penalty of their own, by referee Ken Barratt.

There was the usual big match build up for the semi-final, the photographs and interviews, but for defender Steve Chettle, it was to be harsh introduction to the distorted world of tabloid journalism. Along with a whole load of other facile questions, he had been asked a question about what he had for a pre match breakfast and innocently replied: "Beans on toast." By the time the quote had reached the newspaper it had morphed into: "Barnes on toast." On his day John Barnes the Liverpool winger could be the finest player in the country and the last thing that was needed, was to give him any more incentive to show his skills. Although he was keeping Gary Fleming out of the team, Chettle saw his long term future as a centre half and on this day he was given a real chasing.

Forest were immediately under pressure, defending the Kop End at Hillsborough, where the majority of their fans stood. They were unable to hold out, and conceded an early goal when Chettle hauled down Barnes, for a penalty that Aldridge converted. The first half was virtually all one way traffic, as Liverpool dominated the game, but just couldn't score a second goal.

If Forest thought the pattern of the game might be different after half time, they were in for a shock as Aldridge added a second, volleying in after a fine move. It was only now that Forest got into the game, and there were several fluent moves, before Nigel Clough gave them hope with a sixty sixth minute goal. Indeed, if referee George Courtney had been brave enough to send off Liverpool full back Gary Ablett, after the player had committed another crude foul, only minutes after being booked, the result might have been different.

After losing the semi-final, the last thing that Forest needed was a trip to Anfield just three days later. Forest had their bottoms well and truly spanked, in what was described by many, as Liverpool's best performance for years. Losing Des Walker to an early injury didn't help. But sometimes you just have to praise the opposition. There was nothing the manager could say, they just got on the team coach and went home.

The following weekend, Forest along with fifteen other teams were invited to participate in the Football League Centenary Festival Trophy played at Wembley Stadium, to celebrate one hundred years of the Football League.

The competition was played on a knockout basis, the first two rounds were twenty minutes each way, whilst the semi final and final would be thirty minutes each way. If the scores were level, the game would be settled by sudden death penalty shoot out.
Leeds United provided the first opposition, but little resistance, the 3-0 scoreline was an anomaly in the tournament, as there was generally a lack of goals, the very nature of only playing

Action from the semi-final.

Paul Wilkinson.

Colin Foster.

Beardsley evades this lunge.

F.A. CUP SEMI-FINAL

Hillsborough - 9th April 1988

THE FOOTBALL LEAGUE CENTENARY TROPHY WINNERS

Steve Sutton

Stuart Pearce

Steve Sutton knows how to celebrate!!

a total of forty minutes for a game was never going to lead to a goal rush. The second game against Aston Villa was played at tea-time on the Saturday afternoon, and turned out to be a turgid affair, a 0-0 draw. However Forest progressed via a penalty shoot out, courtesy of Stuart Pearce, in what was to be a feature of the tournament, as eight of the matches were also settled by penalty shoot outs.

Despite the presence of sixteen teams, the first day attracted only 40,000 supporters to Wembley, but Sunday's figures were even worse, just 17,000 scattered around the stadium. The event was not helped by the fact that no London based teams had been invited to play.

The Sunday morning encounter between Forest and Tranmere Rovers was by far the best game of the weekend, with just enough passion and spark to make it interesting. The Reds were twice behind, their final equaliser came with only two minutes left on the clock. Another Stuart Pearce sudden death penalty sent Forest through to the final.

If many of the qualifying games had been poor, they had nothing on the final itself. That was absolutely dire. Their opponents Sheffield Wednesday were lumbering and pedestrian, but disciplined enough to stop Forest playing. The hour that the game lasted, seemed to go on for an eternity, but at least Forest had the satisfaction of winning the competition and a cheque for £75,000. Neil Webb had had the honour of delivering the coup de grace, in yet another penalty shoot out, to an awful Sheffield Wednesday team.

Brian Clough had taken the fortunate decision not to attend, so it was left to the players and in particular Stuart Pearce to comment on what winning the club's first silverware for many years meant, and he said: "I am super competitive, I want to win at everything. Never under estimate the value of winning that trophy at Wembley, as far as I am concerned it could set us on our way."

Steve Sutton was continuing to have a fantastic season, it had been virtually a one man show when he had attempted to defy Liverpool at Anfield, and it was his penalty saves at Wembley that helped win the trophy. So when he was voted player of the month by supporters, (for an unprecedented fourth time in a row), it was fully merited. He then celebrated the award by keeping his eighteenth clean sheet of the season with a 0-0 draw at Upton Park, eventually ending the season with twenty in total, a figure only beaten by Peter Shilton during the championship year of 1978.

After overcoming the disappointment of being knocked out by Liverpool, Forest ended the season with another unbeaten run, this time of six games, made all the more creditable as they were missing Pearce and Walker through injury. Steve Chettle had moved across to partner Colin Foster in central defence, allowing Gary Fleming to return at right back. The manager also seemed to have finally lost patience with Paul Wilkinson and he lost his place to Lee Glover.

Forest ended the season in third place, on seventy three points, just behind Manchester United, but 17 points behind runaway champions Liverpool.

Nigel Clough top scored again with twenty goals, whilst Neil Webb made the most appearances with forty eight. Webb had now matured into a fine all rounder and was also a valuable member of the England squad.

The major problem now facing Brian Clough was keeping hold of his best players, already there were ominous noises coming from Old Trafford. Were they about to raid the City Ground once more?

FOREST

APPEARANCES TEAM LINE-UPS

Aug 15th, A, v Charlton Athletic, W, 2-1, Scorers Clough, Glover, AT 6,021. Sutton, Fleming, Pearce, Walker, Foster, Campbell, Carr, Webb, Clough, Wilkinson, Glover.
Aug 19th, H, v Watford, W, 1-0, Scorer Pearce (P), AT 14,527, Sutton, Fleming, Pearce, Walker, Foster, Campbell, Carr, Webb, Clough, Wilkinson, Glover.
Aug 22nd, H, v Everton, D, 0-0, AT 20,445, Segers, Fleming, Pearce, Walker, Foster, Campbell, Carr, Webb, Clough, Wilkinson, Glover.
Aug 29th, A, v Newcastle United, W, 1-0, Scorer Clough, AT 20,111, Segers, Fleming, Pearce, Walker, Foster, Campbell, Carr, Webb, Clough, Wilkinson, Glover.
Sept 2nd, H, v Southampton, D, 3-3, Scorers Pearce, Webb, Clough, AT 14,173, Segers, Fleming, Pearce, Walker, Foster, Campbell, Carr, Webb, Clough, Wilkinson, Glover. SUBS Wilson, Chettle.
Sept 5th, A, v Chelsea, L, 3-4, Scorers Foster, Webb, Clough, AT 18,414, Segers, Fleming, Pearce, Walker, Foster, Campbell, Carr, Webb, Clough, Wilkinson, Glover. SUBS Wilson, Chettle.
Sept 12th, H, v Arsenal, L, 0-1, AT 18,490, Segers, Fleming, Pearce, Walker, Foster, Campbell, Carr, Webb, Clough, Wilkinson, Glover. SUBS Wilson, Starbuck.
Sept 19th, A, v Coventry City, W, 3-0, Scorers Pearce (P), Wilson, Carr, AT 17,519, Sutton, Fleming, Pearce, Walker, Foster, Wilson, Carr, Webb, Clough, Wilkinson, Rice. SUB Campbell.
Sept 23rd, LC, H, v Hereford United, W, 5-0, Scorers Carr, Webb (2), Clough, Wilkinson, AT 11,617, Sutton, Fleming, Pearce, Walker, Foster, Wilson, Carr, Webb, Clough, Wilkinson, Rice. SUBS Chettle, Glover.
Sept 26th, A, v Norwich City, W, 2-0, Scorers Webb (2), AT 13,755, Sutton, Chettle, Pearce, Walker, Foster, Wilson, Carr, Webb, Clough, Wilkinson, Rice. SUB Glover.
Oct 7th, LC, A, v Hereford United, D, 1-1, Scorer Clough, AT 3,905, Sutton, Chettle, Pearce, Walker, Foster, Wilson, Carr, Webb, Clough, Wilkinson, Rice.
Oct 10th, A, v Derby County, W, 1-0, Scorer Wilkinson, AT 22,394, Sutton, Chettle, Pearce, Walker, Foster, Wilson, Carr, Webb, Clough, Wilkinson, Rice.
Oct 17th, H, v Sheffield Wednesday, W, 3-0, Scorers Carr, Clough, Wilkinson, AT 17,685, Sutton, Chettle, Pearce, Walker, Foster, Wilson, Carr, Webb, Clough, Wilkinson, Rice. SUB Osvold.
Oct 24th, H, v Tottenham Hotspur, W, 3-0, Scorers Carr, Webb, Clough, AT 23,543, Sutton, Chettle, Pearce, Walker, Foster, Wilson, Carr, Webb, Clough, Wilkinson, Rice. SUB Osvold.
Oct 27th, LC, A, v Manchester City, L, 0-3, AT 15,168, Sutton, Chettle, Pearce, Walker, Foster, Wilson, Carr, Webb, Clough, Wilkinson, Rice. SUBS Osvold, Starbuck.
Oct 31st, A, v Manchester United, D, 2-2, Scorers Pearce, Wilkinson, AT 44,669, Sutton, Chettle, Pearce, Walker, Foster, Wilson, Carr, Webb, Clough, Wilkinson, Rice. SUBS Osvold, Starbuck
Nov 14th, H, v Portsmouth, W, 5-0 Scorers, Wilson, Webb, Clough, Wilkinson, Rice, AT 15,851, Sutton, Chettle, Pearce, Walker, Foster, Wilson, Carr, Webb, Clough, Wilkinson, Rice. SUBS Glover, Starbuck.
Nov 21st, A, v West Ham United, L, 2-3, Scorers Webb, Clough, AT 17,216, Sutton, Chettle, Pearce, Walker, Foster, Wilson, Carr, Webb, Clough, Wilkinson, Rice. SUBS Gaynor, Starbuck.
Dec 5th, A, v Wimbledon, D, 1-1, Scorer Clough, AT 5,170, Sutton, Chettle, Pearce, Walker, Foster, Wilson, Plummer, Webb, Clough, Gaynor, Rice.
Dec 12th, H, v Queens Park Rangers, W, 4-0, Scorers Clough (3) (1P), Gaynor, AT 18,130, Sutton, Fleming, Pearce, Walker, Foster, Wilson, Plummer, Webb, Clough, Gaynor, Rice. SUB Starbuck.
Dec 19th, A, v Oxford United, W, 2-0, Scorers Plummer, Rice, AT 7,891, Sutton, Chettle, Pearce, Walker, Foster, Wilson, Plummer, Webb, Clough, Gaynor, Rice. SUB Starbuck.
Dec 26th, A, v Arsenal, W, 2-0, Scorers Pearce (P), Wilson, AT 31,211, Sutton, Chettle, Pearce, Walker, Foster, Wilson, Plummer, Webb, Clough, Gaynor, Rice. SUB Starbuck.
Dec 28th, H, v Coventry City, W, 4-1, Scorers Wilson, Gaynor (2), 1(OG), AT 31,061, Sutton, Chettle, Pearce, Walker, Foster, Wilson, Plummer, Webb, Glover, Gaynor, Rice. SUBS Fleming, Starbuck.
Jan 1st, H, v Newcastle United, L, 0-2, AT 28,534, Sutton, Chettle, Pearce, Walker, Foster, Wilson, Plummer, Webb, Glover, Gaynor, Rice. SUBS Fleming, Starbuck.
Jan 3rd, A, v Everton, L, 0-1, AT 21,680, Sutton, Chettle, Pearce, Walker, Foster, Wilson, Carr, Webb, Starbuck, Gaynor, Rice. SUBS Fleming, Wilkinson.
Jan 9th, FAC, A, v Halifax Town, W, 4-0, Scorers Pearce, Wilson, Plummer, Wilkinson, AT 4,013, Sutton, Chettle, Pearce, Walker, Foster, Wilson, Plummer, Webb, Glover, Gaynor, Rice. SUBS Fleming, Wilkinson.
Jan 16th, H, v Charlton Athletic, D, 2-2, Scorers Plummer, Webb, AT 15,363, Sutton, Chettle, Pearce, Walker, Foster, Wilson, Plummer, Webb, Glover, Gaynor, Rice. SUBS Crosby, Wilkinson.
Jan 23rd, A, v Watford, D, 0-0, AT 13,158, Sutton, Chettle, Pearce, Walker, Foster, Wilson, Plummer, Webb, Glover, Wilkinson, Rice.
Jan 30th, FAC, A, v Leyton Orient, W, 2-1, Scorers Plummer, Glover, AT 19,212, Sutton, Chettle, Pearce, Walker, Foster, Wilson, Plummer, Webb, Glover, Wilkinson, Gaynor.
Feb 3rd, SC, A, v Reading, L, 1-2, Scorer Webb, AT 9,096, Sutton, Chettle, Pearce, Walker, Foster, Wilson, Plummer, Webb, Glover, Wilkinson, Rice. SUBS Starbuck, Fleming.
Feb 6th, H, v Chelsea, W, 3-2, Scorers Foster, Crosby, Clough (P), AT 18,203, Sutton, Fleming, Pearce, Walker, Foster, Wilson, Crosby, Webb, Clough, Gaynor, Rice. SUBS Starbuck, Chettle.
Feb 13th, A, v Southampton, D, 1-1, Scorer Clough, AT 13,314, Sutton, Fleming, Pearce, Walker, Wassall, Wilson, Crosby, Webb, Clough, Wilkinson, Osvold.
Feb 20th, FAC, A, v Birmingham City, W, 1-0, Scorer Crosby, AT 34,494, Sutton, Fleming, Pearce, Walker, Foster, Wilson, Crosby, Webb, Clough, Wilkinson, Rice.
March 5th, A, v Sheffield Wednesday, W, 1-0, Scorer Webb, AT 19,509, Sutton, Fleming, Pearce, Walker, Foster, Wilson, Crosby, Webb, Clough, Wilkinson, Rice. SUB Gaynor.
March 12th, FAC, A, v Arsenal, W, 2-1, Scorers Wilkinson, Rice, AT 51,570, Sutton, Chettle, Pearce, Walker, Foster, Wilson, Crosby, Webb, Clough, Wilkinson, Rice.
March 16th, A, v Queens Park Rangers, L, 1-2, Scorer Clough, AT 8,316, Sutton, Chettle, Pearce, Walker, Foster, Wilson, Crosby, Webb, Clough, Wilkinson, Rice.

March 19th, H, v Manchester United, D, 0-0, AT 27,598, Sutton, Chettle, Pearce, Walker, Foster, Wilson, Crosby, Webb, Clough, Wilkinson, Rice.
March 26th, A, v Tottenham Hotspur, D, 1-1,

1987 - 1988 DIVISION 1 TABLE

TEAMS	P	W	D	L	F	A	W	D	L	F	A	PTS
1 Liverpool FC	40	15	5	0	49	9	11	7	2	38	15	90
2 Manchester U	40	14	5	1	41	17	9	7	4	30	21	81
3 Nottingham F	40	11	7	2	40	17	9	6	5	27	22	73
4 Everton	40	14	4	2	34	11	5	9	6	19	16	70
5 Q.P.R	40	12	4	4	30	14	7	6	7	18	24	67
6 Arsenal	40	11	4	5	35	16	7	8	5	23	23	66
7 Wimbledon	40	8	9	3	32	20	6	6	8	26	27	57
8 Newcastle U	40	9	6	5	32	23	5	8	7	23	30	56
9 Luton T	40	11	6	3	40	21	3	5	12	17	37	53
10 Coventry C	40	6	8	6	23	25	7	6	7	23	28	53
11 Sheffield W	40	10	2	8	27	30	5	6	9	25	36	53
12 Southampton	40	6	8	6	27	26	6	6	8	22	27	50
13 Tottenham H	40	9	5	6	26	23	3	6	11	12	25	47
14 Norwich C	40	7	5	8	26	26	5	4	11	14	26	45
15 Derby Co	40	6	7	7	18	17	4	6	10	17	28	42
16 West Ham U	40	6	9	5	23	21	3	6	11	17	31	42
17 Charlton A	40	7	7	6	23	21	2	8	10	15	31	42
18 Chelsea	40	7	11	2	24	17	2	4	14	26	51	42
19 Portsmouth	40	4	8	8	21	27	3	6	11	15	39	35
20 Watford	40	4	5	11	15	24	3	6	11	12	27	32
21 Oxford U	40	5	7	8	24	34	1	6	13	20	46	31

WHO? WHAT!

FACTFILE

RESULTS LEAGUE TABLE

Scorer Clough, AT 25,306, Sutton, Fleming, Chettle, Walker, Foster, Wilson, Crosby, Webb, Clough, Wilkinson, Rice.

March 30th, H, v Derby County, W, 2-1, Scorers Clough (2), AT 25,017, Sutton, Chettle, Pearce, Walker, Foster, Wilson, Crosby, Webb, Clough, Wilkinson, Rice.

April 2nd, H, v Liverpool, W, 2-1, Scorers Webb, Hansen (OG), AT 29,188, Sutton, Chettle, Pearce, Walker, Foster, Wilson, Crosby, Webb, Clough, Wilkinson, Rice.

April 4th, A, v Portsmouth, W, 1-0, Scorer Wilson, AT 17,528, Sutton, Chettle, Pearce, Wassall, Foster, Wilson, Crosby, Webb, Clough, Wilkinson, Glover.

April 9th, FAC, N, v Liverpool, L, 1-2, Scorer Clough, AT 51,627, Sutton, Chettle, Pearce, Walker, Foster, Wilson, Crosby, Webb, Clough, Wilkinson, Rice.

April 13th, A, v Liverpool, L, 0-5, AT 39,535, Sutton, Chettle, Pearce, Walker, Foster, Wilson, Crosby, Webb, Clough, Glover, Rice. SUB Wassall.

April 20th, H, v West Ham United, D, 0-0, AT 15,775, Sutton, Fleming, Pearce, Chettle, Foster, Wilson, Crosby, Webb, Clough, Carr, Rice. SUBS Gaynor, Wassall.

April 30th, H, v Wimbledon, D, 0-0, AT 14,341, Sutton, Fleming, Williams, Chettle, Foster, Wilson, Carr, Webb, Gaynor, Parker, Rice.

May 4th, H, v Norwich City, W, 2-0, Scorers Webb, Glover, AT 11,610, Sutton, Fleming, Williams, Chettle, Foster, Wilson, Carr, Webb, Clough, Glover, Rice. SUBS Wilkinson, Parker.

May 7th, H, v Oxford United, W, 5-3, Scorers Carr, Webb (2), Clough (2), AT 12,762, Sutton, Fleming, Williams, Chettle, Foster, Wilson, Carr, Webb, Clough, Glover, Rice.

May 13th, A, v Luton Town, D, 1-1, Scorer Glover, AT 9,018, Sutton, Fleming, Williams, Walker, Chettle, Wilson, Carr, Webb, Clough, Glover, Crosby. SUB Foster.

May 15th, H, v Luton Town, D, 1-1, Scorer Webb, AT 13,106, Sutton, Fleming, Chettle, Walker, Foster, Wilson, Carr, Webb, Clough, Glover, Rice. SUB Crosby.

There were a hat-trick of winners in a recent Junior Reds half time prize draw. Andrew Cartwright (Doncaster), Darryl Boot (Codnor) and Jamie Marshall (Mansfield) receive sweatshirts from Andrew Dolloway (second right), of Nottingham Sports Promotions and our youngster Steve McLoughlin is on hand to help out with the presentation.

WHERE! WHEN!

SEASON 1988-89

Back row L to R: Brian Laws, Gary Fleming, Garry Parker, Steve Chettle, Darren Wassell, Brian Rice, Steve Hodge.
Middle row L to R: Liam O'Kane (Trainer), Tommy Gaynor, Terry Wilson, Steve Sutton, Hans Segers, Colin Foster, Neil Webb, Brain Clough (Manager)
Front row L to R: Nigel Clough, Lee Glover, Des Walker, Stuart Pearce, Franz Carr, Gary Crosby.

The coming season of 1988-89 was to be the club's most successful for a decade, but it was also to be one tainted by an association with the biggest tragedy to happen in the history of English football. If anybody had thought that football could possibly sink any lower in the estimation of the British public after the events of 1985, they were in for a rude awakening and once more it would involve Liverpool Football Club.

Over the past couple of years, Brian Clough had been carefully assembling a squad of players that at the very least would compete for cup success, but if they could avoid injuries or losing their best players, they might just surprise a few people in the League as well. The manager had not been resting on his laurels post season and it was clear where he thought that the team could do with strengthening.

When Forest were considering signing a player, the process often began in a similar style. Brian Clough would obtain the telephone number of the intended target and then call him: "Now young man, how would you like to play for Nottingham Forest?" This is how Brian Laws remembers his first conversation with the manager that he still adores. Laws had fallen out with Middlesbrough manager Bruce Rioch and was looking for a way out of Ayresome Park when the call came. The message was clear: "Then get yourself down here and bring your wife and your children," Clough told him.

The pair met up at the City Ground a few days later, and after the usual Clough put downs: "Can you play?" etc., they finally got down to business. In front of the player, the manager asked Ronnie Fenton how much Middlesbrough wanted: "Between 4 and 500,000 boss." Cloughie's response being: "No way am I paying that," then turning back to the player he said: "I will tell you now son, you can sign that contract, but if we have to pay any more than £100,000, you can forget it."

The difference between the two clubs valuation of the player was so great, that the matter went to a tribunal. This was to be an anxious wait for the player, particularly because the tribunal wasn't due to meet until July, just after pre-season training had been due to commence. Laws, Fenton and Rioch all attended the tribunal held at Highfield Road Coventry, where the matter would be resolved. After hearing evidence from all parties, the panel announced that the fee would be £125,000, Laws heart sank. However after Fenton had spoken to the manager, he agreed to pay the extra and the deal went through.

There was to be another convoluted transfer that July, this time involving the return of an 'old boy'. Steve Hodge had enjoyed some success since leaving the club, first at Aston Villa, before he quickly moved on to Tottenham. He had become an England regular and had played in the infamous, 'Hand of God', World Cup match against Argentina in Mexico, even bagging Maradona's shirt in the process, but in truth he had never settled in London. The Spurs' players lived miles apart and socially there wasn't the same team camaraderie that he was used to back in Nottingham. As the previous season had drawn to a close, he put the word out via friends to let Liam O'Kane know that he would be open to a move home, and soon Hodge heard back that Forest would be interested if the price was right. Steve went to see Spurs boss Terry Venables, to see what sort of fee they might ask for him. After a discussion, Venables said that he would recommend to his board that they should accept £550,000 for his transfer, but once more Clough

Steve Hodge is a happy man on his return to the City Ground.

Ron Fenton pictured alongside new signing Brian Laws and family.

said they would only go to half a million. (The manager was renowned for looking after the club's money, particularly when it came to wage rises!) Meanwhile Derby County came in with an offer but Hodge definitely wasn't interested, but was shrewd enough to realise it might be useful during contract talks if Forest knew that he did have other options open to him. Eventually Clough relented and agreed to pay Tottenham the extra £50,000. So the way was now clear for the player to go up to Nottingham along with his advisor, to discuss personal terms. Now Steve was fully aware that he didn't have the strongest hand for bargaining, because the manager knew that he was desperate to return to Nottingham, but Clough's first question took him by surprise: "Son, are you homosexual?" - "No I am just a shy lad that can't pull a good looking bird," Steve replied.

When they finally began to talk about money, Clough offered less than the player was on at Tottenham, Hodge refused, he wanted to be valued by the club and knew what he could bring to the team, so he walked out and went to his parents house just outside Nottingham. Ten minutes after arriving there, the phone rang, it was the manager: "Get back here and let's get it sorted." The outcome was that Clough gave him a wage rise and a three year deal as well.

Forest began their pre-season with a week in Nottingham to shake off the cobwebs, including some running around Wollaton Park. It was here that Brian Laws was introduced to the way things were done at the club: "We were running, jogging and walking, I was just dying for it to speed up a bit, to show what I could do, when I was joined by skipper Stuart Pearce who said, 'Who the f**k are you, and what do you think you are doing? Hang fire, get back here and just watch what the rest of us do'. And after training had finished, Pearce hammered me again. 'That's the hardest session we've had, because of all your pushing at the front'. I didn't do that again."

Laws was to learn quickly, that at Forest, the ball did all the work and you didn't have to be the fittest team. Training was built around 6 a-side, short and sharp, and by the time the season had got going, every team's fitness levels were virtually the same anyway, because of all the games that were played.

Forest set off for Denmark minus one player, Paul Wilkinson. Although Paul was a willing worker, he was missing that final bit of quality that distinguishes good players from the very good. Also he wasn't deadly enough in front of goal and Nigel Clough needed another forward to take some of the scoring burden off his shoulders. Paul left to join Watford for £300,000, with the club's best wishes.

Brian Clough had already earmarked his successor, Lee Chapman from Sheffield Wednesday, but he was to be disappointed initially, when the player chose to join French club Niort instead. They were offering him a massive contract that he just couldn't turn down.

It really doesn't need to be said, but pre-season followed the usual routine. Opponents were again semi-professional Scandinavian outfits, these were really just an excuse to get match play into the legs, before culminating in a couple of harder games. This year Pescara from Italy and Cologne provided the opposition in a mini tournament held in Italy, before they returned home to face Notts County in the County Cup for the final warm up game.

As Clough had feared, Manchester United came in with a late bid for Neil Webb. The transfer fee would have been the highest that the club had ever received, but the manager was delighted when the player said that he wasn't interested in a move at this time. This was a mature approach from the mid-fielder, on one hand he knew that the money he would receive from United could be life changing, but he also knew that he wasn't the finished article and as we saw with Garry Birtles who had made the same move, there were plenty of potential pitfalls.

The contrast in the strength of the squad with previous years was clear. New signings Garry Parker and Brian Laws couldn't even force their way in to the squad immediately. Steve Chettle continued at right back and Parker was competing with either Gary Crosby or Brian Rice for a wide role. So apart from Hodge wearing the number ten shirt instead of Wilkinson, the team was virtually the same as that which had finished third

Steve Sutton welcomes new signing Lee Chapman to Nottingham Forest.

the previous season.

Forest began their campaign at Carrow Road against a Norwich side who turned out to be the surprise package in the league that year, hovering around the top four all season.

On a beautiful sunny day, using a ploy that he had employed many times before, Clough requested that the coach driver drop them off about a mile from the ground, where they joined with spectators making their way to the stadium. Steve Hodge had immediately settled back in to the old routine, but the manager made him aware that he wasn't coming back as top dog, when he told him to get the ball to Neil Webb, or as he put it: "Give it to a good player." The 2-1 defeat however, was an inauspicious start to the season.

Although the Reds had won the Football League Centenary Trophy at Wembley the previous April, the League decided that wasn't enough recognition of that important event, and so they announced that there would be another competition called The Mercantile Trophy, that had to be squeezed into an already congested fixture list. With the absence of European football, the games' hierarchy were always looking at extra ways to increase club's revenue. The manager never liked to lose any fixture, but I don't think even he was too disappointed to go out at the first stage to Liverpool, but the 4-1 scoreline would have concerned him.

The slow start to the campaign continued with four consecutive 1-1 draws, Sheffield Wednesday, Everton, Derby and Aston Villa. All of the games were winnable, but the lack of a target man up front was clear. Tommy Gaynor had been drafted into the side, but he wasn't able to make much of a difference, and was unable to add to his goals tally.

They did manage a scoring spree in their next game though, but that was only a Littlewoods Cup tie against Third Division Chester City. There were five different scorers, Pearce, Clough, Webb, Hodge (his first since returning) and Gaynor, but this was followed by another draw, this time 0-0 away at Luton.

Hans Segers had by now realised that he was not going to regain his place in the team, and with several young keepers like Mark Crossley emerging, decided his future lay elsewhere. So he left to join Wimbledon for a fee of £180,000, good business as far as Forest were concerned.

England played Denmark in a friendly international at Wembley in September and when Des Walker came on to replace Tony Adams, it meant that Nottingham Forest had four players on the pitch, not only more than any other club, but an event not even achieved by the legends of the 1970's. It is amazing how quickly the Reds' line up had changed from the mid eighties, when they were dependant on ageing stars such as Todd, Young and Bowyer to keep the team afloat, to the new vibrant wearers of the Garibaldi.

They finally broke their drawing sequence at Loftus Road against Queens Park Rangers, 2-1. This time the game was played on a regular grass surface after the home side had decided to dispense with their artificial pitch. The plastic pitch had been controversial since the time it had been laid. The first few games played on the surface had been chaotic, long kicks from the goalkeeper were bouncing twenty feet in the air. They tried to remedy this by applying tonnes of sand in an attempt to 'deaden' the pitch, but the ball continued to behave as if it was filled with helium. The other concern had been the burns grazes you received if you fell on the pitch, or simply forgot and attempted a slide tackle. After two years, even the Rangers' players had been calling for an end to the experiment.

The thinking behind the introduction of plastic pitches was sound enough, the surface offered far more commercial opportunities than a grass pitch with other events, pop concerts etc., but the technology was just not advanced enough to warrant its introduction and it clearly gave the home team an advantage. It is significant that in the thirty years since, despite vast improvements in the technology, no top flight club in England has ever seriously considered asking for permission to install one.

Although Clough's pursuit of Lee Chapman had initially ended in failure, the Reds continued to monitor the situation, and when it was revealed by the player, that the financial obligations to him had not been met, they sensed that the

WOW

Webb blasts home the winner against Liverpool.

Gaynor with the sixth against Chester City.

Hodge with the fourth goal.

Des Walker in search of his first Forest goal.

Brian Rice with a rare headed goal against Liverpool.

Action from the recent Coventry City encounter.

Nigel Clough is foiled by the Coventry keeper Ogrizovic.

Colin Foster in action against Sheffield Wednesday.

RICK HOLDEN
WATFORD
FRANZ CARR
FOREST
SHIPSTONES
Fine Beers

SUPER LEE

1. Nigel Clough's shot is blocked by the Arsenal defence.

2. But Pearce follows up to score.

Franz Carr is foiled by the Leicester keeper, Cooper.

Stuart Pearce along with the mascots away at Southampton.

Gary Crosby is foiled by this late block from a Coventry defender.

Lee Chapman on target against Middlesbrough.

Lee Chapman adds his second against Middlesbrough.

Gary Crosby evades this challenge from Liverpool's Gary Gillespie.

player would now be open to a return to England.

The story of his transfer to Nottingham Forest was to reveal the unscrupulous side of Derby County chairman Robert Maxwell, as Forest tried to honour the wishes of the player and bring him to the City Ground.

When Lee Chapman realised the situation at Niort, he had quickly got in touch with Alan Hill, who told him Forest were still interested. Forest then contacted the French club and agreed a fee. In the meanwhile, Derby contacted the player, to be told he only wanted to go to Nottingham.

Brian Clough himself then called the player: "Do you want to play for me? Yes, OK, then sit tight and stick to your guns."

It was then that Derby began to pressurise the player in to changing his mind. First Arthur Cox the Rams' boss, followed by Peter Shilton the keeper, then Cox once more before Ian Maxwell, the chairman's son called to say Derby had done a deal for the player and Niort were now insisting that Chapman could only sign for Derby. Lee continued to restate that he was only interested in joining Forest and there was nothing that Derby could offer that would change his mind.

An hour later Chapman picked up the phone to hear the booming voice of Robert Maxwell on the other end of the line: "I want you to sign for Derby, we will pay you all of the money, do you need a car, have whatever you want. I understand your wife is in show business, I can get her a job presenting on television." The offers were now getting so fantastic, that Lee felt he really should discuss them with his wife, as he was potentially turning down a fortune. It was a short discussion, they both decided that the move to Forest was the better option. On hearing this it seemed as if Maxwell had finally accepted the situation and wished the player well.

Not so, as a man accustomed to winning, this then became a personal crusade for Robert Maxwell, as he threatened Niort, Forest and Chapman, and then even tried to buy the Niort Football Club itself. He just couldn't bear the thought of losing to anyone.

On this occasion he would have to, as Forest closed the deal and the player was officially unveiled as a Red on October 19th. There were not too many unhappy faces years later, when it was revealed that Robert Maxwell was a crook and had been pilfering The Mirror Groups' pension scheme for his own benefit.

Chapman made his debut away at Millwall in a 2-2 draw, but Forest let slip a two goal lead after dominating the game. In the final reckoning, these drawn games would cost the Reds the League title.

However, the team now began to hit their stride, they looked strong and well balanced all over the pitch and with Chapman's height and heading ability, they now had another weapon to hurt opponents with. This was perfectly illustrated in the home encounter with Liverpool as Forest showed no fear and took the game to the Scousers. It might only have finished 2-1, but in reality they saw the game out comfortably despite the much vaunted Liverpool attack.

For Lee Chapman it was great to be concentrating on his football once more. He had quickly settled into the team and didn't have to wait too long for his first goal. It turned out to be a valuable one as it proved to be the only one of the game in a 1-0 victory away at Newcastle United.

Lee had been thought of only as a target man, even he himself saw his role as to win the high ball and bring others into play. Clough and his coaching staff saw something else in the player. Training at Forest consisted of a lot of 6 a-side, short sharp passing, ball control and awareness, and after even just a few weeks, the player's touch and instincts began to improve. The manager was also able to pass on small tips that would help the player. He was previously expected to stay at the 'far post,' win the high ball, but Clough showed him the benefit of near post runs, to unsettle the defence, and he was to score many goals from this.

The League Cup was later to provide Forest with their first serious silverware for nine years, but it was not to be without it's scares along the way. In the second round, they twice had to come from behind, before they eventually overcame Coventry 3-2 at the City Ground. Injuries meant that Gary Charles made his debut as a right winger alongside keeper Mark Crossley, who had made his bow a couple of weeks earlier against Liverpool.

Steve Hodge relates a strange tale about a visit he made to the Baseball Ground with the manager the following evening to watch a reserve fixture. After the game, they had gone into the dressing room, because Brian Clough had seen something that he didn't like. Brian Clough always wanted to beat Derby County, he didn't care whether it was first team, reserves or youth team. So when Jemson had gone on as a late substitute

SHIPSTONES
SHIPSTONES
FOREST
COLIN FOSTER / DES WALKER

The London Royal Ballet pictured on a recent visit to the City Ground.

with the Reds winning, and selfishly gone for goal, rather than killing time he was incensed. Approaching Nigel Jemson who was seated, he asked the player: "Have you ever been punched in the stomach son?" And proceeded to punch him. "Well you have now."

Nigel Clough had developed into the fulcrum of the team, everything seemed to go through him in much the same way that everything was channelled through John Robertson ten years previously. He might not have been the quickest mover, but he was most definitely the quickest thinker, like a chess player always a couple of moves ahead. He was also one of the bravest, playing with his back to goal in an era when the tackle from behind had not been outlawed, and players such as Graham Roberts of Tottenham and Terry Hurlock of Millwall fouled with impunity. There was also Tony Adams and Steve Bould of Arsenal who seemed to delight in trying to kick Nigel out of the game whilst his father looked on. When Arsenal visited the City Ground and left with a 4-1 victory, Brian Clough was incensed that referee Derek Hutchinson let the visitors get away with murder.

To the manager, it didn't matter who you were. If you didn't follow his instructions, he acted. The next game away at West Ham provided a perfect example of this. Forest were leading, when Stuart Pearce played a poor pass that was intercepted, leading to a United goal. A fuming Clough turned to substitute Brian Laws saying: "Lawsy, can you play left back? - Well, then get stripped." Up went the number 3 board and Pearce slowly made his way off the pitch glowering at his manager, who made a point of ignoring him. The rest of the game you could hear him shouting: "Great play Lawsy, that's how to play left back."

When the players reached the dressing room at the end of the 3-3 draw, they knew what to expect. It was great fun, if you weren't on the end of it. Pearce refused to sit down, stood his ground, not even reacting when the boss rabbit punched him. But he had proved his point as well.

After a hard fought 0-0 draw away at Leicester City in the Third Round of the League Cup, all the better because Forest were forced to play virtually the whole of the second half with 10 men after Pearce was sent off, they travelled up to Middlesbrough for the Saturday game.

It would be fair to say, that up to this point, Lee Chapman was still adapting to the Forest way. Not only the style of play, but also the little things such as days off and not meeting on a home match day until 45 minutes before a game. However, when he read that morning's paper, and the manager's criticism of him, he feared he was about to be dropped. He wasn't, and in fact this game proved to be the turning point in his season. After a spell of only one goal in nine games, he scored two that day, and so began his lethal partnership with Nigel Clough.

However, the side was still inconsistent. Further points were dropped to Southampton, Wimbledon and Manchester United, but sandwiched between these defeats they did make progress in the League Cup, as Leicester were disposed of in the replay.

Brian Laws had by now tied down the right back spot, as Steve Chettle was left out, only deputising in centre defence if there were injuries. In another managerial masterstroke, Terry Wilson, who had lost his midfield place, returned to play alongside Des Walker. Wilson was a competitive player, good on the ball, and he was to keep out Colin Foster, who fell right out of favour.

Garry Parker who had joined the previous season had found his first team opportunities limited. He considered himself to be primarily a central midfield player, but with those positions occupied by Neil Webb and Steve Hodge, it looked as if injuries would provide his only route through to the team. Right footed, it was a surprise therefore when he found himself in the number eleven shirt playing wide left, but his ability to drift inside proved invaluable as the season wore on and he soon cemented his place in the line-up.

There was a thought that Forest never hit their straps until Christmas, by which time their fitness levels had caught up with everyone else's. So it wasn't altogether a surprise when they embarked on a long unbeaten run, with the away form particularly striking.

After ending the year on a high, beating Sheffield Wednesday 3-0, the New Year saw a run of 6 cup games out of the next eight fixtures. Second Division Ipswich Town were swept aside in the FA Cup, before the Reds travelled South to Stamford Bridge to take on Chelsea in the Simod Cup. Although it was nicknamed the 'Mickey Mouse' Cup, Clough took it seriously, after all there was a final to be played at Wembley. So it was a full strength Forest side that prevailed over the Blues, after an energy sapping extra time 4-1 victory, on a rain swept night in London.

They were back in London five days later and returned with all the points after defeating Spurs 2-1, an especially pleasing result for Steve Hodge. It is well worth noting that the attendance at White Hart Lane was only 16,903!

The League Cup game against Queens Park Rangers on the following Wednesday should have been noteworthy only for the scoring exploits of Lee Chapman, who bagged four in a 5-2 victory, but instead of his name being plastered over the back pages, it was his manager Brian Clough instead.

Tommy Gaynor rounds the Everton keeper Neville Southall to score.

Pearce scores against Ipswich Town in the Simod Cup.

Parker against Chelsea in the Simod Cup.

Hodge stoops to flick the ball past Spink the Villa keeper.

A Pearce rocket thunders in to the Villa net.

LITTLEWOODS CUP 4th ROUND

NOTTINGHAM FOREST 5
QUEENS PARK RANGERS 2

Chapman celebrates his hat-trick.

Chapman goal number 1.

Clough goal number 3.

Chapman goal number 2.

Chapman goal number 4.

Chapman goal number 5.

Forest heroes, Clough and Chapman.

A different view of Chapman's first goal.

Hodge turns away in celebration.

Chapman went close to adding his fifth goal.

As the game finished, several hundred Reds' supporters spilled on to the pitch to congratulate the players. The manager who was known for his quick post game getaways to the sanctuary of the dressing room, found his way blocked by well wishers. Nobody can say for certain what went through Brian Clough's mind as he lashed out, catching several young supporters around the face, but it was captured by a local news crew, and before long it was a national story.

Back in his office, it was beginning to sink in just what he had done. Speaking with Ron Fenton he said: "I've really done it now." Fenton went outside and returned with the news that things didn't look too good.

Surprisingly Brian Clough received support. The Chief Superintendent of Sheffield for one, and then Neil Kinnock, head of the Labour Party commented: "Who hasn't wanted to do the same to these hooligans." There is no doubt that the game of football was suffering from hooliganism, but it has to be said that this incident should never have been viewed in the same context. The pitch invasion was pure joy. That some apologists for the manager tried to claim that he was standing up for his beliefs, that the pitch was his work place and he was defending it, was frankly pathetic.

Anyway, a hurriedly arranged meeting with the 'injured' youths, ended with them apologising to the manager, getting a kiss and 15 minutes of fame. While the FA doled out a £5,000 fine and a touchline ban to the boss.

Brian Clough had even considered at one stage whether he should resign, but the following letter laid out the club's position.

Dear Brian,
On behalf of my board of directors, I am writing to inform you that we are not prepared to accept your resignation, and I would be obliged if you could arrange to meet me to discuss an extension to your contract....

As Jimmy Greaves would say: "Funny old game isn't it." The team meanwhile carried on their exceptional form. Another of Steve Hodge's old teams Aston Villa, were battered 4-0, Ipswich were knocked out of another cup, the Simod, before a full house saw Leeds tamely surrender 2-0 in the FA Cup at the City Ground.

After the team's tenth successive win at Kenilworth Road, 3-2 over Luton Town, (their first ever victory on an artificial surface as well), Forest were up to 4th place in the table, but another drawn game against Queens Park Rangers, infuriatingly halted the run.

The next four fixtures were all cup games across 3 competitions. Starting with the first leg of the semi-final of the League Cup against Third Division Bristol City. City weren't mugs, they had Steve McClaren in midfield and a forward line including Joe Jordan. They deservedly held a 1-0 lead until late in the game, when a John Pender own goal, gave Forest a lifeline.

Steve Hodge recalls lying in the bath ruminating over the poor display, when the manager came in and said: "Harry, come on darling, you can't do anything about it now, soon be Saturday."

And he was right, except that on this occasion it was Sunday, and a live TV FA Cup game at Vicarage Road against Watford, with the outcome a serene 3-0 victory.

By now Forest were also in the semi-final of the Simod Cup, where they would face Crystal Palace in Nottingham. Not so Mickey Mouse now, over 20,000 turned out to watch Forest win 3-1 and book their first Wembley Final appearance for 9 years, (Mercantile Credit Trophy not withstanding).

As the games came thick and fast, the chance to secure a second Wembley visit came just four days later at Ashton Gate. The playing conditions for this game were horrendous, strong wind and rain. Stuart Pearce described it as the coldest he had been on a pitch. But after battling hard for ninety minutes, even surviving a late scare when City hit the post in the last minute of regulation time, the Reds prevailed 1-0, after Parker fired home what proved to be the winner.

Jubilation all round. None more so than for the manager, who having waited on the touchline for the players to return after saluting the drenched supporters, persuaded Pearce to accompany him back over to take the plaudits, in a rare display of unbounded joy, but who could blame him?

It had been a long journey back for Brian Clough. Those that had sneered that he was nothing without Peter Taylor, would now have to stay silent. He had built a whole new team, more youthful and perhaps more expressive than the previous one. Old Big Head was back.

Stuart Pearce in particular was so proud that he was the captain of the team that was taking Clough back to Wembley.

There was still much to play for. They were still in contention in the League, and had a massive FA Cup game at Old Trafford to look forward to. Would the daunting playing schedule catch up with the players? Two games a week. Even

Brian Clough and Archie Gemmill.

with the manager's policy of plenty of rest, the team remained virtually unchanged, leading to some erratic results. They followed up an impressive 3-1 victory at Highbury against Arsenal, with a lack lustre performance at home against soon to be relegated Newcastle. They could perhaps be excused this however, as the Manchester United encounter loomed.

The FA Cup was United's only chance of success this season. In fact their fans were demanding it. But Forest arrived ready to burst their bubble.

Clough had learnt over the years, that a tense and under pressure player, couldn't perform, so he would do anything in his power to ensure that this didn't happen, often to his own detriment.

Maurice Roworth, the chairman often popped into the dressing room to wish the lads well, before the manager inevitably told him to piss off. On this occasion, Steve Hodge was visiting the toilets, when he found Roworth lying prostrate on the floor unable to breathe due to an asthma attack. After the medics were called, Clough strolled by and on seeing him said: "Mr. Chairman, if you are going to die, could you hurry up because I've got a game to play in 10 minutes."

Before the same game, Brian Clough, who often had a red face, asked Graham Lyas the physio, if he had any cream: "Over there on the table," was the reply. Clough then proceeded to give his team talk before shouting: "Why is my face burning?" It turned out that he had put 'Deep Heat' on by mistake. The players were in hysterics. When they strode out alongside the United team, who were deep in serious mode, their players couldn't believe it.

The game turned out to be the perfect away performance. Controlling the game, striking quickly on the counter attack, they limited United to a few chances, before Parker clinically finished off a flowing move to score what turned out to be the games only goal.

Des Walker had perfected the way to play United's main goal threat Mark Hughes. Hughes was a tough physical player, so Des decided never to rile him, convinced that he was a lesser player if he wasn't playing on 'the edge'. Also, he didn't play tight, preferring to sit off and deal with him when he turned. Despite a couple of scares, they were through to another semi-final.

Gordon Strachan, Manchester United's right winger, was asked how was it to play against Forest: "Once they get a lead they are so difficult to break down. They play with intelligence and stay on their feet," he said. The 12,000 Forest fans who had made the journey to back the team were in dreamland.

The 18 match unbeaten run however, came to an end just a few days later, when Tottenham lowered their colours, but even then it took a 90th minute Samways' goal after a seventy yard run from Chris Waddle to do it.

Normal service was resumed next game, and they couldn't have chosen a better place for it to happen, the Baseball Ground, where Lee Chapman showed the Rams exactly what they had missed out on, when he headed home the second goal, in an easy 2-0 win.

It was the end of March, but Forest still had a possible 14 games to fit in, and the chance of an unprecedented three cup finals at Wembley. So the challenges were coming thick and fast. Manchester United were still a big draw, and over 30,000 were in Nottingham to see a 2-0 win that could, and should have been six. Steve Hodge remembers the boss taking him to one side before the game: "Robson's shot it, he said,

Terry Wilson.

LITTLEWOODS CUP
SEMI FINAL 1nd LEG

NOTTINGHAM FOREST	1
BRISTOL CITY	1

Chapman arm raised, as Forest equalise.

Another view of the Forest goal.

CLOUGHIE'S BACK AT WEMBLEY *Again!*

Forest stand firm at Ashton Gate.

Stuart Pearce.

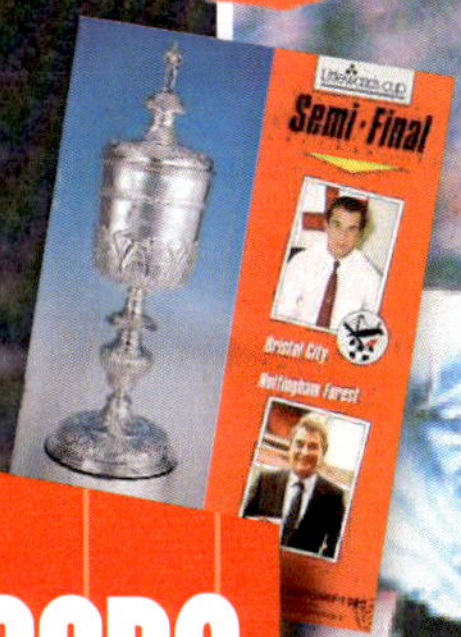

LITTLEWOODS CUP
SEMI FINAL 2nd LEG

BRISTOL CITY	0
NOTTINGHAM FOREST	1

Franz Carr.

Garry Parker puts the real Reds ahead at Old Trafford.

Steve Sutton to the rescue.

F.A. CUP

QUARTER FINAL

MANCHESTER UTD	0
NOTTINGHAM FOREST	1

The Forest players cannot hide their delight.

Lee Chapman is in determined mood.

Neil Webb.

Forest's winning goal at Old Trafford, as Franz Carr lays it on a plate for Garry Parker.

his legs have gone, run him off the pitch."

Although the Reds seemingly had no problem with the top divisions footballing sides, their Achilles heel re-appeared once more when they came up against an ultra physical side in Wimbledon. They had only conceded 6 goals in the previous eleven games, but they shipped four in this one game. There was also another incident involving the manager, who although was banished to the directors box, still couldn't stop himself from getting involved, particularly as on this occasion, he was watching his team fall apart. Some of the occupants of the box were not pleased at some of the language coming from his direction, so a policeman was summoned. Clough, not realising who was tapping him on the shoulder, told the person to piss off, which obviously didn't go down too well. A senior officer was called, and the result was that the manager watched the remainder of the game from the Police Control area.

Forest's preparations for this particular game had been disrupted by a freak domestic accident involving Brian Laws the night before. Whilst attempting to separate two glasses when washing up, he unluckily severed an artery in his hand. After spending the night in hospital, he awoke the next morning, not only to find a 'pot' on his hand, but also with all of his fingers wired up.

The first thing the player thought of was the League Cup final only eight days away. The surgeon was clear, there was no chance he would be able to play, but he hadn't reckoned on the determination of Brian Laws. He had not spent years working towards this moment to then go and miss out.

The player called in to see the manager on the Monday afternoon. Clough asked him: "Are you going to be fit?" "Yes boss," was the reply.

The team had another mid-week league match to fit in whilst preparing for the final. Laws took off to the dressing to join in training, but even running was agony, let alone taking a throw in or taking a blow. The player couldn't even sleep properly.

Laws decided to go and visit the surgeon once more to sound him out. After he was told that playing might have serious consequences, Brian said he was prepared to take that risk, and as a result the player's fingers were stitched together, and a piece of plastic tubing inserted between to provide some rigidity.

The next day, Laws was doing some light running, the pain was easing but still there, when the manager appeared, threw a ball at him, and told him to take a throw in, which he did. "Good, you're playing."

Forest stayed at their usual London hotel, the Post House, nice surroundings, but the players really were just wanting to get on with it. Steve Hodge had played at Wembley a few years before with Tottenham, and of course a few of the lads had appeared there for England, but the experience gained the previous year when they won the Mercantile Trophy, would be invaluable to the squad.

Although Brian Laws had overcome his injury to regain his place, you must spare a thought for Steve Chettle, who dropped out, but at least he had the satisfaction of a place on the bench. Brian Rice was not so lucky. Having already made five appearances en route to the final, he not only missed out on playing, but also the £10,000 that would come with winning the trophy. Steve Hodge for one thought this was unfair,

Nigel Clough has scored Forest's third goal, and Luton's Ashley Grimes and Dave Beaumont know it's the end of a dream.

Nottm. Forest.......3
Luton Town...........1

LITTLEWOODS CUP FINAL SOUVENIR

NICE O
N

Farewell Fozzie – Clough scores his second goal.

The 1989 Littlewoods Cup winners: Nottingham Forest.

NE, GEL

SON SHINES FOR BRIAN

Nigel Clough offered the best evidence yet that he possesses the skill, speed of thought, temperament and eye for goal needed for an England call-up with a Cup-winning performance for Nottingham Forest at Wembley earlier this month.

Young Nigel, constantly overlooked by England manager Bobby Robson when he names his senior squads, emerged as the star of the show as Forest smashed Luton's defence of the Littlewoods Cup.

He scored twice and helped create another goal for midfielder Neil Webb to confirm not only his emergence in the game, but that of this exciting new Nottingham Forest side.

Mick Harford opens the scores – but is a loser this time.

Neil Webb caps a fine display with this goal.

Nigel sends Luton 'keeper Les Sealey the wrong way from the penalty spot – and Forest are back in it.

. . . and now for the goals

Things did not go exactly according to plan when we met Luton in the Littlewoods Cup final last month.

At half time we were trailing to a headed goal by Mick Harford and we clearly needed inspiration from some quarter.

We got it when Steve Hodge's penetrating run into the box led to him being floored by Luton keeper Les Sealey and Nigel Clough reliably scored the equaliser from the spot (top).

Then Tommy Gaynor got in on the act by setting up goals for Neil Webb (middle) and Nigel (below) and, as the saying goes . . . all's well that ends well.

Steve Sutton pictured alongside skipper Stuart Pearce, with the Littlewoods Cup.

particularly as his place was taken by a Clough favourite, Lee Glover.

Although Forest were odds on with the bookies, the first half did not go according to plan. After Chapman had a goal chalked off for offside, Luton went ahead through Mick Harford, and in fact were quite comfortable.

As is so often, there are two versions of what happened in the dressing room at half-time. Either Brian Clough was quite controlled, a few little pointers here and there, or he read the riot act, making the point that all their family and relatives were in the stands watching, so get out there and do better. Whichever version is true, it was a different Reds team that came out for the second half.

In the 53rd minute, Steve Hodge fastened on to a through ball and burst into the Luton area, where the Hatters' keeper Les Sealey stormed out and brought him down. Hodge remembers being amazed when this happened, because Sealey had committed exactly the same offence on him only four weeks before in a league game.

Brian Clough knew how hard it was to score, even from the penalty spot, so as a rule, he insisted that another player retrieve the ball, place it on the spot, whilst the penalty taker prepared himself.

Stuart Pearce and Nigel Clough had often shared the spot kick duties, usually changing after one of them had missed. On this day, it was down to Nigel to bring the Reds level, which he duly did. Forest were now right on top, further goals followed from Neil Webb fifteen minute later, and another from Clough soon after.

The League Cup was coming back to Nottingham after a 10 year absence. The manager allowed himself a small moment of celebration, before he slipped away, allowing the players to take their well earned lap of honour.

Post match, the atmosphere in the dressing room was quite subdued, the sense of a job well done, and after all there were still three other trophies to compete for.

Just three days later they had to play Southampton, a routine 3-0 win, before another big test and a date with destiny at Hillsborough on April the fifteenth. A match now set in history, with the consequences of that day still reverberating 30 years later. I don't propose here, to comment about what happened.

After that day, there were a couple of matters that had to be decided. The first was out of the club's hands. Should the FA Cup for the season continue? And were the Forest players in the right frame of mind to play their next fixture away at Middlesbrough. The Forest players might not have been directly touched by the tragedy, but they had witnessed the scenes, and some of the players had ventured outside after the crowds had been dispersed.

The decision was left to the players, who decided to go ahead. As an antidote for what had happened, it couldn't have been better, as both sides put on a feast of football, with Forest running out winners 4-3.

The club's second Wembley final took place 8 days later on the Sunday, when they took on Everton, (who had already booked their return in the FA Cup after wining the other semi-final). The competition obviously hadn't grabbed their attention, as their fans were heavily outnumbered in front of a healthy crowd of over 46,000.

However, Forest played their part in lifting spirits as the game once more finished 4-3 after extra time, two goals from Lee Chapman in over-time proving to be the difference between the two sides. Both teams were applauded off the pitch after an exhilarating game of football.

In a fitting end to the day, and in a break with tradition, Brian Clough himself led the players up to collect the trophy, and after kissing FA secretary Ted Croker, he held the trophy aloft.

The Football Association, after a period of consultation, had decided to continue with the competition, and re-arranged the Forest- Liverpool tie for May 7th at Old Trafford. Forest knew they were on a hiding to nothing, for the vast majority of the country saw a Liverpool-Everton final as the only fitting climax. Forest had considered withdrawing from the competition, but were persuaded to carry on.

In professional sport, where small percentages can make a huge difference, many of the players had no real desire to play the game. Stuart Pearce was the exact opposite. He held a grudge against Scousers for denying him European football after Heysel, and thought that if they were playing the game, they should try and win it. But he was in a minority.

Although the build up to the game was low key, as the players lined up to kick off, it was clear that Liverpool were determined to win, their fans demanded it, whilst there was almost an air of apology for being there from Forest supporters, as if they were the uninvited guests. Just do the right thing, make enough effort, but lose.

Liverpool took the lead with an early goal from John

Ronnie Whelan and Stuart Pearce before the game.

Saturday 15th April 1989

The F.A. Cup Semi-Final between Liverpool and Nottingham Forest was abandoned at 15.06 with the score at 0 - 0.

£I.R. 0.69 (inc VAT);
Australia – $1.25;
New Zealand – $1.85 (inc. G.S.T.);
Malaysia (by air) – $2.70;
Italy – L3,000;
Denmark – Kr.12.50.
HILLSBOROUGH:
SPECIAL REPORT
Shoot!
MAGAZINE
45p
29th April, 1989
YOU'LL NEVER WALK ALONE
SHOOT!
DISASTER
APPEAL
Buy a star's shirt and boost the fund
INTERVIEWS:
Neil Webb: Tommy Coyne
Kerry Dixon: Pat Nevin
Kevin Richardson
In colour: FALKIRK
GERAINT WILLIAMS
MARK HUGHES

Cheeky Chappy Clou

Garry Parker blasts Forest back into contention with this stunning volley then celebrates his second equaliser (below).

Lee Chapman nudges Forest into the lead, but Everton hit back.

ghie

SIMOD CUP FINAL SOUVENIR

Forest hit four but Brian grabs the glory

Nottingham Forest created history when they became the first club ever to win two domestic cups in the same season at Wembley.

Forest boss Brian Clough kept a low profile as his side beat Luton to win the Littlewoods Cup.

But after a thrilling Simod Cup Final against Everton that ran into extra-time, the game's most colourful manager led his side up the steps and collected the trophy from former FA chief Ted Croker.

Forest twice came from behind as Garry Parker cancelled out goals from Tony Cottee and Graeme Sharp. Cottee then equalised a glorious goal from Lee Chapman before the big Forest striker wrapped it up.

Chapman finally settles a seven-goal thriller two minutes from the end of extra-time.

LEE CHAPMAN
FOREST
JOHN LUKIC
ARSENAL

Liverpool and Forest players line up before the semi-final replay at Old Trafford.

Aldridge, before Forest surprisingly equalised with one of their rare forays forward, when a deflected shot from Neil Webb deceived Grobelaar. The game ebbed and flowed a little more from then on, but the Merseysiders, particularly through Barnes looked the more threatening.

Liverpool went up a gear in the second half attacking their fans in the Stretford End, and Steve Sutton was forced into a number of fine saves, but it was only a matter of time before they succumbed, Aldridge restoring their lead. Pre-match, Forest might have made all the right noises of respecting the game, going there to win etc., but with the evidence of their own eyes, supporters could see that there wasn't the same fire in their players.

To Forest players however, the whole occasion was tainted in the 72nd minute by one thoughtless act by a Liverpool player. Brian Laws whilst attempting to clear, only succeeded in turning the ball past Sutton for Liverpool's third goal. Whilst the player sat there disconsolately, John Aldridge ran past and ruffled the player's hair. Laws didn't react, it was only afterwards when he saw the footage and when his team-mates discussed it afterwards that he became angry. Now Laws was fuming, Pearce was fuming and so was Clough. Pearce thought that Laws should have chinned him there and then, but sense prevailed with the player. Forest fans drifted away and left Liverpool to celebrate. I wonder if Kenny Dalglish, who was the last to leave the field, appreciated the irony when a jubilant fan who had ran on to the pitch, placed a Juventus hat on his head? Perhaps not.

Brian Laws wouldn't have to wait long for a chance to exact revenge, for, as in the previous season, the Reds were scheduled to play Liverpool in a league game just four days later at Anfield. Aldridge made a show of seeking out Laws before the game to apologise, but he was having none of it. In the dressing room, Brian Clough made a point of telling him to do what he had to do, whilst Pearce had his own vendetta with Steve McMahon to sort out. Laws spent the whole game trying unsuccessfully to kick the player, in fact the only time he caught up with Aldridge he fouled him, giving away a penalty and the winning goal. Whilst Pearce, earned the wrath of the home fans when he smashed a ball in anger into the crowd, knocking out a spectator. All in all, not the best way for a successful season to draw to a close.

There were three league games still to fit in, and another third place to fight for with Norwich. On the day that Forest beat Charlton Athletic 4-0, Norwich were falling at Luton Town, thereby conceding their position to the Reds.

The curtain final fell on the eventful season, with a 2-1 home defeat to West Ham who were in an ultimately unsuccessful attempt to avoid relegation. It was to be Neil Webb's final competitive appearance in the Garibaldi.

The team had more than lived up to expectations. If they had acquired the services of Lee Chapman in August, would they have won more games? If the game with Liverpool at Hillsborough had continued, what would the outcome have been? We can only speculate. As the players, particularly Stuart Pearce acknowledged, Liverpool were stronger in a couple of positions, but on their day, Forest were their equals.

Ultimately they were to lose Neil Webb, but what if they could have kept him and added to the squad. John Sheridan, the player they brought in to replace him didn't last long, and there were also another couple of additions in Nigel Jemson, Gary Crosby and Toddi Orlygsson, but although they were good players, they were never going to be good enough to help mount a Championship challenge. And when Brian Clough was forced to sell Lee Chapman mid-way through the next season, for no other reason than the player needing the signing on fee to settle a tax bill, they were significantly weaker. So with the players available, Forest were always going to be seen as a cup team.

A decade that had begun with another European Cup victory, and the seemingly unbreakable partnership between Brian Clough and Peter Taylor, ended with Cloughie back on top and Taylor in retirement, although destined to die in October 1990, and their friendship never repaired after the fall out from the John Robertson transfer.

In between, Clough had navigated the declining financial position of the club, even reaching another semi-final in the UEFA Cup, where they were cheated by a 'bent' referee. And then built another team, based not only on youth, but perhaps also one with more attacking flair. The satisfaction that this gave the manager was immense, and finally put to bed the absurd notion that he was dependant on Taylor, and couldn't hack it on his own. The enormous pressure that he was under ultimately contributed to his own health problems and his well documented problems with alcohol, but the sight of him striding up the Wembley steps to get his hands on another trophy, is an image that lives on.

However, perhaps his greatest pleasure would have been the sight of his own son wearing the number 9 shirt for club and country, and performing in a style and manner that was befitting of the Clough name.

FOREST

APPEARANCES TEAM LINE-UPS

Aug 21st, CC, A, v Notts County, D, 1-1, Scorer Pearce, AT 6,932, Sutton, Chettle, Pearce Walker, Foster, Wilson, Crosby, Parker, Glover, Hodge, Rice. SUB Wassall.

Aug 27th, A, v Norwich City, L, 1-2, Scorer Chettle, AT 13,48, Sutton, Chettle, Pearce Walker, Foster, Wilson, Crosby, Webb, Clough, Hodge, Rice. SUB Carr.

Aug 29th, MERC CREDIT A, v Liverpool, L, 1-4, Scorer Webb, AT 20,100, Sutton, Chettle, Pearce Walker, Foster, Wilson, Crosby, Webb, Clough, Hodge, Rice. SUB Carr.

Sept 3rd, H, v Sheffield Wednesday, D, 1-1, Scorer (OG), AT 18,963, Sutton, Chettle, Pearce Walker, Foster, Wilson, Crosby, Webb, Clough, Hodge, Rice. SUB .

Sept 10th A, v Everton, D, 1-1, Scorer Webb, AT 30,003, Sutton, Chettle, Pearce Walker, Foster, Hodge, Crosby, Webb, Clough, Gaynor, Rice. SUB .

Sept 17th, H, v Derby County, D, 1-1, Scorer Foster, AT 24,818, Sutton, Chettle, Pearce Walker, Foster, Hodge, Crosby, Webb, Clough, Gaynor, Rice. SUB Carr.

Sept 24th, A, v Aston Villa, D, 1-1, Scorer Carr, AT 23,029, Sutton, Chettle, Pearce Walker, Foster, Hodge, Crosby, Webb, Clough, Gaynor, Rice. SUB Carr.

Sept 28th, LC H, v Chester City, W, 6-0, Scorer Pearce, Hodge, Webb, Clough(2), Gaynor, AT 11,958, Sutton, Chettle, Pearce Walker, Foster, Hodge, Crosby, Webb, Clough, Gaynor, Rice. SUB Fleming.

Oct 1st, H, v Luton Town, D, 0-0, Scorer AT 15,340, Sutton, Chettle, Pearce Walker, Foster, Hodge, Crosby, Webb, Clough, Gaynor, Rice. SUB Carr.

Oct 8th, A, v Queens Park Rangers, W, 2-1, Scorer Foster, Clough(P) AT 11,295, Sutton, Chettle, Pearce Walker, Foster, Hodge, Carr, Webb, Clough, Gaynor, Crosby. SUB

Oct 12th, LC, A, v Chester City, W, 4-0, Scorer Gaynor(3),Crosby, AT 4,747, Sutton, Fleming, Pearce Walker, Foster, Hodge, Carr, Webb, Gaynor, Crosby, Rice, SUB Glover.

Oct 22nd, A, v Millwall, D, 2-2, Scorer Hodge(2), AT 16,074, Sutton, Chettle, Pearce Walker, Foster, Hodge, Crosby, Webb, Clough, Chapman, Gaynor. SUB

Oct 26th, H, v Liverpool, W, 2-1, Scorer Webb, Rice, AT 29,755, Crossley, Chettle, Pearce Walker, Foster, Hodge, Crosby, Webb, Clough, Chapman, Rice. SUB

Oct 29th, A, v Newcastle United, W, 1-0, Scorer Chapman, AT 24,765, Crossley, Chettle, Pearce Walker, Foster, Hodge, Crosby, Webb, Clough, Chapman, Rice. SUB Wilson.

Nov 2nd, LC, H, v Coventry City, W, 3-2, Scorer Foster, Hodge, Clough, AT 21,301, Crossley, Chettle, Pearce Walker, Foster, Hodge, Charles, Wilson, Clough, Chapman, Rice. SUB

Nov 6th, H, v Arsenal, L, 1-4, Scorer Clough, AT 19,038, Sutton, Chettle, Pearce Walker, Foster, Hodge, Charles, Wilson, Clough, Chapman, Rice. SUB Starbuck.

Nov 12th, A, v West Ham, D, 3-3, Scorer Hodge,Clough(2), AT 21,682, Sutton, Chettle, Pearce Walker, Foster, Hodge, Starbuck, Wilson, Clough, Chapman, Rice. SUB Crosby, Laws.

Nov 19th, H, v Coventry City, D, 0-0, Scorer AT 17,250, Sutton, Chettle, Pearce Walker, Foster, Hodge, Crosby, Webb, Clough, Chapman, Rice. SUB Wilson.

Nov 26th, A, v Charlton Athletic, W, 1-0, Scorer Pearce, AT 6,411, Sutton, Chettle, Pearce Walker, Foster, Hodge, Starbuck, Webb, Clough, Chapman, Rice. SUB Wilson.

Nov 30th, LC A, v Leicester City, D, 0-0, Scorer AT 26,704, Sutton, Chettle, Pearce Walker, Wassall, Hodge, Starbuck, Webb, Clough, Chapman, Rice. SUB Wilson.

Dec 3rd, H, v Middlesbrough, D, 2-2, Scorer Chapman(2), AT 17,742, Sutton, Chettle, Pearce Walker, Foster, Hodge, Carr, Webb, Clough, Chapman, Rice. SUB

Dec 10th, A, v Southampton, D, 1-1, Scorer Clough, AT 15,259, Sutton, Laws, Pearce Chettle, Foster, Parker, Carr, Webb, Clough, Chapman, Rice. SUB

Dec 14th, LC H, v Leicester City, W, 2-1, Scorer Clough,Chapman AT 26,676, Sutton, Laws, Williams Chettle, Foster, Parker, Carr, Webb, Clough, Chapman, Rice. SUB Hodge

Dec 18th, H, v Wimbledon, L, 0-1, Scorer AT 16,247, Sutton, Chettle, Williams Walker, Foster, Parker, Carr, Webb, Clough, Chapman, Rice. SUB Hodge, Laws.

Dec 26th, A, v Manchester United, L, 0-2, Scorer AT 39,582, Sutton, Laws, Williams Walker, Wilson, Hodge, Carr, Webb, Clough, Chapman, Rice. SUB Gaynor, Starbuck.

Dec 31st, A, v Sheffield Wednesday, W, 3-0, Scorer Hodge, Webb, Gaynor, AT 20,470, Sutton, Laws, Pearce Walker, Wilson, Hodge, Carr, Webb, Gaynor, Chapman, Parker. SUB Starbuck.

Jan 2nd, H, v Everton, W, 2-0, Scorer Hodge, Webb, Gaynor, AT 20,470, Sutton, Laws, Pearce Walker, Wilson, Hodge, Carr, Webb, Gaynor, Chapman, Parker. SUB Starbuck.

Jan 7th, FAC, H, v Ipswich Town, W, 3-0, Scorer Gaynor, Chapman, (OG), AT 20,743, Sutton, Laws, Pearce Walker, Wilson, Hodge, Carr, Webb, Gaynor, Chapman, Parker. SUB

Jan 10th, Simod, A, v Chelsea, W, 4-1, Pearce(P), Gaynor, Chapman, Parker, AT 8,457, Sutton, Laws, Pearce Walker, Wilson, Hodge, Carr, Webb, Gaynor, Chapman, Parker. SUB Clough.

Jan 15th, A, v Tottenham Hotspur, W, 2-1, Scorer Clough, Parker, AT 16,903, Sutton, Laws, Pearce Walker, Wilson, Hodge, Carr, Webb, Clough, Chapman, Parker. SUB Chettle.

Jan 18th, LC, H, v Queens Park Rangers, W, 5-2, Scorer Chapman(4), Clough(P), AT 24,065, Sutton, Laws, Pearce Chettle, Wilson, Hodge, Carr, Webb, Clough, Chapman, Parker. SUB Crosby.

Jan 21st, H, v Aston Villa, W, 4-0, Scorer Laws, Pearce, Hodge, Parker, AT 22,622, Sutton, Laws, Pearce Chettle, Wilson, Hodge, Carr, Webb, Clough, Chapman, Parker. SUB Crosby.

1988 - 1989 DIVISION 1 TABLE

TEAMS	P	W	D	L	F	A	W	D	L	F	A	PTS
1 Arsenal	38	10	6	3	35	19	12	4	3	38	15	76
2 Liverpool FC	38	11	5	3	33	11	11	5	3	32	15	76
3 Nottingham F	38	8	7	4	31	16	9	6	4	33	27	64
4 Norwich C	38	8	7	4	23	20	9	4	6	25	25	62
5 Derby Co	38	9	3	7	23	18	8	4	7	17	20	58
6 Tottenham H	38	8	6	5	31	24	7	6	6	29	22	57
7 Coventry C	38	9	4	6	28	23	5	9	5	19	19	55
8 Everton	38	10	7	2	33	18	4	5	10	17	27	54
9 Q.P.R	38	9	5	5	23	16	5	6	8	20	21	53
10 Millwalll	38	10	3	6	27	21	4	8	7	20	31	53
11 Manchester U	38	10	5	4	27	13	3	7	9	18	22	51
12 Wimbledon	38	10	3	6	30	19	4	6	9	20	27	51
13 Southampton	38	6	7	6	25	26	4	8	7	27	40	45
14 Charlton A	38	6	7	6	25	24	4	5	10	19	34	42
15 Sheffield W	38	6	6	7	21	25	4	6	9	13	26	42
16 Luton T	38	8	6	5	32	21	2	5	12	10	31	41
17 Aston Villa	38	7	6	6	25	22	2	7	10	20	24	40
18 Middlesbrough	38	6	7	6	28	30	3	5	11	16	31	39
19 West Ham U	38	3	6	10	19	30	7	2	10	18	32	38
20 Newcastle U	38	3	6	10	19	28	4	4	11	13	35	31

WHO? WHAT!

FACTFILE

RESULTS LEAGUE TABLE

Jan 24th, Simod A, v Ipswich Town, W, 3-1, Scorer Pearce, Hodge, Crosby, AT 16,498, Sutton, Laws, Pearce Chettle, Wilson, Hodge, Carr, Webb, Clough, Chapman, Parker. SUB Crosby.

Jan 28th, FAC, H, v Leeds United, W, 2-0, Scorer Chapman, Parker, AT 28,017, Sutton, Laws, Pearce Chettle, Wilson, Hodge, Carr, Webb, Clough, Chapman, Parker. SUB Starbuck.

Feb 4th, A, v Luton Town, W, 3-2, Scorer Clough(P2) Parker, AT 10,465, Sutton, Laws, Pearce Chettle, Wilson, Hodge, Carr, Webb, Clough, Chapman, Parker. SUB

Feb 11th, A, v Queens Park Rangers, D, 0-0, Scorer AT 19,690, Sutton, Laws, Pearce Chettle, Wilson, Hodge, Carr, Webb, Clough, Chapman, Parker. SUB Starbuck.

Feb 15th, LC H, v Bristol City, D, 1-1, Scorer (OG) AT 30,016, Sutton, Laws, Pearce Chettle, Wilson, Hodge, Carr, Webb, Clough, Chapman, Parker. SUB

Feb 19th, FAC, A, v Watford, W, 3-0, Scorer Laws,Webb, Chapman, AT 18,044, Sutton, Laws, Pearce Walker, Wilson, Hodge, Carr, Webb, Clough, Chapman, Parker. SUB

Feb 22nd, Simod, H, v Crystal Palace, W, 3-1, Scorer Pearce,Webb(2), AT 20,374, Sutton, Laws, Pearce Chettle, Wilson, Hodge, Carr, Webb, Clough, Chapman, Parker. SUB

Feb 26th, CC, A, v Bristol City, W, 1-0, Scorer Parker, AT 28,084, Sutton, Laws, Pearce Walker, Wilson, Hodge, Carr, Webb, Clough, Chapman, Parker. SUB

Mar 11th, A, v Arsenal, W, 3-1, Scorer Clough, Carr, (OG), AT 39,369, Sutton, Laws, Pearce Walker, Wilson, Hodge, Carr, Webb, Clough, Chapman, Parker. SUB

Mar 15th, H, v Newcastle United, D, 1-1, Scorer Clough(P), AT 20,800, Sutton, Laws, Pearce Walker, Wilson, Hodge, Carr, Webb, Clough, Chapman, Parker. SUB

Mar 18th, FAC A, v Manchester United, W, 1-0, Scorer Parker, AT 55,052, Sutton, Laws, Pearce Walker, Wilson, Hodge, Carr, Webb, Clough, Chapman, Parker. SUB

Mar 22nd, H, v Tottenham Hotspur, L, 1-2, Scorer Parker, AT 23,098, Sutton, Laws, Pearce Walker, Wilson, Hodge, Carr, Webb, Clough, Chapman, Parker. SUB

Mar 25th, A, v Derby County, W, 2-0, Scorer Hodge Chapman, AT 25,174, Sutton, Laws, Pearce Walker, Wilson, Hodge, Gaynor, Webb, Clough, Chapman, Parker. SUB Chettle.

Mar 27th, H, v Manchester United, W, 2-0, Scorer Pearce Chapman, AT 30,092, Sutton, Laws, Pearce Walker, Wilson, Hodge, Gaynor, Webb, Clough, Chapman, Parker. SUB Chettle.

Apr 1st, A, v Wimbledon, L, 1-4, Scorer Clough, AT 7,687, Sutton, Chettle, Pearce Walker, Wilson, Hodge, Gaynor, Webb, Clough, Chapman, Parker. SUB

Apr 5th, A, v Norwich City, W, 2-0, Scorer Clough, Pearce AT 19,782, Sutton, Laws, Pearce Walker, Wilson, Hodge, Gaynor, Webb, Clough, Chapman, Parker. SUB Foster.

Apr 9th, LC, N, v LUTON TOWN, W, 3-1, Scorer Clough(2,1P), Webb AT 76,130, Sutton, Laws, Pearce Walker, Wilson, Hodge, Gaynor, Webb, Clough, Chapman, Parker. SUB

Apr 12th, H, v Southampton, W, 3-0, Scorer Clough(P), Pearce, Gaynor, AT 18,948, Sutton, Laws, Pearce Walker, Wilson, Hodge, Gaynor, Webb, Clough, Chapman, Parker. SUB Rice.

Apr 15th, FAC N, v Liverpool, Abandoned, AT , Sutton, Laws, Pearce Walker, Wilson, Hodge, Gaynor, Webb, Clough, Chapman, Parker. SUB

Apr 22nd, A, v Middlesbrough, W, 4-3, Scorer Webb, Chapman(2), Parker, AT 20,778, Sutton, Laws, Pearce Walker, Wilson, Hodge, Gaynor, Webb, Clough, Chapman, Parker. SUB Chettle.

Apr 30th, Simod N, v Everton, W, 4-3, Scorer Chapman(2), Parker(2), AT 46,608, Sutton, Laws, Pearce Walker, Wilson, Hodge, Gaynor, Webb, Clough, Chapman, Parker. SUB Chettle, Carr.

May 3rd, H, v Millwall, W, 4-1, Scorer Hodge,Gaynor, Parker, AT 15,982, Sutton, Laws, Pearce Walker, Wilson, Hodge, Carr, Webb, Clough, Gaynor, Parker. SUB

May 7th, FAC N, v Liverpool, L, 1-3, Scorer Webb, AT 38,000, Sutton, Laws, Pearce Walker, Wilson, Hodge, Gaynor, Webb, Clough, Chapman, Parker. SUB Glover, Starbuck.

May 10th, A, v Liverpool, L, 0-1, Scorer AT 39,793, Sutton, Laws, Pearce Walker, Wilson, Rice, Carr, Webb, Clough, Chapman, Parker. SUB Gaynor.

May 13th, H, v Charlton Athletic, W, 4-0, Scorer Wilson, Carr,Webb, Chettle. AT 17,637, Sutton, Laws, Pearce Walker, Wilson, Rice, Carr, Webb, Clough, Chapman, Parker. SUB Gaynor, Chettle.

May 15th, A, v Coventry City, D, 2-2, Scorer Webb, Clough. AT 14,003, Sutton, Laws, Pearce Walker, Wilson, Rice, Carr, Webb, Clough, Chapman, Parker. SUB

May 18th, H, v West Ham, L, 1-2, Scorer Chapman. AT 21,003, Sutton, Laws, Pearce Walker, Chettle, Hodge, Gaynor, Webb, Clough, Chapman, Parker. SUB

WHERE! WHEN!

Thanks and Credits

As with any book of this detail, there have been a great many people involved in all aspects of its creation. We would like to start by thanking the many organisations who have allowed us to painstakingly work our way through their archives, collecting images and topics of interest. Many thanks to those ex-players and supporters who have allowed us use of images from their private collections. Special thanks particularly to the Evening Post (Trinity Mirror) and John Sumpter.

The list is endless, but if we have left anyone out, it was totally accidental, we would like to thank (in no particular order): Ian Bowyer, Liam O'Kane, Frank Clark, John Robertson, Trevor Francis, Colin Barrett, John Lawson, Andy Smart, Peter Gibson, Alan Hill, Steve Chettle, Johnny Metgod, Larry Lloyd.
Simon Meakin, Design Associate
Adele Dolloway, Assisting Editor

Picture Credits

In particular John Sumpter of JMS Photography, PA Images, Getty Images, Evening Post (Trinity Mirror), Football Post, The Pedigree Group Ltd, Haymarket Media Group, Color Sport. Supporters archive collection and the author's own collection. We have also made use of various players' own collections.

Book Quote References and Research

Nottingham Forest, The Official Statistical History, Smales K. (1991)
The Forest Who's Who, Matthews T. (2004)
Kicking with Both Feet, Clark F. (1999)
Clough, A Biography, Francis T. (1987)
Clough, The Autobiography, Sadler J. (1994)
His Way, The Brian Clough Story, Murphy P. (1993)
With Clough, By Taylor, Taylor P. (1980)
Archie Gemmill, Both sides of the Border, Gemmill A. (2005)
From Bo'ness to the Bernabeu, McGovern J. (2012)
First Among Equals, Anderson V. (2010)
Inside Soccer, Woodcock T. (1985)
Laws of the Jungle, Laws B. (2012)
More than a Match, Chapman L. (1992)
Psycho, Pearce S, (2000)
The Man with Maradona's Shirt, Hodge S. (2010)
A Game of Three Halves, Swain K. (2013)
Hard Man,Hard Game, Lloyd L. (2009)
Super Tramp, Robertson J & Lawson J. (2011)
My Magic Carpet Ride, Birtles G. (2011)
Peter Shilton-The Autobiography, Shilton P. (2004)
Justin Fashanu, The Biography, Read J. (2012)

Nottingham Forest programmes (1979-1989)
Nottingham Forest handbooks (1979- 1989)
Football Post Guides (1970-1974)
Various newspapers